No one has ever written about the preparation and serving
of meals as an expression of the Buddhadharma, nor have
any teachers taught concerning these matters....
Why must it be so?

—Dogen Zenji

Boredom arises from the loss of meaning, which in turn comes in part from
a failure of "religio" or connectedness with one another and with our past.
This book is a modest plea for the realization that absolutely nothing
is intrinsically boring, least of all the everyday, ordinary things.
These, today, are after all what even we are prepared
to admit we have in common.

—Margaret Visser, *Much Depends on Dinner*

Veggiyana

THE DHARMA OF COOKING:
With 108 Deliciously Easy Vegetarian Recipes

Sandra Garson
Illustrations by Michelle Antonisse

Wholesome Food from the Whole Wide World

WISDOM PUBLICATIONS • BOSTON

Wisdom Publications
199 Elm Street
Somerville MA 02144 USA
www.wisdompubs.org

Library of Congress Cataloging-in-Publication Data

Garson, Sandra.
  Veggiyana : the Dharma of cooking : with 108 deli-
ciously easy vegetarian recipes : wholesome food from
the whole wide world / Sandra Garson ; illustrations
by Michelle Antonisse.
    p. cm.
  Includes bibliographical references and index.
  ISBN 0-86171-636-1 (pbk. : alk. paper)
1. Vegetarian cooking. 2. International cooking.
3. Dharma (Buddhism) I. Title.
  TX837.G32 2011
  641.5'636—dc23
                    2011022677

ISBN 978-086171-6364
eBook ISBN 978-086171-8818

15 14 13 12 11
5 4 3 2 1

Cover and "Dharma fork" design by Phil Pascuzzo.
Illustrations by Michelle Antonisse.
Author photo by Peter Sutherland.
Interior design by Gopa & Ted2, Inc.
Set in Arno Pro 11.25/15.

Wisdom Publications' books are printed on acid-free
paper and meet the guidelines for permanence and
durability of the Production Guidelines for Book Longevity of the Council on Library Resources.

Printed in the United States of America.

The paper used in the printing of this book is FSC® certi-
fied. For more information, please visit www.fscus.org.

To the very venerable and incomparable
Khenchen Thrangu Rinpoche
and to the children
at his Shree Mangal Dvip Boarding School

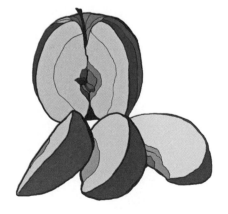

Table of Contents

*The purpose of any religion, any culture, any way of life,
always has been to take care of the body and the mind.*
—TAI SITU RINPOCHE

*It was a common belief throughout much of the world ... that food was more
than mere nourishment. Its own qualities were closely linked to the
physical and moral qualities of those who prepared or ingested it.*

—REAY TANNAHILL, *Food in History*

Preface: The Veggiyana

The Buddha acted on the insight that whatever truth a person may reach is reached best by a healthy body and mind.

—John Daido Loori

ABOUT 775 YEARS AGO, the seminal Zen Buddhist teacher Dogen Zenji noted in one of his most important teachings, *Instructions to the Monastery Cook*, that taking diligent care in the kitchen enables all members of the community to fulfill their lives in the most stable way. Hunger, fatigue, and sickness, he said, are powerful distractions, and a cook who truly understands the meaning of a kitchen has the power to prevent them. This is still true.

Just after all the hoopla of the new millennium fizzled, I went to Nepal to study Dharma. While there, I visited the boarding school my teacher had established for lay children from high Himalayan villages, Tibetan refugee camps, and the squalid sprawl of Kathmandu. It was an overcrowded, vibrant hive out of which black-haired children poured as word spread that a "yellow hair" had come. I was quickly engulfed in a sea of smiles. But around those gleaming white grins were runny noses, and the hands reaching out to me revealed rashes and unhealed scratches. Then I noticed how scrawny all these kids were. I immediately wanted to feed them.

At the end of the next teaching, with more gumption than I'd realized I had, I jumped up and shouted to the crowd of about a hundred people that I knew they were all going to go spend a dollar on a beer or a pot of Nepali chai at lunch. And I also knew they could live without it. So if they would give *me* that dollar instead, I would buy the kids at Rinpoche's school a pantry full of food to help give them the gift of good health—which they quite literally couldn't live without. In ten minutes I had $120. That's how the Veggiyana began.

The monks thought I had gone mad when I made them take me food shopping all over the valley, but that afternoon I stocked the storeroom with fifty-kilo sacks of nutritious beans, unadulterated cooking oil, jars of ghee, iodized salt, raisins, peanuts, cornmeal, and fifty kilos each of popping corn and granola. The following year when I returned, every one of the three hundred kids in that school remembered me.

I was so flattered I spent a very long day cooking them three big meals in a kitchen that had no electricity, no water, no flooring above the packed down earth, no tables, and no stove—only a mudded pile of stone into which three men shoved or withdrew a tree trunk to send varying heights of fire up through a hole at the top. "You must be very happy," three teenaged girls said, giggling, while they watched me through the doorway. "Why?" I asked, for by now it was me who had begun to think I'd gone mad. "Because," one started to say when another interrupted with more giggles, "you're making *us* very happy!"

Each of the next two years, during my three-week visit to study Dharma, I dragged two or three monks shopping with me. I joked that while others came to Kathmandu for the Buddha, I now came for what amounted to a hill of beans. Back in America, from time to time I'd send a few hundred dollars to help the steward monks keep buying fresh fruits and high-quality dhal. The improvement in the children, their energy and their immunity, had started to become so obvious the stewards didn't dare backslide. They and their cohorts at the monastery actually began to complain I was ignoring *them*—the grown-ups—and that, they whined ever so slightly, wasn't fair. So I bought them ten kilos of peanut butter, a pickup truck–load of apples, and fifty kilos of popping corn.

I then set up a learning program in which every Saturday—the only day the children had vacation from classes—a dozen kids went into the kitchen and cooked lunch for the whole school. I wanted to teach the children to do what I did so they could spread the gospel of good food from their own experience—personal understanding being the time-honored way that Dharma has been propagated. And they certainly have done that. The Saturday cooking class is still going strong; in fact, it has become so prestigious and popular it has no shortage of volunteers, no shortage of monks and nuns who show up to eat, no shortage of school graduates who, from wherever in the world they are now studying, write to say how much it steadies them to know how to appreciate the food they find there.

Ten years after that spontaneous shopping spree, it's not only the children who've bloomed. The magnificent new monastery in the ancient village of Namo Buddha, about an hour's drive beyond Kathmandu, has a huge terraced vegetable garden and an orchard to supply its kitchen, which serves soy beans and fava beans so fewer monks visit the medical clinic with rashes, digestive disorders, and fatigue. The 250 nuns at the abbey in the Syambu section of Kathmandu who, two years ago, were fainting from malnutrition now tend their own vegetable garden, fruit tree collection, and bird sanctuary and have joined an environmental cleanup squad that not only collects trash in the famed Syambu stupa area but promotes composting and recycling in the residential neighborhood abutting it. The schoolchildren are composting, growing lettuces, learning the basics of vitamins and working with Jane Goodall in her international children's environmental and animal protection program, "Roots and Shoots." In the summer of 2010, Thrangu Rinpoche, the great benefactor of all this activity, consecrated the Thrangu Monastery Canada in Vancouver, where ninety fruit trees were planted out back and a community vegetable garden laid in on one side. All in all, the bright glow on the full faces of those in his care has become so noticeable that other teachers are asking for food help too. World-renowned sacred chanters Deva Premal and Miten, as well as Philadelphia flutist Marianne Sutin, have sent profits from CDs and concerts to help. A full-fledged charity has been set up so everyone can join in too. The whole story of how I deliberately learned Himalayan cooking, answered calls to make meals for traveling Tibetan gurus to keep their strength and spirit up, cooked for enough Dharma retreats to get the Tibetan name *Hayong Trukhen Lakpa* ("dishpan hands"), and cooked at Rinpoche's school—and how that all became the Veggiyana—is available online with photos, blog entries, and a smorgasbord of useful information at veggiyana.org.

The simple message of that website and this book is that ordinary food is extraordinarily powerful. With right aspiration, the impact of a few peanuts can be immeasurable. Who knows how many lives the schoolchildren will benefit as they mature, how many people have been comforted by the monks and nuns who embody Dharma, how prolonged the lives of our great teachers are now—thanks to a healthier diet. That spontaneous collection of $120 has evolved into a Veggiyana, a vegetable path that leads to liberation from unnecessary physical suffering, freeing people to engage positively with the world, since those who feel good can do good. It's a path everyone, Buddhist or not, can get on. Its noble truth is simply that a strong body is the key to a strong mind. Hunger, fatigue, and sickness prevent all of us from aiming at our dreams, accomplishing our aspirations, helping others. Certainly, if we love someone—our selves included—we don't want him or her to be shunted to the sidelines by that unnecessary suffering; we want our loved ones to be powerful enough to live their dreams and reach their stars. Since that means fueling their bodies with the right food, the kitchen is where the real generosity of love stirs and compassion is served. That's why Dogen Zenji said: "Just working as the cook is the incomparable practice of the buddhas."

Taking hope and taking action will transform things.

—Dzigar Kongtrul Rinpoche

Do not take lightly small good deeds,
Believing they can hardly help;
For drops of water, one by one,
In time can fill a giant pot.

—Patrul Rinpoche

Introduction

What glorious flavors there are in the world!
Once you start eating, you can hardly stop.... Oh sweet nectar of life!
—NIKOLAI GOGOL, *Evenings on a Farm Near Dikanka*

THIS IS NOT so much a book about vegetarian cooking as it is a statement, an accounting of riches. I wanted to offer an eye-opening reminder that all of us are heirs to the world's greatest wealth: the wisdom of survival. It's that magical mix of science and art dished out every day in tiffins, reed baskets, bento boxes, and blue plate specials that we take so for granted that iPhones and jet planes seem more wondrous inventions than chocolate and yogurt. Yet, because we never escape the need to eat, what comes out of the kitchen is far more essential than any gadget. If we had not inherited the way to preserve milk as yogurt or leach toxins out of soybeans, boil bread (which is the original description of making noodles), or avoid the poisonous leaves of the rhubarb plant while stewing its nutritious stems—if all this knowledge had been hoarded, monopolized, or buried like other treasure, instead of being freely shared, none of us would be here now, enjoying life with all its gadgets.

"The discovery of a new dish," Jean Anthelme Brillat-Savarin said in *The Physiology of Taste*, "does more for human happiness than the discovery of a star." So this book is a reckoning of the joy in our world. It's an accounting of the marvelous ingenuity we have inherited so that we can eat and be well. Some of its line items explain how we got this priceless gift, revealing why the cow is sacred, how pasta was invented, what the word *recipe* means, and why Ali Baba said "Open Sesame!" These are tidbits you can serve for good table talk.

Most of the essays, like the quotes scattered around as spice, are flavored with Buddhism. This is partly because Buddhist teachings are designed to heighten awareness, but mostly because while the need to eat has imbued all religions with faith in the almighty power of food—fasts like Islam's Ramadan, feasts like Judaism's Seder, proscriptions like the Hindu taboo on eating beef, prescriptions like proper food for Lent—Buddhism's core teachings seem to show the most concern for food. Perhaps that's because it was actually launched by a meal. Struggling to reach the gleaming pinnacle of enlightenment through the harsh austerities prescribed by the great yogis of his day, Prince Siddhartha reached only death's door by following the ascetic path of near starvation. With nothing gained and nothing left to lose, he accepted a dairymaid's offering of what's sometimes described as yogurt, and sometimes as milk and rice. His body reinvigorated by nourishment, he sat down under a ficus tree, strong enough to meditate through the night, to become Buddha, one who is awake to absolute reality. The strong link between the Buddhist teachings and eating is vividly illustrated in the first words of the *Abhidharma*, the logical scientific treatise that underlies the Buddha's teaching: *sabbe satta aharatthitika*, "All beings exist on food." More than two millennia later, the Zen patriarch Dogen declared, "Dharma is eating and eating is Dharma."

Since recipes are the universal food processor, I offer 108 delightful and healthful vegetarian favorites, one for every bead on a Buddhist *mala*—each an example of how necessity has been kneaded into delight. I gathered them from kitchens all over the planet to impart the flavor of a neighborhood cookbook, to show how, despite geography or politics, everyone brings something to the table. Eating unites us in a truly worldwide web, the ultimate food chain of interdependence, and one of its greatest comforts is the reminder that we are never alone in the kitchen. Thousands of years of cooking have brought us to this day where we have taste buds that blossomed from our own experience, generations of family tradition in our blood, guidance from cookbooks in our brain, cooks past and present on every continent of the planet cueing our imagination. The foods we eat and the spices we enliven them with, like the words we use to talk about them, reveal our interconnectedness and interdependence with each other. "When we acknowledge that the food we eat comes from the efforts of all sentient beings past and present," contemporary Zen master John Daido Loori said, "we immediately identify with that Great Net of Indra." That legendary net covering the entire universe, each knot or node a jewel reflecting every other jewel, perfectly captures our interwoven kitchens.

I chose the recipes in this book because they are, as my friend Nancy calls her favorite clothes and plates, "reach-fors": beloved items she chooses again and again because they can always be trusted to be just right. Hopefully these will make it much easier to do the compassionate work of giving and saving life by feeding yourself and others. I also selected them because they embody what I think of as G-U-S-T-O:

> The recipes represent Generosity because they contain no ingredients whose harvesting inherently causes harm or whose ingesting will harm your body.

(Do of course modify them further in accordance with your own allergies or medical needs).

They illustrate Universality by containing no exotic, super-expensive ingredients you will have to hunt down and ship in from thousands of miles away, then never use again; everything should be at your local supermarket or health food store, and all of it reasonably priced.

The dishes are pure Simplicity, for you don't have to get a graduate degree in molecular gastronomy, buy exotic equipment, or sacrifice three days to make any of them; one hour, a few ordinary pans, and a little willingness will work just fine.

They are Tasty to the tongue and attractive to the eyes.

And finally, they are all worthy of being an Offering to yourself, your loved ones, and the Buddha that the Dharma promises is in you, just waiting to be nourished.

In Turkey, people toast someone who has cooked a wondrous meal with "health to your hands!" To everyone who eats a meal, my toast is "wealth to your body and mind."

We do not realize often enough that we are dependent on one another;

at the simplest material level, we are all interdependent for our

daily needs, and in this way we owe a debt to all beings.

—Kalu Rinpoche

The Salad Bowl

YOU CAN DISPLAY all or a few of these mouthwatering salads to create a memorably picturesque table. French and Roman restaurants serve lots of temptations like these side by side on a colorful buffet table as *hors d'oeuvres variés* or *antipasti misti*, respectively, to launch a merry meal. The Greeks would add a bowl of olives, some crusty bread, and tasty cheese to a half-dozen such dishes and make a hot-weather meal of *mezes*. My favorite hot-weather lunch or light supper is three salads festively served with exquisite bread or fresh corn tortillas, a yogurt condiment such as one from the Dhal Bhat section, and perhaps something salty like nuts or brined olives. Any salad in this section will stand alone or as an excellent accompaniment to any of the cooked dishes in this book—and all will leave room for dessert.

Crops on the farm are the cure for poverty....
Give more away in gifts, and you will never be hungry.

—JETSUN MILAREPA

Armenian-Style Green Beans

Green beans, which were known as string beans before the string was bred out, are related to those nutrient-rich beans known as *dhal*. They are grown for the pod itself, not the beans inside, but are themselves rich in nutrients like vitamins K, C, and A, as well as iron, manganese, and calcium. This traditional eastern Mediterranean recipe is a popular and very tasty way to swallow all that.

SERVES 6–8.

2 lb. green beans (e.g. Kentucky Wonder or Blue Lake), ends trimmed

1 cup olive oil

5 garlic cloves, peeled and minced

1 large red onion, sliced into thin rings

1 tsp. dried oregano

2 tsp. dried thyme

3 Tbs. chopped fresh parsley

1 tsp. freshly ground or cracked black pepper

⅛ tsp. salt

3 medium tomatoes, seeded and chopped

⅓ cup chopped fresh dill

▶ Cut the beans into a uniform length, between 3 and 4 inches long. Try to keep them in one direction now and when cooking, so that they look attractive when served.

▶ Heat the olive oil in a heavy-gauge casserole. Add the garlic and then the onion and sauté over medium heat until the onion is soft but not yet browning.

▶ Add the beans. Add the rest of the ingredients except dill. Cover, lower heat to simmer, and cook 20–30 minutes until the beans are tender.

▶ Remove from heat. Stir in dill and cool uncovered.

▶ Serve at room temperature. (You can store the dish in the refrigerator for several days until ready to serve.)

Bhutanese Cucumber Salad

This Bhutanese condiment, used to cool the palate after eating chilies, is surprisingly rich for a salad with no dressing.

SERVES 4.

1 English cucumber
(the long skinny kind)

1 small red onion, peeled and finely diced

½ cup crumbled feta or farmer's cheese or ricotta salata

½–1 (depending on your preference) small hot red pepper, seeded and minced

⅛ tsp. salt

⅛ tsp. freshly ground black pepper

2 Tbs. chopped fresh cilantro

▶ Peel cucumber and slice it in half lengthwise. Scoop out seeds and halve it lengthwise again. Cut it crosswise to make bite-sized pieces. Put into serving bowl.

▶ Add the remaining ingredients and mix well. Add salt to taste. Serve.

Never feel aversion toward plain ingredients.

—DOGEN ZENJI, *Instructions to the Monastery Cook*

Cauliflower Puttanesca

Italians named their sassy (thanks to the hot peppers) and sharp (due to the anchovies) spaghetti sauce *puttanesca*, after a slang term for "prostitute." I found its vibrancy a perfect foil for cauliflower, which is so bland. After years of pasta puttanesca with cauliflower, I put aside the pasta and created this salad.

SERVES 8.

1 head cauliflower, cored and broken into large florets

4 Tbs. high-quality olive oil, divided

½ dry pint cherry tomatoes (about 2 dozen), halved

24 pitted Kalamata or similar olives, chopped

1 Vidalia or other sweet onion, peeled and diced

1 Tbs. capers, drained

1 tsp. red pepper flakes or 1 serrano chili, seeded and minced

¼ tsp. salt

½ cup chopped fresh parsley

2 garlic cloves, minced

1 Tbs. balsamic vinegar

⅛ tsp. Dijon-style mustard

¼ tsp. black olive paste or tapenade

1 Tbs. grated Parmesan cheese

▶ Preheat oven to 450°F. Line a small baking sheet with foil and place the cauliflower florets on it. Cover with 1 Tbs. olive oil and a pinch of salt. Roast 12–15 minutes, until florets start to show spots of brown. Cool.

▶ Cut florets into smaller pieces. In a large serving bowl, combine roasted cauliflower, tomatoes, olives, onion, capers, hot pepper, salt, and parsley. Mix well. Season with black pepper to taste.

▶ In a small cup or cruet, whisk together garlic, balsamic vinegar, mustard, olive paste, and 3 Tbs. high-quality olive oil. Pour over salad. Sprinkle grated cheese on top to serve.

The Edible Truth of Suffering

What is there
like fortitude! What sap
went through that little thread
to make the cherry red!
—Marianne Moore

WHY VEGETABLES GROWN in the stony, alluvial soils of freezing Maine have significantly more flavor than the photogenic ones produced in the year-round sunshine of California was a mystery until Maine's renowned chef Sam Hayward went to a culinary cook-off at a northern California winery chosen for its perfect vegetable beds. Invited to pick whatever he needed to create a signature meal, Sam found himself running back to those beds again and again. No matter how many zucchini or beans or tomatoes he grabbed, he couldn't achieve the intense flavor he was used to. "That produce looked gorgeous," he reported, "but it had no taste."

Sam was so perplexed that, when he got home, he went to his favorite farm and got exactly the amount of vegetables he'd picked the first time in California. Some of them were small and some a little bruised, yet when that produce hit the pot, flavor flowed. Sam took this news back to Frank the farmer and the two eventually figured out that the boulders shattered annually when the late winter thaw rudely heaves them from Earth's depths continually aerate and enrich Maine's soil with minerals. Melting snow, cresting rivers, and spring rains then irrigate it. This perfect setting is unfortunately followed by a growing season so short and erratic it becomes a survival marathon in which plants must overcome volatile extremes of hot or cold, dry or wet, in ever-changing combinations that breed unpredictable arrays of fungi and insects. Unavoidable self-defense requires vegetables to produce all the hormones and chemical compounds they can—and these are the very sources of their flavor. So, in the garden, difficulties become blessings.

This truth of suffering was confirmed a decade later at a northern California winery famous for producing incomparable zinfandel and infamous for not producing enough to satisfy demand. The sign on its unmarked gate said, "One bottle per group." I showed up on a chilly, damp February day with no grapes growing and nobody else in sight, so the proprietor himself came out. When I asked how he managed to make unique wine in the midst of so many neighborhood competitors, he said, "I am the only one who doesn't irrigate. I make my grapes fight to survive. That makes them fire up all the chemical compounds they've got. The hard time they have makes them flavorful and that flavor goes into my wines." After I told him Sam Hayward's theory of why hard-won Maine vegetables are superior to those with the easy life of California, he gave me three bottles of wine. Ever since, I have really tried not to resent but to instead appreciate indignities and small sufferings as the flavor-enhancing spices of life.

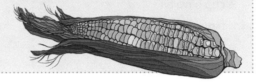

Monique's Marinated Mushrooms from Provence

Decades ago, before there was any "development," I spent several weeks on the Mediterranean coast of Turkey, where on a fishing boat I met Monique and her husband, Andre. They lived in Andre's native village on France's rugged Breton coast but Monique had been born and raised in Provence. So when I later took up her invitation to visit and rode the train from Paris through Nantes, I arrived to a Mediterranean meal that started with this "company's coming" recipe her mother had given her when she got married and moved away.

SERVES 8–12 AS AN HORS D'OEUVRE.

½ cup olive oil

⅛ tsp. red wine vinegar

½ cup dry white wine

1 Tbs. dried thyme

1 Tbs. dried tarragon

½ cup raisins

⅛ tsp. salt

1 tsp. whole black peppercorns

1 Tbs. minced fresh parsley

16 pearl onions, peeled

1 lb. whole button mushrooms, washed

2 Tbs. tomato paste

▶ Combine oil, vinegar, and wine in a heavy stockpot or large heavy-gauge casserole. Add spices, raisins, salt, and pepper. Add parsley, onions, and mushrooms.

▶ Add just enough water to barely cover the ingredients. Stir in tomato paste.

▶ Bring to a boil. Lower heat and simmer 5 minutes. Turn off heat.

▶ Cool and refrigerate overnight.

▶ Serve at room temperature with toothpicks. (In autumn I have hollowed out a small pumpkin to use as a serving bowl and studded it with toothpicks.)

We all have to eat. It is a basic requirement of being alive. Unfortunately, there are few daily activities that are so loaded with pain and distress, with guilt and shame, with unfulfilled longing and despair than the simple act of putting energy into our bodies. When we learn to eat mindfully, our eating can be transformed from a source of suffering to a source of renewal, self-understanding and delight.

—Jan Chozen Bays, *Mindful Eating*

Madame Segard's Carrot Salad

Mme. Segard, a Parisian *bonne femme*, is my French "mother." She adopted me when her daughter Marie-France brought me home after we'd met in Tunisia. Marie-France, a stewardess, wanted nothing to do with cooking because her mother had "spent her whole life just doing that and never gets out of the kitchen to learn something important." When she told me how sad her mother was that the only food her only child kept in the refrigerator were leftovers from first-class airline cabins, I volunteered to be the daughter her mother could pass her culinary expertise to. It was win-win because it got Marie-France off the hook and reinvigorated her mother, who took to cooking with new passion. Of all she taught me, this simple salad speedily whipped up for lunch while we prepared the traditional seven-course Christmas Eve feast is my favorite.

SERVES 6.

7 medium-large carrots, peeled and grated

1 bunch curly parsley, stems removed, leaves minced

½ tsp. salt

¼ tsp. freshly ground or cracked black pepper

2 Tbs. fresh lemon juice

¼ cup walnut oil or fruity olive oil

▶ Combine carrots and parsley in a serving bowl. (You can do this a half day before serving and store, covered tightly, in the refrigerator.)

▶ Mix in salt and pepper.

▶ Combine lemon juice and oil in a small cup, shake well, and pour over the carrots.

▶ Serve immediately.

Food shapes us and expresses us even more definitively than our furniture or houses or utensils.

—MARGARET VISSER, *Much Depends on Dinner*

Corn Salad with Green Olives and Pumpkin Seeds

This homage to Mexico features the foods Columbus discovered in the new world, garnished with ingredients brought from the old one by those who settled here after him. The mix is rich in vitamins, protein, and fiber, with the seeds also providing vital zinc.

SERVES 6–8.

SALAD

1 lb. corn kernels (6–8 fresh ears or one bag of frozen), cooked

1 (15-oz.) can pinto beans, rinsed and drained

½ cup green Spanish olives stuffed with pimento

18–20 cherry tomatoes, cleaned

½ large avocado, peeled and diced

¼ cup roasted pumpkin seeds (*pepitas*)

½ green bell pepper, seeded and diced

DRESSING

3 tsp. fresh lime juice

1 Tbs. olive oil

dash of Jerez (Spanish sherry) or balsamic vinegar

¼ tsp. dried oregano

¼ tsp. freshly ground or cracked black pepper

pinch chipotle chili powder

pinch salt

GARNISH

⅓ cup chopped fresh cilantro

¼ tsp. red pepper flakes (optional)

▶ In a large serving bowl, combine corn, beans, olives, tomatoes, avocado, pumpkin seeds, and bell pepper.

▶ For the dressing, whisk together the lime juice, olive oil, and vinegar. Whisk in the oregano, black pepper, chipotle, and salt.

▶ Pour dressing over corn salad and gently toss. Taste and adjust salt if necessary.

▶ Garnish with chopped cilantro and optional red pepper flakes.

Sesame Seeds

IN MARCH 2007, during the lunch break of a Dharma talk, I went to visit my teacher's nuns in the Syambu neighborhood of Kathmandu. Since nobody was expecting me, the abbey courtyard was empty, but before long, a young woman in maroon robes appeared. I called out to introduce myself, and not wanting her to disappear, asked if she had taken secular classes at our teacher's boarding school. "Yes," she said, but she had graduated.

"Well," I said, "when you were there, did you like the lunches?"

She smiled brightly.

"I am *America machen* ['American cook,' the nickname the school kids gave me], who started them. I have come to help the nuns eat better too. Is the abbess here?"

As if on cue, the elder nun in charge appeared. She invited me to the office for tea, and in the halting question-and-answer conversation that followed, the abbess tearfully confessed that almost all the money being raised went into building, and of course the statues, texts, and *thangkhas* for the new buildings. Miniscule amounts were allocated for ephemera like food. Some of her 250 young charges had fainted from weakness, and, she said with tears, she had had to "take them off the Path."

"I will fix that." I heard myself say and departed realizing I had no idea how. I worried myself out of a night's sleep, stewing over the karmic repercussions of not keeping a pledge. Two days later, while I was with the boarding school's steward in a tiny shop piled to the ceiling with one-kilogram bags of raisins, nuts, and grains, I saw an opportunity. "I want ten kilos of sesame seeds," I said to the shopkeeper, and turned to the steward. "You must take them to the nuns and tell the cook to put them on everything." Frankly, I was thinking only about the oil that would put sorely needed fat in those female bodies, and of course the terrific bargain of getting twenty-two pounds of sesame for the same price as four and a half pounds of raisins. I had no idea how mighty and magical sesame seeds could be—but most of the world's people are not so ignorant.

Sesame is the oldest, most treasured seed on Earth. Over 5,000 years ago, the Chinese burned its oil not only for light but to make the soot necessary for calligraphy ink-blocks. The earliest recorded mention of the seed as edible is an Assyrian stone tablet on which a creation myth is written, claiming the gods indulged in sesame wine the night before they created the earth. By the first Christian millennium, sesame was so common in Arab culture, those two little words, *Open sesame!*, famously chanted by Ali Baba to gain access to the cave packed with riches, symbolized thousands of years of human delight at the sight of the sesame pod bursting with a pop that sounds exactly like that of a lock being sprung, releasing nutritious treasure. Broadly speaking, sesame seeds are 25 percent protein and loaded with zinc, calcium (more than three times the amount in milk), the crucial B vitamins (including folic acid), omega-6 fatty acids, phosphorous, magnesium, potassium, and as much iron as a piece of liver. Plus they contain a unique natural preservative that keeps their oil from turning rancid. Sesame oil is still the main source of cooking fat in Asia. In Buddhist ritual, sesame seed represents earth, one of the five life-sustaining essences. As one of the five grains that symolize human activity, it stands for destruction—of the unwholesome.

Sesame seeds are routinely ground into a butter best known as the Middle Eastern staple *tahini*, and into a drier paste that's the basis of the dense fudge-like sweet known as *halvah*. Spoonfuls of sesame paste are added to thicken Nepali sauces, salads, and chutneys—the way European cooks add breadcrumbs. The Chinese coat their fried pastries in sesame seeds. The Japanese crush toasted seeds and combine them with salt to make their signature condiment *gomashio*. Because *goma*, the Japanese word for sesame, is the most crucial ingredient to *shojin ryori*, the exquisite vegan cooking developed in Zen monasteries hundreds of years ago, a meal prepared in that tradition will frequently begin with *goma-dofu*, an ultra silky tofu made from sesame seed paste fortified by starch. The wild sesame plant is thought to be native to sub-Saharan Africa, whose peoples all called it *benne*, and brought the name and the ingredient with them on slave ships to the American South. Eastern Europeans bake sesame seeds into bagels. Moroccans sprinkle them on their breads. And, of course, today they sit like jewels on top of American hamburger buns.

The familiar white sesame seeds popular in the Western world are hulled ones, softer than those with their ecru, brown, or yellowish skin left on. The nuttier tasting, slightly smaller black sesame seeds are prized in China and Japan. It seems somehow fitting that the founding father of the vast Kagyu lineage of Buddhism, the one who unlocked the treasured teachings for the Tibetans, is known as Tilopa, which in Sanskrit means "sesame grinder."

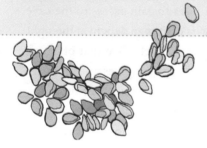

Sesame Broccoli

This nutritional bonanza features a common Korean flavor combination of soy sauce, sesame seeds, and sesame oil. Like the Japanese, Koreans have an esteemed tradition of vegetarian cooking that started in Buddhist monasteries. This vegan dish—without the garlic—would fit right in.

SERVES 4–6.

1 Tbs. white sesame seeds

1½ lb. broccoli

1 Tbs. peanut oil

2 tsp. sesame oil

2 tsp. soy sauce

2 garlic cloves, peeled and minced (optional)

▶ Lightly toast the sesame seeds in a dry frying pan over medium heat for 3–5 minutes. Cool.

▶ Cut the broccoli florets from the stems. Slice the stems on the diagonal into thin oblong pieces. Blanch these and the florets in heavily salted boiling water for 2 minutes. Immediately drain and rinse with cold water. Drain completely.

▶ In a serving bowl, combine the sesame seeds, peanut oil, sesame oil, soy sauce, and garlic (if desired). Add broccoli and toss to coat in the dressing. Put in the refrigerator to chill at least an hour. (You can make this a day ahead and chill overnight in the refrigerator.) Serve at room temperature.

Rainbow Slaw with Tangy Dressing

Here in confetti form are all the colors of autumn leaves with a hint of evergreen—and lots of bittersweet tang. In its more simple form, grated cabbage and carrot, it is the one and only Tibetan salad, known simply in that meat-based culture as *tangtse*, "cold vegetables." But what vegetables! The carrot is loaded with vision-enhancing vitamin A, the green cabbage has anti-inflammatory chemicals that calm ulcers. The red cabbage added here has powerful antioxidants that fight cancerous cells, and the bell pepper provides vitamin C.

SERVES 10–12.

SALAD

2 large carrots, peeled

1 large daikon, peeled

1 small celeriac bulb, peeled

1 small red/purple cabbage, core removed

½ small green cabbage, core removed

1 large red bell pepper, stem off and seeded

1 bunch dill, washed and finely chopped

¼ tsp. salt

½ tsp. freshly ground or cracked black pepper

DRESSING

3 garlic cloves, minced or mashed

1 tsp. dried tarragon

½ tsp. Dijon-style mustard

½ tsp. caraway seeds

½ cup vinegar; I mix balsamic vinegar, rice wine vinegar, and plain red wine vinegar (you can also use apple cider vinegar for a slightly sweeter taste)

¼ cup olive or corn oil

salt to taste

▶ With a hand grater or food processor, shred carrots, daikon, and celeriac. Combine in a large bowl and stir to blend colors.

▶ Shred or grate the two cabbages into thin, soft strips and add to the bowl.

▶ Slice red pepper into very thin strips, cut strips in half, and add to the mix. Add dill, salt, and pepper. Carefully mix everything so all colors show evenly. (Mixed vegetables can be refrigerated, covered, until ready to dress and serve.)

▶ Combine all ingredients of the dressing and whisk to blend. Pour over vegetables, stirring carefully to blend.

Raw Kale Salad

Kale is a gift to those who live in chilly climates and a traditional staple of European kitchens from Ireland to Portugal. It is about as perfect as food gets: a medicine chest packed with vitamins, iron, calcium, and minerals.

SERVES 4.

4 cups chopped curly kale (little more than half a bunch)

1 Tbs. dried cranberries

2 Tbs. pine nuts, lightly toasted

2 Tbs. currants

2 Tbs. pumpkin seeds (*pepitas*), salted and toasted

1 heaping Tbs. grated or minced lemon peel

¼ tsp. freshly ground or cracked black pepper

pinch salt

1 tsp. sesame oil

1 Tbs. fruity olive oil

2 Tbs. fresh lemon juice

½ tsp. minced fresh ginger

▶ Chop kale into bite-sized pieces and put it in a serving bowl.

▶ Combine cranberries, pine nuts, currants, pumpkin seeds, and lemon peel in a small bowl. Spread mixture over the kale. Sprinkle on black pepper and a pinch of salt.

▶ To make the dressing, combine sesame oil, olive oil, lemon juice, and ginger in a spouted cup. Let mixture sit for 5 minutes so the ginger flavors the liquids. Pour over the kale salad and serve.

Understand that a simple green has the power to become

the practice of the Buddha.

—DOGEN ZENJI, *Instructions to the Cook*

Here and There:
The World Wide Web of Food

*For most of human history, we have spent a much longer portion
of our lives worrying about food, and plotting, working, and fighting
to obtain it, than we have in any other pursuit.*
—MARGARET VISSER, *Much Depends on Dinner*

GLOBALIZATION IS NOT an amazing new twenty-first-century wonder brought to us by supersonic jets and supercharged electronics.
The worldwide ebb and flow of food is almost as ancient as the human
appetite for something tasty. Archeologists excavating along the Euphrates
in Syria found cloves in a ceramic urn at the site of a house dated to 1721
BCE. Since cloves only grow on five remote, tropical, volcanic cones in the
Pacific Ocean, that means more than a millennium before the Buddha, Con-
fucius, or Moses, without benefit of compasses, radios, or printed maps, somebody shipped from what we call the Moluccas to the Mediterranean reaches of
Mesopotamia. They must have known those tiny cloves, the dried bud of an
evergreen tree, were a mild anesthetic, a remarkable anti-inflammatory, an antibacterial agent, and a rich source of minerals and vitamins. Similarly, a huge
underground mound of amphora shards also tells archeologists that—1,700
years after those cloves were taken from those islands—Rome imported an
estimated 1.6 billion gallons of olive oil, mostly from Spain. It also imported
walnuts from Persia, pepper from southern India, spices from China, and grain
from Africa. "Roman citizens everywhere," Sara Murray says in *Moveable Feasts*,
her study of portable food, "were accustomed to the fact that what they ate had
been hauled in from all over the empire." Similarly, noodles moved from Central Asia's steppes to China, Vietnam, and Palestine. Today Basmati rice, native
to the Himalayas, is growing in Texas and California.

Humans are not naturally *locavores*, content to eat only food grown nearby.
The borderlines of the globe have been set, shifted, sabotaged, and secured by
worldwide hunger for tastes like salt (Neolithic settlements were at salt springs,

caravans trekked the Sahara trading salt ounce-for-ounce for gold, and British taxes aimed at salt starvation instigated Gandhi's successful overthrow of the Raj), coffee (carried by competing colonial powers from Ethiopia and Yemen to Central America, East Africa, and Indonesia), and sugar (transplanted from India to the Caribbean Islands, where huge plantations shipped cane back to Europe and up to North America). Bananas are native to Southeast Asia and are thought to have been first domesticated on the island of New Guinea, from which they spread to the Malaysian peninsula. Somebody who found them there liked them enough to tote a few to India, where they are mentioned in early Buddhist texts, and where Alexander the Great evidently tasted them, for around 327 BCE he sent bananas from India home with his troops to Greece. Someone not so identifiable sailed them across the Indian Ocean to Madagascar, where slave-trading Arabs happened upon these finger-like "fruits"— *banaan* is the Arabic word for finger—and took up trafficking in them as an equally lucrative enterprise. At the start of the fifteenth century, Portuguese sailors fell for the bananas Arabs had brought to Africa's west coast and turned their nearby Canary Islands into a plantation. A century later, a Portuguese monk stowed some plants on board the ship carrying him to Santo Domingo in the Caribbean. Bananas now cover a huge portion of Central American land along the Caribbean, are grown in 107 countries, and are the world's most exported fruit.

Our pantries have made all of us far more polyglot than we assume. *Gourmet* and *gourmand* are French terms my word processor recognizes as perfectly normal English, just like spaghetti, bialy, pâté, tortilla, and curry. Our English word *yogurt* is Turkish; the Japanese word for *bread* is Portuguese because the Japanese had no bread until Portuguese sailors brought theirs ashore. The words *alcohol, apricot, artichoke, candy, lemon, marzipan, orange, saffron, sesame, spinach, syrup,* and *tarragon* are essentially Arabic. Americans who think Chinese is just too foreign for words need only open the refrigerator and look at the name of their favorite tomato-based condiment, an Anglicization of the spicy Cantonese sauce *ke tsiep*.

The United States was forged in part not by religious fanatics but by highly financed fishermen feeding Catholic Europe's need for salt cod on meatless Fridays and the month of Lent. Spanish explorers didn't find the fountain of youth but those who followed them did find huge profit in using the residue from Caribbean sugar cane—and the molasses spun out of it during the refining process—to make rum. Spice also reshaped the world. "The Asian empires of Portugal, England, and the Netherlands," author/scholar Jack Turner wrote, "might be said with only a little exaggeration to have sprouted from a quest for cinnamon, cloves, pepper, nutmeg, and mace, and something similar was true of the Americas.... Columbus, Vasco da Gama, and Magellan, the three standard-bearers of the Age of Discovery, were spice seekers before they became Discoverers." Columbus sailed the ocean blue in 1492 looking for a shortcut to East Asia so the Spanish king could cut out middlemen Arabs who monopolized overland spice routes. The Italian navigator did not bring back galleons filled with gold or ginger, a profound and almost life-threatening disappointment, but he did inadvertently hit a jackpot far richer, and more world shattering than anyone suspected. The discovery of America was the discovery of potatoes, tomatoes, corn, beans, chilies, pumpkins, squashes, avocados, cassava (tapioca), quinoa, and chocolate. These foods turned out to be a nutrition bonanza, adaptable to almost every terrain and kitchen. Since they were purloined from the Americas, they have immigrated to almost every corner of the planet, and have kept most of the world alive.

Although the benchmark of authenticity in the U.S. is being as "American as apple pie," apple pie crossed the Atlantic in the cookery notes of English colonists whose "native" apples originated in the Caucasus. Potatoes aren't Irish any more than they are Russian; they come from Peru. Carrots came to Italy from Afghanistan. The salt cod that is featured on so many Caribbean menus seems to be indigenous but represents a taste acquired from Yankee traders who offloaded New England barrels of it in exchange for molasses and rum. In the long-hidden kingdom of Bhutan, nobody eats anything not slathered in chili peppers, which are native to Central America. The plethora of spinach-like greens the Chinese stir-fry were given to them by the ruler of Nepal in 647 CE; a millennium later, the British took tea from China to Nepal and turned the hill town of Darjeeling into a synonym for it. Arguably the apotheosis of all this food fusion is Italy's signature dish, spaghetti with tomato sauce. First the Romans imported olive oil and learned to plant its trees. Then the Arabs pioneered dried pasta, and several centuries later Columbus shipped home the tomato, a reddish yellow orb thought by dazzled Italians to be a golden apple: *pomodoro*.

Claims have even been made that the Mahayana Buddhist tradition of putting food on the altar of deities originated in Greek practices brought to India by Alexander the Great in the third century BCE. In Japan, red beans are called *ingenmame*, after the Zen Buddhist roshi Ingen, who brought beans to Japan from China. California became the continental capital of grape growing because Catholic missionaries from Spain had to bring vines with them in order to assure wine for Communion. The same missionaries brought wheat and olive trees to Mexico and California. If there is tofu now in unlikely places, it's because the flower children of 1960s America brought it over the Pacific from Japan alongside meditation practice, just before a tsunami of those little packages of instant ramen flooded the entire planet.

Romanian Eggplant

This dish came into my life when someone showed up at my house with it while my family was in mourning. It perked me up so much, I asked the woman to come back and teach me how to make it. It's crunchier and greener than Mediterranean eggplant salads like *baba ganoush*, and is commonly served smeared on "Jewish" rye bread. (I sold it that way once when I had a food stand at a summer fair and it drew mobs.) In Romania, eggplant used to serve as a meat substitute, inspiring dishes like "eggplant steak" on the menus of delis in New York.

SERVES 6.

1 large eggplant

½ large or 1 small green bell pepper, cut into thin strips

1 small garlic clove, peeled

¼ cup high-quality olive oil

¼ tsp. salt

▶ The eggplant can either be roasted or grilled.

▶ To roast, preheat oven to 450°F. To grill, get the fuel hot and smoky. Make 3 or 4 deep slits lengthwise in the eggplant, and wrap it tightly in aluminum foil. Roast for about 40 minutes or grill for about 30 minutes, until it feels soft all over. Either way, once it is cooked, open the foil, drain off juices that leached out, and cool.

▶ Combine eggplant, green pepper, and garlic in the bowl of a food processor and use the pulse button 4 or 5 times to coarsely chop. The green pepper pieces should remain large enough to see and have crunch. (That crunch and the salt added just before eating are the hallmarks of this dish.)

▶ Put the mix in a serving bowl. Slowly pour in olive oil, stirring to blend. Continue to add oil until it stops soaking in.

▶ Add salt to taste (the dish is meant to taste quite salty) and serve with crusty rye bread. Traditionally, this salad is salted after it is spooned onto a piece of bread.

Tell me what you eat, and I will tell you what you are.

—JEAN ANTHELME BRILLAT-SAVARIN

Sweet Potato Salad

Sweet potatoes and yams are commonly conflated or confused, one a seemingly perfect stand-in for the other. As it happens, they are quite different, each with its own botanical roots. Sweet potatoes have thinner, smoother skin, are shorter, stubbier, and more tapered than the long, cylindrical yam. They also come firm or soft, and because the soft ones often have vibrant orange flesh, they get mistaken for the common yam. Both vegetables are highly nutritious, but the sweet potato is unsurpassed for its beta-carotene content and is, well, sweeter.

SERVES 8–10.

3 orange-fleshed sweet potatoes, peeled and diced

1½ tsp. olive oil

3 navel oranges, peeled and segmented

peel of one orange, grated

1 cup pecan halves, toasted (if you prefer smaller pieces, break the halves in half)

½ cup dried cranberries

1 bunch scallions, cleaned and sliced into thin disks

GARNISH

¼ cup chopped fresh flat-leaf parsley

DRESSING

1 garlic clove, peeled and minced

½-inch piece fresh ginger, peeled and grated or minced

1 tsp. soy sauce

3 Tbs. Valencia orange juice*

¼ cup olive or vegetable oil

¼ tsp. salt

¼ tsp. freshly ground or cracked black pepper

¼ tsp. ground cinnamon

pinch ground allspice

✳ Valencia is the most sour orange juice. If you don't have Valencia oranges, add ¼ tsp. Jerez (Spanish sherry) or balsamic or cider vinegar to ordinary orange juice.

- ▶ Heat the oven or toaster oven to 400°F. Line a baking sheet with foil and spread the diced sweet potatoes on it. Coat with 1½ tsp. olive oil and roast for 30–35 minutes, until lightly toasted. Remove from oven and cool.

- ▶ While potatoes roast, make the dressing by combining all listed ingredients in a small bowl or large measuring cup and blend well. Let it sit so the flavors blend.

- ▶ When ready to serve, cut orange segments in half. Combine in a large serving bowl with sweet potatoes, orange peel, pecans, dried cranberries, and scallion.

- ▶ Pour on as much of the dressing as you like. You may not use all of it. Garnish with the chopped parsley and serve.

Good eating habits must be accompanied by good thoughts and healthy exercise. No matter how nutritious the food, it cannot be digested unless the mind's thoughts, the heart's desires and the body's well-being are sound.

—MICHAEL SASO, *A Taoist Cookbook*

Turkish Bean Salad

Turkish housewives make protein very colorful in authentic dishes like this simple one, which includes careful old-fashioned instructions to use not an ordinary permeable wooden bowl but a ceramic or glass one where vinegar is involved. The saltiness provided by capers and olives can help the body in its struggle to retain moisture on sweaty, hot summer days.

SERVES 6.

2 (15-oz). cans cannellini or great northern beans, drained

¾ cup plus 2 Tbs. wine vinegar (or plus 1 Tbs. vinegar and 1 Tbs. fresh lemon juice)

1 red onion, peeled and sliced into thin disks

¼ tsp. salt, divided

½ bunch parsley, finely chopped

freshly ground black pepper

1 large or 2 small tomatoes

12–15 pitted kalamata or other black olives

3 hard-boiled eggs, peeled

2 tsp. capers, drained

¼ cup olive oil

▶ Put beans in a ceramic or glass bowl and cover with ¾ cup of vinegar. Let them soak for 3 hours, then drain and put into a large serving bowl.

▶ Cut onion disks in half, and then half again, and then separate the rings of each quarter to make thin slivers. Put these on a plate and cover with ⅛ tsp. salt. Rub the salt into the onion, pressing. Then wash the onions and drain well.

▶ Add onion and parsley to the beans, mixing well. Add a pinch of salt and pepper to taste.

▶ Cut tomato into thin slices, cut each slice in two and decoratively place around the outside of the bowl in a circle. Use as much tomato as you need to make a full circle and toss any juices left from cutting onto the beans. Fill the center with olives.

▶ Cut eggs in half, then cut each half into three wedges. Arrange these around the center of the bowl, like flower petals reaching toward the tomato. Season with black pepper and sprinkle the capers around the top.

▶ In a small measuring cup or spouted bowl, blend 2 Tbs. vinegar, olive oil, and ⅛ tsp. salt. Pour over the salad when ready to serve.

On the Back Burner: Stovetop Cooking

When we take a meal, we enter into the process of
merging with everything that surrounds us.

—JOHN DAIDO LOORI, *The Metaphysics of Eating*

Buddha's Delight:
The Meaning of a Classic Chinese Dish

BUDDHA'S DELIGHT, the standby proudly listed in the vegetarian offerings of nearly every Chinese restaurant and take-out joint, is not exactly as ordinary as it seems. Rather than a freewheeling vegan composition of vegetables and tofu, it's actually a sacred Buddhist dish formulated centuries ago in Chinese monasteries to symbolize purity and the promise of enlightenment. The ingredients of the original creation are supposed to cleanse, charge, and purify the body the way Dharma cleans, charges, and purifies the mind. The name in Chinese, *Luohan zhai*, literally means "vegetarian food of the accomplished ones."

No matter how or where it is composed, the defining ingredient of Buddha's Delight has always been symbolism. Those sometimes maddeningly endless bean thread or cellophane noodles represent long life; bamboo shoots symbolize new chances. Carrots sliced into disks look like gold coins and signify wealth. Since its peas stay in the pod, snow peas typify unity, and the shriveled black wood-ear fungus is a reminder of longevity. Mushrooms epitomize opportunity, the multileaved cabbage prosperity. Tofu, a highly nutritious food created by the alchemy of fermentation, exemplifies blessings. The black moss, which looks like hair, is thought to be especially crucial since its name, *fat choi*, is exactly the same as the word for wealth in the common Chinese New Year greeting: *Gung hay fat choi*, "May you get rich!"

The stubborn ubiquity of this stir-fry, even in eateries that distinguish themselves as purely Szechuan, Cantonese, or Shanghainese, is testament to the flourishing of Buddhism in China for more than a millennium before the Cultural Revolution extirpated all forms of religious practice, leaving this telltale culinary remnant. On the mainland and across the worldwide Chinese diaspora, families continue to celebrate their premier ethnic and national holiday, Chinese New Year, by preparing this vegan dish. Refraining from killing on the first day of the year honors their Buddhist tradition of nonharming. The restraint reminds them of the possibility of renewal and change.

Since the Chinese consider the number eighteen to be lucky, many authentic recipes require eighteen ingredients, but nowadays nine is often a Chinese housewife's limit. Fortunately, an exact, inflexible list was never set in any monastery stone, but the apparently indispensible components are "cellophane" noodles, tofu, snow peas, water chestnuts, wood-ear mushrooms, black moss, bean curd skins (cut into sticks), and bamboo shoots. Excepting perhaps the black moss, these are the ingredients most commonly stir-fried into the Buddha's Delight of Chinese restaurants catering to foreigners. (Ironically, in recent years in locations far from the monasteries where this dish was invented, dried oysters have sneaked in.) Chinese cabbage, carrots, shiitake mushrooms, and/or peanuts may be added as further indications of the bounty of good fortune, or perhaps, more likely, of local grocers. When making this dish at home, you may want to substitute them for the harder to find or more exotic, traditional ingredients like gingko nuts, lotus root, arrowhead (an aquatic tuber), bamboo fungus, wheat gluten (*seitan*), and jujubes (red Chinese dates). Dried lily buds, also known as "golden needles" or "yellow flower vegetables," seem to be available these days on the Chinese shelf in the supermarket.

No utterly genuine recipe would include garlic, onions, leeks, or chives since eating these pungent "smelling foods" was strictly forbidden for Chinese Buddhist monks. Monastery cooks would've poured soy sauce, sesame oil, perhaps a splash of rice vinegar, or the acrid red fermented bean curd known as *sufu* or *fu shung* (sometimes called in English "Chinese cheese") into the wok for seasoning.

Buddha's Delight with rice is likely to be the main meal of New Year's Day in a majority of ethnic Chinese homes. I've been told it's also served on the first day of every month by the more devout. The profusion of dried ingredients, if diligently soaked overnight, can be assembled quickly and stir-fried in a wok while hungry revelers munch roasted melon seeds. When all eighteen traditional components are included, the dish unites the four cosmic elements that sustain human life—earth (peas, carrots, and bamboo shoots that grow out of the soil), water (moss, lotus root, and arrowhead), fire (fermented products like tofu), and air (mushrooms that depend upon the wind to spread their spores).

Buddha's Delight

1½ Tbs. corn oil

1 cube red fermented bean curd (*fu shung*) or 1 tsp. miso paste

2 oz. tofu (extra firm is good, pressed is better, sticks are most authentic), cut into thin strips

1 oz. wood-ear or shiitake mushrooms (soaked, if dried; reserve soaking water)

¾ cup dried golden needles (lily buds), soaked overnight; reserve soaking water

½ dozen peeled gingko nuts or raw, shelled peanuts

10 snow peas, cleaned

10 canned water chestnuts, drained and halved

⅓–½ cup bamboo shoots

ANY ONE OF THE FOLLOWING

¼ cup jujubes (red Chinese dates), soaked overnight and pitted; reserve soaking water

⅓ cup black Chinese moss (*fat choi*), soaked overnight; reserve soaking water

1 small lotus root, peeled and cut into thin disks

1 carrot, peeled and cut into thin disks

6.5–7 oz. cellophane noodles, soaked in boiling water for 2 minutes and drained just before you start; reserve soaking water

2 Tbs. soy sauce, or more to taste

2 Tbs. sesame oil

1 Tbs. rice cooking wine or vinegar

▶ Combine all reserved soaking water.

▶ Heat oil in a wok or large skillet over a hot flame. Add fermented bean curd or miso paste, whichever you have located, and stir to blend. Fry tofu strips for one minute till crisp.

▶ Add mushrooms, lily buds, nuts, snow peas, water chestnuts, bamboo shoots, and whichever of the final ingredients you chose. Stir-fry for 1 minute.

▶ Add noodles and ½ cup of the soaking water. Try to separate the noodles and mix into the other ingredients. Stir-fry 2–3 minutes, adding soaking water in ¼ cup increments as needed to prevent sticking or burning and create steam.

▶ Add soy sauce, sesame oil, and vinegar, stirring vigorously to blend (Chinese cooks often use a single chopstick for stirring like this). Continue to stir-fry 1–2 minutes, making sure there is always some liquid in the bottom of the pan.

continued on next page

- Remove from heat and serve.

- Nontraditionally, you can garnish with chopped fresh cilantro and or grated ginger.

While eating I meditate

and during this eating where eating is meditating

I know eating and drinking to be ritual feasting.

—JETSUN MILAREPA, *Turning Daily Behavior into a Practice*

Chickpea and Cauliflower Ragout with Okra and Apricots

Chickpeas are popular, ancient protein providers beloved across the globe from Nepal, where they're called *kabuli channa* or "dhal from Kabul," through Italy, where they're *ceci*, to Mexico, where they're known as *garbanzos*. By cheating with canned chickpeas, you can make this hearty, fragrant ragout quickly.

SERVES 8–10.

2 bay leaves

1 cinnamon stick

5 cardamom pods, cracked

6 whole cloves

12–14 whole black peppercorns

3½ cups vegetable broth

5 large garlic cloves, peeled

3-inch piece fresh ginger, peeled

4 Tbs. olive or vegetable oil

2 serrano chilies, seeded and chopped (or 1 habanero, Scotch bonnet, or tiny Thai chili, seeded and chopped, if you can't find serranos)

1 large red onion, finely chopped

½ tsp. salt

1 tsp. ground cumin

½ tsp. ground coriander

¼ tsp. ground turmeric

⅛ tsp. ground nutmeg

3 (15-oz.) cans of chickpeas (garbanzos), drained and rinsed

1 cup chopped tomatoes, in their juices

8 dried apricot halves

1 large cauliflower, cored and cut into florets

½ lb. okra, halved lengthwise

juice of 1 lime

¼ cup chopped fresh mint

¼ cup chopped fresh flat-leaf or curly parsley

▶ Combine the bay leaves, cinnamon stick, cardamom pods, cloves, and peppercorns in a piece of cheesecloth, a spice bag, or perhaps a tea leaf filter bag, and tie it tightly with non-plastic string.

▶ Put the spice bag in the bottom of a large casserole or medium soup pot. Add the vegetable broth. Cover, and simmer on medium heat for 10–12 minutes.

▶ In a mini food processor, or by hand, chop and blend the garlic and ginger into a paste.

continued on next page

- Heat a medium skillet and add the olive oil. When it is hot, add the garlic/ginger paste, serrano chilies, and diced onion. Brown over medium heat for about 5 minutes. Add salt, cumin, coriander, turmeric, and nutmeg. Stir-fry 1 minute until mixture is fragrant.

- Pour this onion mix into the broth, carefully stirring as you do. Add chickpeas, tomatoes, and apricots. Cook uncovered over medium heat for 5 minutes. Add cauliflower and continue cooking until it is almost tender, 5–8 minutes.

- Add okra and continue cooking 5 minutes.

- Remove the spice bag. Add the lime juice. Taste and adjust salt. Garnish with mint and parsley and serve over couscous or quinoa, perhaps with a yogurt condiment such as one of those from the *achar* part of the Dhal Bhat section.

- This tastes even better the next day, especially if you leave the spice bag in overnight.

Good living is an act of intelligence,

by which we choose things which have an agreeable taste

rather than those which do not.

—Jean Anthelme Brillat-Savarin

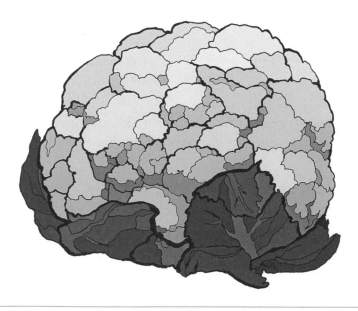

Gnocchi with Fava Bean Puree: A Spring Fling from Apulia

The people in the bottom of the boot of Italy may be economically down at the heels but they know how to eat well for nothing but a little effort. They have a genius for combining very simple, earthy foods into highly nutritious and surprisingly delicious meals. They are particularly skillful with protein-packed fava beans, sometimes combining them mashed with chicory greens and cheese for a luscious lunch, or in the way shown here, as sauce for potatoes transformed into gnocchi.

SERVES 8.

GNOCCHI

(You can buy fresh gnocchi in lieu of making it yourself.)

3 large russet baking potatoes (approximately 3 lb.)

2 cups all-purpose or durum/semolina flour

4 oz. pecorino or Parmesan cheese, grated

⅓ cup finely chopped fresh chives

⅛ tsp. salt

1 egg

FAVA BEAN PUREE

3 cups shelled fava (broad) beans* (about 3½ lb. of pods)

5 Tbs. high-quality olive oil, divided

1 medium onion, peeled and diced

4 garlic cloves, peeled and minced

¼ tsp. freshly ground or cracked black pepper

1 cup or handful of a chopped fresh bitter green like dandelion, chicory, or arugula

2½ cups vegetable broth

¼ tsp. salt, or to taste

1 Tbs. fresh lemon juice

GARNISH

½ cup chopped fresh flat-leaf parsley

✳ Try to buy freshly picked, small-pod beans to save labor, because as fava beans age on the vine and enlarge inside the pod (that is itself growing bigger and fuzzier), each develops its own individual casing. This has to be removed by a second, very tedious round of peeling. You can also avoid all of that by using a 30–32 oz. can of cooked fava beans. These are dried beans that, having been rehydrated through boiling, look like brown peas. They will slightly change the color and taste of the puree but using them will simplify and speed the preparation of an equally delicious dish.

▶ Boil potatoes whole in a large pot until they are soft to the touch, about 40 minutes. Drain and, while still warm, peel and grate or pass through a ricer into a large bowl or pasta board.

▶ Fill a large pasta or soup pot ⅔ with water, cover, and bring to a boil over high heat.

▶ Make a well in the center of the potatoes. Cover everything evenly with flour, then cheese. Add the chives. Put salt in the center of the well, then the raw egg. Using a fork, stir the egg into the flour and potato until dough starts to form. Then, using your hands (which you may want to glove), knead gently until you have a ball of dough. Continue to knead until the dough is no longer sticky, about 3–4 minutes. Add a Tbs. of flour at a time, if it continues to feel sticky.

▶ Break the dough ball into smaller balls, each about the size of an ice cream scoop or tennis ball. Roll these each into a snake about ¾ inch thick. Using a fork's tines, cut off pieces about ½–1 inch long and drop them into the boiling water.

▶ Cook until they float (1–2 minutes). Remove and keep warm on a covered plate.

▶ If you want to store these for a day, immediately put them into a large bowl of iced water for a few minutes, then drain and put in a large shallow dish. Pour ½ cup light olive or canola oil over them and cover tightly. Keep in the refrigerator. Reheat in salted boiling water for 1 minute.

▶ If using fresh beans, shell them and blanch the beans in boiling water for 1 minute. Drain and rinse with cold water. If the beans are large like lima beans and have a light green covering, you will have to remove the covering bean by bean at this point to release the rich green bean inside. (Hint: squeeze it and the bean should emerge.)

▶ If using canned beans, drain and rinse.

▶ In a large skillet, heat 2 Tbs. olive oil over medium-high heat. Add onion and sauté until it is soft and translucent. Add garlic and black pepper and continue to sauté for 30 seconds.

▶ Reduce heat to medium. Add the greens and beans, mix well, and continue to sauté until these are hot, a minute or two. Add broth and continue to cook for 5 minutes. Stir in salt and lemon juice and remove from heat.

▶ Pour the skillet contents into a food processor or blender and puree. Add 3 Tbs. olive oil and blend. Taste and adjust for salt.

TO SERVE

▶ Spoon enough hot puree to thickly cover the bottom of a shallow soup bowl, season with a turn of the pepper mill, and place 6–8 gnocchi in the center. Drizzle your finest olive oil over everything and lightly sprinkle chopped parsley.

▶ Serve with a bowl of black olives, a green salad, a platter of cheeses, and crusty bread.

Imam Bayildi

The name of this classic Turkish eggplant dish literally means "the imam fainted." The rumors as to why are legion: the cleric fainted from the sublime taste, or when he realized how much expensive olive oil had been used on his behalf, or from sheer delight at the extravagant food put before him at somebody else's expense.

SERVES 8.

4 small eggplants, the large Japanese kind work fine (about 1½–1¾ lb.)

Salt

¼ cup olive oil

¼ cup plus 2 Tbs. high-quality olive oil

2 medium onions, peeled, halved lengthwise, and thinly sliced

6 large garlic cloves, peeled and minced

2 ripe tomatoes, peeled and chopped

¼ cup chopped fresh parsley (about ⅓ bunch)

2 Tbs. chopped fresh dill

¼ tsp. freshly ground black pepper

juice of ½ lemon

▶ Cut stems off eggplants and peel strips of skin off at 1-inch intervals, for a striped effect. Cut each eggplant in half lengthwise. Make a deep slit lengthwise through the fleshy side of the eggplant (the non-skin side), being careful not to cut all the way through and puncture the skin. If any of the halves do not lie perfectly flat on the skin side, slice off a tiny, thin piece so they do. Salt the exposed flesh, turn upside down and drain on paper towels for 30 minutes. Rinse and dry.

▶ In a very large skillet, heat the ordinary olive oil over high heat until it's crackling or smoking. Put in the eggplants, flesh side down, and fry until golden brown, about 4–6 minutes depending on heat capacity, burner size, and size of pan. Remove and drain on paper towels. Lightly salt.

▶ In the same skillet, heat ¼ cup high-quality olive oil over medium-high heat. Add onions and garlic. Sauté, stirring frequently, until the onions are soft and translucent, about 5 minutes.

▶ Pour the contents of the skillet into a medium bowl. Add tomatoes, parsley, dill, pepper, pinch of salt, and 1 Tbs. high-quality olive oil. Blend well.

- ▶ Arrange eggplant halves slit side up in the skillet. Carefully stuff each slit with as much onion mixture as you can and then cover all exposed eggplant with it. Sprinkle lemon juice over all eggplants.

- ▶ Put 1 Tbs. high-quality olive oil into the skillet. Add ½–¾ cup water, enough to cover the entire bottom so nothing will burn.

- ▶ Cover the skillet (use foil or a cookie sheet if you have no lid) and simmer over low heat until eggplants are soft, about 50–65 minutes. Check every 10–15 minutes, adding water if necessary.

- ▶ Cool to room temperature. Pour any remaining skillet juices over the eggplants to serve.

To Romans, such as Cicero, how and what you ate were issues of the utmost ethical importance. Diet was a yardstick of, and in some sense shaped, moral worth.

—JACK TURNER, *Spice: The History of a Temptation*

Perfecting Perception:
Chocolate as Dharma Practice

BY ARI GOLDFIELD OF WISDOM SUN

ON THIS PATH of wisdom that the Buddha taught, that you come to know for yourself as true, we are encouraged to look at what we perceive…to look into our circumstances using something that is called pure perception, direct perception, to find out the difference between what appears and what is real. The way this practice works is that we take a look at how our sense consciousnesses perceive something and see the difference between what we actually perceive and what we think we perceive.

One very good way to practice direct perception is eating. You can rest in the inexpressible experience of pure taste. Chocolate is a great tool for this. When you think about the experience of eating chocolate, it is ultimately indescribable. What I mean is, suppose you are eating chocolate and somebody who has never eaten chocolate before asks you: "What is it like to eat chocolate?" and you say: "Well, it's rich. It's creamy. It's sweet." Then the other person asks: "But what is rich, creamy, and sweet like? What are they actually?"

Now you have to move from ordinary language to what in Tibetan is called *nyong tsik*, meaning "experiential vocabulary," because you can only say something like: "Mmmmmm, that's what it's like." We are leaving ordinary words and getting closer to the experience itself. It is still not the experience itself, however, because if this person then asks, "Well, what is *Mmmmm*? What's that like?" at this point you cannot answer. And that is where you are in the essence of the experience of eating chocolate, beyond words, beyond thoughts' ability to conceive. Beyond the reach of thinking is the actual experience of eating. And when you rest in that inexpressible experience, you are free of judgment, free of shame or embarrassment, free of any clinging at all. So it is an experience of eating that is inexpressibly relaxed and delightful.

Moroccan Squash, Sweet Potato, and Lentil Tagine

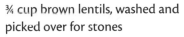

Aroma and vivid color make this one of my most popular recipes. It's brimming with vitamins, minerals, even a bit of protein from the lentils and iron from the raisins.

SERVES 6.

¾ cup brown lentils, washed and picked over for stones

2 whole cloves

2 Tbs. butter

3 Tbs. olive oil

3 garlic cloves, peeled and minced

1 large red onion, peeled and diced

1 cinnamon stick

1 tsp. ground ginger

1 tsp. ground turmeric

½ tsp. ground cumin

¼ tsp. ground cayenne

2 Roma tomatoes, diced

¼ tsp. salt

2 cups vegetable broth

⅛ tsp. saffron

¼ tsp. orange flower water or orange peel finely grated

1 small butternut squash, peeled, seeded, and cubed

2 medium red sweet potatoes, peeled and cubed

¼ cup dark raisins

▶ Put the lentils and cloves in a small saucepan and cover with 3 cups salted water. Bring to a boil over medium-high heat. Reduce heat to medium and cook 20 minutes, skimming off any foam. Remove from heat and drain. Remove cloves.

▶ Combine the butter and olive oil in a medium heavy-gauge casserole and heat over medium heat until the butter melts. Add the garlic and cook for 30 seconds. Add the onion, stir, and cook another 30 seconds. Add the cinnamon stick, ginger, turmeric, cumin, and cayenne, stirring to blend. Continue to sauté over medium heat until the onion is soft.

▶ Add the tomatoes and salt. Cook another minute over medium-low heat.

▶ Add the vegetable broth, the saffron, and the orange flower water or peel. Increase heat to medium and bring to a boil. Add the squash, sweet potato, raisins, and lentils. Cover and simmer on medium-low heat for 20 minutes or until the squash is tender.

▶ Remove from heat and stir in cilantro. Serve with pine nut–studded couscous.

Maghreb Couscous
with Seven Vegetables

Couscous with meats, sweets, and vegetables is one of the most traditional and legendary dishes of North Africa. The specific dish "couscous with seven vegetables" comes from the glorious Moroccan city of Fez, where seven is considered a lucky number. Perhaps that's why grand preparations have seven components: dairy (butter), spices, vegetables, meats, sweets (raisins), heat (*harissa*, a fiery tomato paste), plus the couscous itself. This particular meatless version blends Tunisian and Moroccan recipes.

SERVES 8–10.

4 Tbs. butter or ghee

2 onions, peeled and quartered

2 cinnamon sticks

½ tsp. ground turmeric

⅛ tsp. saffron, pulverized

¼ tsp. allspice

2 tsp. freshly ground or cracked black pepper

1 chili pepper, seeded and diced

4 tomatoes, blanched and skinned

1 tsp. salt

⅓ cup fresh parsley and cilantro, mixed, not chopped

1 lb. turnips, peeled and sliced into disks

1 lb. carrots, peeled and cut into 1½-inch lengths

1 quart vegetable broth

1 lb. zucchini, about 4 medium squashes

1 (15-oz.) can cooked fava beans, brown beans, or chickpeas

¼ cup raisins, preferably dark for color contrast

4 Tbs. mashed pumpkin

1 lb. couscous (packaged is okay)

► In a large heavy-gauge casserole or soup pot, melt the butter or ghee over medium heat. Add onions, cinnamon, turmeric, saffron, allspice, black pepper, chili pepper, tomatoes, salt, and parsley and cilantro. Sauté 10 minutes, shaking the pot a few times so the butter touches everything.

► Add turnips, carrots, and vegetable broth. Bring to a boil, then reduce heat to simmer and cover. Simmer 30 minutes.

► Add zucchini, cooked beans, and raisins. Cover and continue simmering 20 minutes. Stir in mashed pumpkin (this slightly thickens the broth). Cover and simmer 10 more minutes.

- Prepare couscous according to package instructions.

- Mound couscous on a very large serving platter. Press a well in the center and fill it with the vegetables removed from the pot with a slotted spoon to drain them. Ladle broth over the whole platter and serve. (Note: if there is too much broth, pour some into a gravy boat to serve on the side.)

A word about one of the most mysterious things in Morocco . . . a kind of magic called kimia. Kimia, according to those who know, is the power to multiply food. Thus a person with kimia can live on very little; if a man has some couscous and kimia he can presumably multiply his couscous into as much of that grain as he will need in his lifetime, and even into everything else he needs to eat. . . . Kimia is something very personal, something that lies between the person who has it and the universe.

—Paula Wolfert

Peruvian Black Bean and Purple Potato Stew

Serve this dish over quinoa, another gift from Peru, with guacamole and cornbread or tortillas. Or serve it over cornmeal in any of its forms. End the feast with chocolate, and complete this celebration of New World foods.

SERVES 6–8.

2 Tbs. corn oil

1 large onion, peeled and diced

3 large garlic cloves, peeled and minced

2 serrano chilies, seeded and minced

1 poblano pepper, roasted and peeled

2 tsp. ground cumin

½ tsp. ground coriander

1 tsp. dried oregano

2 (15-oz.) cans black beans, drained

2 cups chopped tomatoes in their juices

3 medium-large purple potatoes, peeled and cut into bite-sized pieces

2 cups winter squash (pumpkin, kabocha, butternut, acorn, or red kuri), peeled and cut into bite-sized pieces

⅛ tsp. chipotle chili powder

1 tsp. salt

1 tsp. Jerez (Spanish sherry) or balsamic vinegar

GARNISH

2 Tbs. roasted spiced pumpkin seeds (*pepitas*)

½ cup chopped cilantro

1 cup queso blanco or crumbled feta or ricotta (optional)

▶ Heat oil in the bottom of a large heavy-gauge casserole or soup pot. Add onion and sauté over medium heat 3–5 minutes until it is soft and translucent. Add garlic and peppers. Cook for 2 minutes. Stir in cumin, coriander, and oregano.

▶ Add black beans, tomato, potatoes, squash, chipotle, salt, 2 cups water, and vinegar. Stir to blend everything. Cover and simmer on low heat about 15–20 minutes or until potatoes and squash are tender.

▶ To serve, garnish with pumpkin seeds, cilantro, and crumbed white cheese.

The Incas also had folk wisdom about dietary needs that has been confirmed by modern research. They knew how to combine plants foods to make up for the lack of protein and other nutrients in corn.... The technique of soaking dried corn in water with lime or ashes to peel and soften the corn has been shown to add calcium to it.

—MARIA BAEZ KIJAC, *The South American Table*

Taking "Eat" out of "Meat"

I did not stop eating roast chicken because that was better for me.
I did it because it was better for the chicken.
—ISAAC BASHEVIS SINGER

IT SEEMS to have been easier for Shakyamuni Buddha to reach the firmament of enlightenment than to reach a firm decision on whether or not it is acceptable for a Buddhist—or any human being—to eat meat. His direct quotes in the tales and teachings handed down from his lifetime, as well as in the biographies that followed, conflict with each other on this issue—as, it seems, some of his disciples still do. Nobody denies the Buddha did at times consume animal flesh. Although the story has been questioned, he died supposedly from eating tainted pork rather than distress an innocent host who intended to present a respectful offering. Yet he is quoted in the sutras advising his disciples to restrain all carnivorous urges because meat can only be obtained from a dead animal, and the first precept of Buddhism is to not kill. When asked what he actually believed, the Buddha said: "Abandon every evil deed, practice virtue well, perfectly subdue your mind: this is Buddha's teaching." Elsewhere he added: "Whatever in the other traditions accords with Dharma is to be respected as my teaching."

As it happens, the India Shakyamuni Buddha inhabited was predominately vegetarian because meat was costly. With a tradition of vegetarianism to sustain them, the pious did not find it difficult to give up what scraps of meat they ate from time to time. The same held true in the southern countries to which the Buddha's teachings first spread: in Burma, to this day, the devout let shopkeepers crack their eggs so they themselves do no harm. But China was another culture altogether, a country of voracious omnivores. Not surprisingly, it is the sutras written in China a millennium after the Buddha died that put into his mouth very definite, dire karmic warnings about the horrors of eating animals. "Meat consumption is the source of many evils," he preaches in the

Lankavatara Sutra. "It is wholly destitute of virtues. It is not the food on which the wise sustain themselves. How could I permit my followers to taste of such unwholesome and unfitting nourishment as meat and blood?" That is the question still asked about Tibetan Buddhists, so pious and yet great consumers of meat, lots and lots of meat.

As the cultural anthropologist Marvin Harris pointed out, "Buddhist principles are flexible." Their maddening equivocation in this case may, though, be "accidently on purpose," to give us something meaty to chew on. Shakyamuni Buddha was not a giver of laws, so the precepts of Buddhism are not akin to the commandments of Moses or the edicts of Mohammed. The Buddha claimed only to be a teacher, a spiritual trekking guide able to provide direction and footing. Although this irritates fundamentalists and other certainty-zealots, the Buddha took that stance because his great insight was that one-size-fits-all dictates can't change hearts and minds as long as there are huge variables in the way human beings function. Since we all peer at the world through our own custom-crafted lenses, there is no single certainty about the way we see things and thus no guaranteed one-size-fits-all idea. To reach, open, and liberate differing minds, the Buddha, like a doctor prescribing medicine, consequently gave thousands of different teachings that seem as contradictory and flexible as people but actually say one thing: watch what you are doing.

Some disciples consequently detect in this pragmatic Buddha's teachings three or perhaps four subtle steps to the abolition of meat eating. The first acknowledges, as Marvin Harris puts it, "…animal food plays a special role in the nutritional physiology of our species…. We seem to have descended from a long line of meat-hungry animals." Humans cannot live by bread alone because meat (which includes fowl and fish) efficiently provides missing proteins and essential amino acids. Consequently the first of the Buddha's gradual steps is to at least avoid certain animals of more benefit in other ways: the horse, cow, elephant, camel, dog, cat. He also prohibited monks from eating apes, monkeys, tigers, water birds, hawks, and owls. And he moved to abolish India's widespread tradition of animal sacrifice to please the gods, insisting that gods are not pleased by some of their creatures happily killing other ones. In all, this first step is to minimize the harmful impact of a physical need.

The second step is the *threefold purity.* The Buddha declared that if you eat meat that you did not see, hear, or order killed for yourself—meat you did not willingly and knowingly have murdered for your meal—you will not be afflicted by the negative karma of the killing. This grace is not meant for supermarket shoppers buffeted by the winds of convenience but for those caught in circumstances beyond their control, especially the disciples of the Buddha who found themselves in this predicament every morning as a result of their alms rounds. Monks were required to seek food as charity from local people, most of whom were barely scraping by themselves, so a tidbit of meat set atop a mound of rice was generously offered as a sign of respect. Rejection would have devastated the donor and denied the merit of the offering. The Buddha therefore taught that, when faced with a choice between harms, it's better to accept what's offered without fuss or moral drama. This practice of recognizing the intention behind the offering works to maximize generosity.

The next step delineates the difference between those times you can't avoid eating meat—the times you have to—and those times you just *want* to. After all, it's tasty, nutritious, and efficient. All habits die hard, putting up notorious resistance, and eating habits die the hardest of all. It's silly to belittle immigrants whose suitcases are full of their native food when POWs have died rather than eat the weird food of their captors and great gurus who have climbed many rungs of the bodhisattva's ladder to buddhahood and who are admirably close to omniscience consistently turn out to be stuck in old habits at meal time. A very venerated Tibetan teacher I cooked for kept sending back the salads and vegetables in favor of more meat, the fattier the better. He also indulged in bread with lots of butter and mounds of rice, passing on fruits. Like many of his peers raised on a Tibetan diet, he was diabetic and suffered from high blood pressure. So every time I made the meals he wanted, I stealthily pureed vegetables into the meat gravy, praying that his ticking time bomb of a diet wouldn't prematurely blow away our access to his spiritual wisdom. But in fact it did explode and we almost lost him.

The Buddha's advice on how to break the habit of eating meat was that, to change what gets into your stomach, you first have to change what comes into your mind. Buddhist mind training is the reverse of military brainwashing that makes the enemy inhuman. Its aim is to provoke profound disgust at the thought of killing or eating another living creature by making you feel a bond with it. Through the practice of *lojong*, mind training, you teach yourself to perceive all creatures spinning in samsara beside you, from ants to zebras, as endless reincarnations of past beings, some of whom in your own past being could have been your mother or your child, beloved relatives you wouldn't dream of killing. Gradually you develop unshakable compassion for all beings as relatives and as imprisoned by their own suffering as you are.

This unbreakable connection is the goal, the aspiration. Like wanting to go to Boston from Los Angeles, you have to start where you are and work your way forward, mile after mile, step by step. There will be stops, detours, and breakdowns, but the destination can be reached if you never lose the intention to get there, and as Dzigar Kongtrul Rinpoche likes to say: "The only thing you are truly 100 percent in charge of in this world is your intention." The vegetarianism of Chinese Buddhist monks was a deliberate display of the final goal so that lay Buddhists and ordinary folks didn't lose sight of their intention to eventually reach it, even if only by a lengthy detour. And Chinese people managed to take progressive steps toward avoiding meat. Many still do not eat it on the first day of the New Year, some refrain on the first day of a new month, and those with deep Buddhist roots won't eat it on the sacred fifteenth day of the month either. Tibetans display their aspiration through the practice of "life release," which ranges from annually setting free a yak adorned with special *do not touch* markings to purchasing live birds or fresh caught fish for the specific purpose of putting them back in the wild they were snatched from. My teacher participated in two lobster releases on the coast of Maine.

These activities from restraint to release serve as reminders of the harm we do. Since we are the only creatures on earth able to comprehend the connection between cause and effect, paying careful attention to our eating habits gets to the essence of Buddhism and thus becomes the final step. His Holiness the Seventeenth Karmapa, Ogyen Trinley Dorje, has suggested since we eat three meals a day, seven days a week, fifty-two weeks a year, we have over 1,000 annual chances for change. We could start by eliminating meat from just one meal a week. When that has become an unquestioned habit, progress to two meals a week, then three…advancing onward through time toward the goal of a vegetarian diet normal to the mind and supportive to the body. Even if we don't achieve the goal in this lifetime, every reduction in the demand for meat would reverberate in a reduced need to slaughter animals, because transforming one thing inevitably transforms another. "Fruition," His Eminence Tai Situ Rinpoche says, "is not something that happens with a bang, but is a continuous step-by-step process. . . . Today's practice is tomorrow's fruition."

The permission to eat meat and fish is a teaching that is to be interpreted. For the Buddha declared that if he had forbidden meat from the very start, there were some who would never have entered the teachings. It is with skill, therefore, that he only gradually excluded it. On the other hand, as an antidote for those who claim that the mere abstention from meat is their great and all-sufficient practice, the Buddha declared the contrary by saying that meat eating does not constitute a hindrance on the path. He said this to put straight those who considered that they were superior on account of being vegetarians.

—POTAWA, *The Precious Heap*

Root Vegetable Potpie
with a Polenta Crust

This is about as low as you can go on the food chain: a bunch of roots. I started bringing them together in autumn over two decades ago as a reminder that the earth is packed with nutritious underground edibles, from pungent *Alliums* (good sources of cysteine sulfoxide, an antibacterial amino acid) and flamboyant beets (which are full of folate) to starchy tubers like the yam (a provider of omega-3 fatty acids and potassium). In this potpie, I combined only fifteen of the dozens "down under." The creation turned out to be startlingly and enduringly popular. Dinner guests are impressed by the surprising variety of ingredients, vivid colors, and unique flavor of each bulb or rhizome—something they never realized. Two friends, one in Maine and one from Spain, now make this regularly, sometimes adding jicama or Jerusalem artichoke, proselytizing for roots when they serve it.

SERVES 6.

FILLING

3 Tbs. olive oil or peanut oil

4 large garlic cloves, peeled and minced

2-inch piece fresh ginger, peeled and minced

⅛ tsp. freshly ground black pepper

½ tsp. ground turmeric (also a rhizome!)

1 shallot, peeled and thinly sliced

1 large onion, peeled, sliced into thin disks, then quartered

1 leek, washed and cut into ½-inch disks

1 tsp. ground coriander

¼ tsp. chipotle chili powder or smoked paprika

2 tsp. dried marjoram

1 small rutabaga, peeled and coarsely chopped into bite-sized pieces

1 white turnip, peeled and chopped into bite-sized pieces

3 carrots, peeled and cut crosswise into 1-inch pieces

1 parsnip, peeled and cut into ½-inch disks

1 sweet potato, peeled and sliced into thin disks

1 small daikon, peeled and cut into thin disks

1 small celeriac bulb, peeled and coarsely chopped

6 purple or red round potatoes, washed and quartered

1 tsp. salt

1½ cups vegetable broth or water

½ cup chopped tomatoes

continued on next page

½ cup chopped fresh parsley

CRUST

1 tsp. salt

1 cup dried polenta meal

2 Tbs. plus 1 tsp. butter

½ cup buttermilk

¼ cup grated Parmesan, Romano, or Asiago cheese

pinch ground nutmeg

▶ Heat the oil in a large casserole or small soup pot over medium heat. Add the garlic, ginger, black pepper, and turmeric and stir-fry for 30 seconds. Add the shallot, onion, and leek. Sauté for 3–5 minutes until soft. They will be colored by the turmeric.

▶ Stir in ground coriander, chipotle or smoked paprika, and marjoram. Put remaining root vegetables in the pot. Add salt and broth or water. Raise heat to a boil. Cover, lower heat to simmer, and cook 20 minutes.

▶ Preheat oven to 350°F.

▶ While vegetables simmer, boil 4 cups of water and 1 tsp. salt in a large saucepan. Gradually stir in polenta and 2 Tbs. of butter; stir rapidly to blend, so the polenta doesn't lump up. Continue stirring and cooking the polenta for 4–5 minutes, until it starts to release large bubbles. Remove from heat and stir in buttermilk.

▶ Stir tomatoes and chopped parsley into the vegetables.

▶ Fill a large ovenproof casserole or deep-dish pie pan with the vegetables and their juice, leaving about ¼ inch at the top. Using a large kitchen spoon, spoon the polenta over the top to create a crust, up to ½-inch thick. Be sure to cover the edges and smoothe the top.

▶ Cut the tsp. of butter into tiny pieces and scatter on top of the cooked polenta. Sprinkle on the cheese and the pinch of nutmeg.

▶ Put the potpie in the center of the oven and put a large cookie sheet on the rack below it to catch any spills. Cook for 20–30 minutes, until the top starts to brown and crisp. Remove and let it cool for 5–10 minutes before serving.

▶ Serve with a plain green salad or the Raw Kale Salad on page 21.

A balanced and skillful approach to life, taking care to avoid extremes,

becomes a very important factor in conducting one's everyday life.

—THE DALAI LAMA

Sonia's Vegetable Paella

Although tourists come away from her country certain *paella* means "seafood and rice," my friend Sonia says in Spain it merely means a distinct way of combining rice with other ingredients in a specific pan. She herself can make myriad varieties, but when she gets homesick in San Francisco for her family and their thriving food business outside Barcelona, this is the cozy version she makes. Back home, her family joins forks and sits around the table eating it together right out of the pan.

In Spain Sonia uses fava beans fresh from the garden; here she resorts to canned or frozen lima beans. The artichoke, she says, is indispensible, and too much tomato "robs the flavor." As for that delicate flavor, she keeps a stash of authentic paella rice because "it's what I know, what we've always used at home, what makes this dish taste so good. It's rice you can cook quickly and serve al dente. You have to be careful about that, not overcooking it. This is a dish you make fast."

SERVES 3–4.

4 cups plus 1 Tbs. vegetable broth

2 Tbs. olive oil

2 medium red bell peppers, finely diced

1 artichoke, outer leaves stripped, stem off

1 shallot, peeled and diced

8–10 small asparagus spears or ½ lb. green beans, chopped into 1-inch pieces

2 bay leaves

1 medium tomato, grated (should be a juicy one)

¼ tsp. freshly ground black pepper

4 garlic cloves, minced, divided

1¼ cup Spanish paella rice or short-grain white rice, not starchy

1½ tsp. smoked paprika*

4–5 threads of saffron

½ cup cooked lima or baby fava beans

½ cup peas

¼ cup chopped fresh parsley

2 tsp. salt

1 roasted red pepper, skinned and sliced into thin strips

GARNISH

lemon wedges (optional)

✳ This is a Spanish flavoring that comes in a square tin can becoming prevalent in gourmet markets. If you can't find it, don't worry. Substitute ½ tsp. chipotle chili powder and 1 tsp. Hungarian paprika, which is more widely available.

- ▶ Boil the broth in a large saucepan.

- ▶ In a medium paella pan or flat-bottom sauté pan of similar round shape, heat the oil over medium heat. Add diced red pepper and sauté for 3–5 minutes, lowering heat if it starts to brown.

- ▶ Be sure all the hard outer leaves are off the artichoke and quarter the heart. Remove and discard the hairy choke on all pieces and coarsely chop them. Add to the pan, stirring as you do. Add shallot and asparagus or green beans, stirring.

- ▶ Add bay leaves, tomato pulp, black pepper, and half of the garlic, stirring. Add the rice and smoked paprika, continually stirring. Add the hot broth, saving 1 Tbs., and then the saffron. Stir once to incorporate everything and let the paella cook for 15 minutes over medium heat.

- ▶ Add the beans and peas on top.

- ▶ Combine the remaining garlic, the parsley, and the remaining Tbs. of broth in a small food processor or blender and make a thin puree. Pour over the paella and add a pinch of freshly ground black pepper. Carefully stir to blend and turn off the heat. Remove bay leaves. Test for salt and adjust to taste.

- ▶ Let the paella sit and steam for another 5 minutes while garnishing with the roasted pepper strips, arranging them like the spokes of a wheel, and optional lemon wedges standing up around the outer edge. Serve immediately.

Wild Rice with Mandarins, Cranberries, and Pecans

True wild rice from the lakes of Minnesota is thought to be the most nutritious of all the foods eaten by the original Americans. It is still sacred to the Chippewa, who celebrate the fall harvest with a huge festival. This particular dish is a favorite for Thanksgiving and the December holiday season.

SERVES 6.

4 cups cooked wild rice (can be hot from the pot or room temperature)

1 cup toasted pecan halves (can be warm or room temperature)

2 seedless mandarins or clementines, peeled and segmented

½ cup fresh cranberries, or 2 Tbs. dried cranberries

½ tsp. orange juice or ⅛ tsp. orange flower water

1 tsp. raspberry vinegar or Spanish sherry vinegar

¼ cup fruity olive oil or walnut oil

⅛ tsp. salt

⅓ cup chopped fresh parsley (about 6 sprigs)

▶ Combine wild rice, toasted pecans, citrus segments, and cranberries in a serving bowl.

▶ In a small bowl or cup, combine orange juice or flower water, vinegar, oil, and salt. Whip to blend.

▶ Pour the dressing over the rice mixture and carefully blend. Garnish with chopped parsley. Serve warm or cold.

From the Frying Pan

So when you make an effort to eat mindfully . . .
you find that life is worth much more than you
had expected. . . . You find that life is more sacred. . . .
People found the same thing two thousand
five hundred years ago. They found it and they taught
it to us, and now we are discovering it ourselves.

—CHÖGYAM TRUNGPA RINPOCHE

Arepas: Venezuelan Corncakes

With white cornmeal, *arepas* can also be made into thin pancakes much like Rhode Island johnnycakes. If you toss a handful of wild rice into the batter, you will have Chippewa johnnycakes. If you put a handful of cooked black beans in, you will have the Cherokee version.

SERVES 2; MAKES 4 CAKES.

1 cup precooked, instant cornmeal such as *masarepa* or Harina P.A.N. (white is traditional but yellow works fine too)

½ tsp. salt

½ tsp. chipotle or other chili powder (optional)

1–2 Tbs. grated Parmesan, manchego, or other dry salty cheese (optional)

½ Tbs. butter for frying, divided

▶ Preheat oven or toaster oven to 350°F . Bring 1½ cups water to a boil.

▶ Combine cornmeal, salt, and chili powder (if desired) in a medium bowl. Form dough by pouring the boiling water in a steady thin stream, mixing continually with a fork to prevent lumps from forming. Once dough has formed, mix in the cheese (if desired).

▶ Knead dough 2–3 minutes. Then cover and let rest 10 minutes.

▶ Divide into 4 equal pieces. Roll each into a ball. Flatten each ball into a patty about 2½ inches in diameter and 1 inch thick.

▶ Coat a flat-bottom skillet or frying pan with half the butter. Heat over high heat. Put in the cornmeal patties and fry about 90 seconds or until they get a crust on the bottom. Add the remaining butter and flip the patties. Fry another 90 seconds or until crusty. Remove from skillet and put into oven for 15 minutes.

▶ Serve warm. Sometimes in Venezuela, these are cut in half and stuffed with cheese or peppers or slices of avocado.

continued on next page

Variation: Pancakes

► Divide the dough into 6 or 8 equal pieces. Roll into a ball and flatten into a pancake. Fry in butter for 90 seconds on each side and serve warm with a side of beans and scrambled eggs.

Preparing food is like a craft, like painting a picture,

or making a pot. There's a feeling that really goes into it.

—AGNES DILL, Zuni pueblo leader

Barra:
Newari Mung Bean Pancakes

The Newars, thought to be the original inhabitants of Kathmandu, developed a gracefully nutritious vegetarian cuisine, distinct from other Nepalese and Indian food. Although it is still alive and popular in Kathmandu today, you cannot find their tasty cooking elsewhere—unless you have Newari émigré friends as I so luckily do.

These low-calorie, high-protein pancakes can be eaten with yogurt spiced with nutmeg or cinnamon, or topped with tomato *achar* (page 252), or used as the base of Newari pizza: topped with a sunny-side-up egg.

SERVES 4; MAKES 8 PANCAKES.

1 cup mung beans or split black dhal, soaked at least 6 hours

2 garlic cloves, peeled and minced

¼-inch piece fresh ginger, peeled and minced

½ tsp. ground cumin

¼ tsp. ground coriander

¼ tsp. chili powder

½ tsp. salt

1 small onion, finely diced

1 small-medium tomato, seeded and diced

2 Tbs. olive or canola oil, divided

½ red potato, washed and cut in half

1 egg per pancake (optional)

▶ Before draining the soaked mung beans, run your fingers over them to release some of the skins. This will leave some yellow beans and some green ones—which is perfect. Drain beans and remove discarded skins. Rinse beans again and drain. Carefully grind beans to a paste in a small food processor or mortar and pestle.

▶ Put the bean paste in a medium bowl and stir in the garlic, ginger, cumin, coriander, chili powder, and salt. Add the onion and tomato. Add 1 tsp. oil and the chopped cilantro. Combine all ingredients. If the paste is very thick, add 1 Tbs. water. It should have the consistency of cooked oatmeal.

▶ Heat a flat-bottom frying pan over medium heat. Put the remaining oil in a shallow bowl. Oil the pan using my Newari friend Ram's mother's trick to avoid overdoing it and ending up with greasy pancakes: Attach that ½ red potato at the uncut end with the skin on it

continued on next page

to a long-handled fork. Rub the cut end of the potato in the oil, then rub the oiled potato around the bottom of the fry pan to lightly coat it.

▶ To make 4-inch pancakes, use 2 spoonfuls of batter per pancake. Once the batter is in the pan, edge it with the spoon to keep the pancakes round. Cook over medium heat for 5 minutes, then flip.

▶ At this point you can continue to cook the *barra* as it is for another 3–4 minutes and serve. Or you can break an egg over the top and fry it on the pancake while the pancake continues to cook. For this, it's best to cover the pan. Salt the egg to taste.

▶ Remove from the pan and arrange on a serving platter. (Leftovers can be reheated in a microwave oven, in the frying pan, or in a toaster oven.)

Carrot Rolls
with Lemon Yogurt Sauce

This is fancy food from Istanbul, thought to have come from the kitchens of an Ottoman palace, so it takes a little more effort than most of the other recipes in this book. But you'll be rewarded with an elegant way to make vitamins and protein tempting and tasty. And your effort will be memorable!

MAKES 30 ROLLS.

ROLLS

7 large carrots, peeled and sliced into thin disks

8 dried apricot halves

4–5 scallions, roots off and washed

3 large garlic cloves

5 parsley sprigs, stems short

4–5 mint sprigs, leaves only

1 egg

¼ tsp. salt

freshly ground black pepper to taste

1 tsp. ground medium hot chili powder or Moroccan ras el hanout, or ½ tsp. chipotle chili powder and ¼ tsp. ground cayenne (your choice)

2 Tbs. pine nuts, lightly toasted

4 Tbs. breadcrumbs or matzo meal

¼ cup white flour

¼ cup chickpea flour (if you don't have this, mix 3 Tbs. fine cornmeal with 1 Tbs. flour)

Peanut or sunflower oil for frying

SAUCE

4 Tbs. thick yogurt

juice of 1 small lemon

2 garlic cloves, minced

pinch salt

freshly ground black pepper

2 sprigs fresh parsley, chopped

TO MAKE THE ROLLS

▶ Steam the carrots until soft, about 5 minutes if they were thinly sliced. Drain well.

▶ Mince the apricots, scallions, garlic, parsley, and mint either by hand or in the bowl of a food processor (all together is fine). Add the carrots, egg, salt, black pepper, and hot pepper to the mixture, and hand mash or process lightly to crush into a paste.

▶ Stir in the pine nuts and breadcrumbs. Make a dough. It will be sticky.

continued on next page

- ▶ Combine the two flours in a shallow bowl or dish. Take a large walnut-size portion of the carrot mixture in your hand and mold it into a 2-inch roll. Carefully roll this in the flour to coat it and put it aside on a large platter. Continue doing this until all the carrot mixture is finished. (Try to work steadily so the carrots don't get too warm and sticky.)

- ▶ Pour a ¼-inch layer of oil in a large frying pan and heat on medium high. Put in as many carrot rolls as you can without them touching each other, and fry for 90 seconds. Roll them over to brown on the other side for 1 minute. They should be golden brown. Remove from heat with a slotted spatula or spoon and drain on paper towels. Continue frying the remaining rolls.

TO MAKE THE SAUCE

- ▶ Combine all ingredients in a bowl and whip together. Pour over the rolls if you are serving at the table. Put in a separate small bowl as a dip if you are passing the rolls around.

Tostones: Double-Fried Plantains, Caribbean Style

Plantains are a staple in Africa, Central and South America, and also the Caribbean, where this recipe came from. Normally they are sliced and fried either with garlic or perhaps a pinch of sugar. When flattened to look like flying saucers and crisped through double frying, they are called *tostones*. Plantains are a rich lode of potassium.

SERVES 6–8.

3 large firm plantains	24 oz. corn or peanut oil
¼ tsp. salt	or a combination of both

▶ Cut the ends of plantains and peel them. Cut them crosswise into chunks that are about ½ inch thick.

▶ Heat oil into a deep heavy-gauge pan—it needs to be at least 1 inch deep—over high heat until sizzling. Put in as many plaintain chunks as you can so they don't touch and all are covered in the oil. Fry for about 2 minutes, until they just start to brown. Remove the plaintains from heat and set on paper towels to drain. Continue frying the rest in batches.

▶ Using the back of a heavy cleaver, smash each plantain into a round disk less than ¼ inch thick. Lightly salt and return to the frying pan. Fry for another 2 minutes, then flip and fry another 1–2 minutes, or until the disks are golden brown on both sides and slightly crunchy. Remove from pan immediately and set on paper towels to drain.

▶ Serve plain or with yogurt spiced with cinnamon and honey, sour cream, or your favorite salsa, but definitely alongside the Guatemalan *volteados* on page 82, guacamole, and tortillas for a vibrant and tasty Latin American meal.

Mindful eating is not based on anxiety about the future but by the actual choices that are in front of you and by your direct experiences of health while eating and drinking.

—JAN CHOZEN BAYS

Garlic

THE BUDDHIST CODE for monks and nuns mentions garlic, and sometimes other members of the *Allium* genus (onion, chives, shallot, and leek), as forbidden food. Pungency seems to be the problem, for cut or pressed garlic releases the infamously smelly sulfur. Yet in the body, sulfur morphs into a miracle drug, which explains why the ancients praised garlic for its power over evil spirits, a poetic way of describing the discomforts, delusions, and damages of bacteria and parasites. The problem is that sulfur is never digested in the stomach; it heads straight for the bloodstream and lungs (which is why garlic is considered a remedy for colds) and exits the body through breath and perspiration. Thus the Chinese *Brahma Net Sutra* warns that "the breath of the eater, if reading the sutras, will drive away the good spirits," and to Muslims, Mohammed is reported to have warned those who ate garlic to stay away from the mosque. It's still possible to find ancient signs at the entry to Zen Buddhist monasteries in Japan that say: "No fish or garlic is allowed within." The Indian *Mahaparinirvana Sutra* says: "People who dislike the smell of garlic turn away from those who eat it. What need is there to mention the disadvantages of such food?"

Jains and early Buddhists prohibited eating onions and garlic because they are underground bulbs meant by nature to launch green plants, and their sacred vow to do no harm specifically included not killing a plant or tree by yanking its roots. The original Buddhist rules of discipline actually mandate confession for damaging a living plant this way, especially "the five forbidden pungent roots."

Another rationale for the garlic taboo is a traditional belief that all its potent components overwhelm the body's fragile balance. Ancient Hindus considered it a *rajasic* food, one that overly stimulates and thus unbalances the body. Some Tibetan Buddhist teachers have told me garlic "disturbs the winds." The Seventeenth Karmapa has told others garlic causes drowsiness. Hindus and Jains believe that, by warming the body, garlic increases desire. Apparently, the Buddha agreed, for he forbade his ordained followers to eat it. Chinese Buddhists specifically banned eating garlic, chives, onion, and leeks in the *Shurangama*

Sutra because "Eaten raw they are believed to incite people to anger and disputes; eaten cooked they increase one's sexual desire. Buddhist adepts are advised to avoid them, as their consumption tends to disturb the peacefulness of the mind."

The fear of arousing a different hunger is another reason Chinese Buddhists decided a cook must abandon garlic, chives, onion, and leek. Because these have historically been the very ingredients Chinese cooks relied on in their quest for flavor, their tastiness was taken to be the cause of attraction to and craving for food. Early Chinese Buddhists therefore reasoned that robbing food of the very ingredients that make it delicious would remove the mind's hunger for it. Their *Brahma Net Sutra* says: "A disciple of the Buddha should not eat the five pungent herbs—garlic, chives, leeks, onions, and wild chive. This is so even if they are added as flavoring to other main dishes."

The Buddha taught us to look at the body, to contemplate it
and to come to terms with its nature. We must be able
to be at peace with the body.

—Ajahn Chah

Persian Parsley Omelets

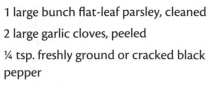

1 large bunch flat-leaf parsley, cleaned

2 large garlic cloves, peeled

¼ tsp. freshly ground or cracked black pepper

6–7 scallions, cleaned

6 eggs

¼ tsp. salt

3 Tbs. olive oil, divided

plain yogurt

▶ Put parsley, garlic, pepper, and scallions in the bowl of a food processor and chop. Or chop each individually, mincing the garlic, and combine.

▶ Whisk the eggs in a large bowl and blend in salt. Whisk in the parsley mixture.

▶ Heat a large flat skillet over medium heat and coat with 1 Tbs. olive oil. When oil is hot, put in 2 Tbs. of egg mixture as though making a pancake. Use a spatula to shape the egg into a circle approximately 2–3 inches in diameter. Do this again 2 or 3 times until the skillet is full but there is space between the omelets.

▶ Cook until the edges start to brown and flip. Cook another minute and remove from heat.

▶ Continue making omelets until the egg mixture runs out.

▶ Serve these warm or at room temperature. They are delicious with a dollop of yogurt and thinly sliced cucumber. For a portable treat, try serving in a lavash.

Purity in food and drink is one of the ten

essential disciplines of life.

—*THE MAHABHARATA*

Potato-Stuffed Paratha

This is standard snack and street food in both India and Nepal. It's also part of a sit-down feast. This particular recipe was given to me by a Kathmandu housewife who shares it with cousins who run a venerable teahouse renowned for its breads and sweets.

MAKES 8 PARATHAS.

STUFFING

2 medium boiling potatoes

2 tsp. ground cumin

1 tsp. ground coriander

½ tsp. ground cayenne

½ tsp. chili powder

¼ tsp. salt

1 Tbs. ghee (or an additional 1 Tbs. oil)

1 Tbs. mustard or sunflower
or corn oil

½ tsp. ground turmeric

1 Tbs. chopped fresh cilantro

DOUGH

4 cups whole wheat flour or
2 cups whole wheat and
2 cups all-purpose flour

2 Tbs. mustard or sunflower
or corn oil

Mustard or sunflower or corn oil
for frying

▶ Boil potatoes in lightly salted water until soft. Remove from heat, drain, cool, and peel.

▶ Meanwhile, make the dough by putting the flour in a large bowl or in a mixer with a dough hook. Pour in oil and work it into the flour. Gradually add 1 cup of water, constantly mixing to form smooth dough. It should not be sticky. (If it is, add 1 Tbs. flour.) Knead dough for 10 minutes and form it into a smooth ball. Coat with ¼ tsp. oil and let it rest, covered in the bowl, for 30 minutes.

▶ While the dough is resting, make the stuffing by chopping the potatoes and putting them into a medium bowl. Add the cumin, coriander, cayenne, chili powder, salt, and ghee or 1 Tbs. oil. Mash the potatoes into a coarse puree, adding 1 tsp. more ghee or oil if you need to. (Do not do this in a food processor as it turns potatoes into paste.)

continued on next page

▶ Heat a medium skillet or coated frying pan over high heat, then lower heat to medium and coat bottom with 1 Tbs. oil. When oil is hot, add turmeric, stirring. Add mashed potatoes in one clump like a large thick pancake and fry in the turmeric for 30 seconds on each side.

▶ Turn off heat, remove potatoes from pan, and put them back in the bowl.

▶ Prepare a flat rolling surface by sprinkling it very lightly with flour. Divide the dough ball into 8 equal pieces. One at a time, with a rolling pin, flatten the ball into a circle 5–6 inches in diameter. Put a heaping Tbs. of mashed potatoes in the center. Gather up the sides, pleating and pinching as you go around the circle to enclose potatoes completely in the dough. Press the top down lightly to seal.

▶ Put the stuffed dough ball on the flat board and carefully roll it into a flat circle, again about 6 inches in diameter. Potatoes should be safely inside. Keep a bit of flour handy if you need to coat the board so the paratha doesn't stick.

▶ Heat the frying pan or skillet on high until it is very hot. Lightly coat the bottom with oil. (A great trick here is to cut a potato, stick a skewer, fork, or long toothpick into the uncut end, coat the cut end in oil, and wipe it around the pan to coat it with oil.) Lower heat to medium. Fry the paratha, shaking the pan so it doesn't stick, and flipping the paratha every 30–40 seconds. The whole process should take maybe 2–3 minutes per paratha. It will develop dark marks in spots.

▶ Remove fried parathas to a plate and keep them covered with foil until ready to serve. Serve warm if you can, otherwise at room temperature. If they get too cool, they can be put into the oven in foil to reheat.

Spanish Tortilla

The Spanish tortilla, a potato omelet, bears no resemblance to the more well-known (in North America) flat disk of cornmeal or wheat wrapped around Tex-Mex burritos and fajitas, except perhaps that in its home country, Spain, it is also beloved as picnic, snack, and comfort food. My friend Sonia shared this recipe, a staple of her family's food shop in the environs of Barcelona. She serves it with artichokes and zucchini grilled and dipped in Romesco sauce (see page 251), which makes an unforgettable meal.

SERVES 4–5.

4 round potatoes about 2 inches in diameter

2 Tbs. olive oil (extra if your pan is large)

1 medium onion, peeled and diced

1 tsp. salt

5 eggs

▶ Cut potatoes in half, then cut the halves in half again, and cut each into uniformly thin slices.

▶ Heat a frying or sauté pan on medium high. When it's hot, coat the bottom with olive oil and heat until it is almost smoky.

▶ Cut heat to low and add potatoes, stir-frying to coat them with the oil. Continue to sauté potatoes 3–5 minutes until they are soft, then cover the pot and continue cooking until they just start to brown, about 5 minutes. (Fresh or new potatoes will cook faster.)

▶ Add onion and salt. Cover the pot and continue to cook on low until onions are soft, 10–12 minutes.

▶ Meanwhile beat eggs in a medium or large bowl. Have ready a flat plate as large as the pan you are cooking in, at least as large as the tortilla will be.

▶ When the onions and potatoes are soft and golden, pour contents of the pan into the scrambled eggs and stir to blend.

▶ Return the emptied pan to the stove and raise heat to high. Add a tsp. of olive oil if necessary.

continued on next page

- When pan and oil are very hot, cut heat to low and pour in the egg mixture. Spread and level it. Cover the pan and cook on low 3–5 minutes, or until the bottom half of the tortilla is firm.

- Put a large plate over the top of the tortilla, remove the pan from the heat and flip it so the tortilla lands on the plate. The cooked side will be up. Slide the tortilla back into the pan with the cooked side up. Cover the pan, return to the heat, and continue cooking another 3–4 minutes until the entire tortilla is firm.

- Immediately invert the tortilla onto a serving plate. Cut into wedges and serve warm.

I particularly enjoyed going over to my parents' house at mealtimes. This was because,
as a young boy destined to be a monk, certain foods such as eggs and pork were
forbidden to me, so it was only at my parents' house that I ever had the chance
to taste them. Once, I remember being caught in the act of eating eggs
by one of my senior officials. He was very shocked, and so was I.
"Go away!" I shouted at the top of my voice!

—THE DALAI LAMA, *Freedom in Exile*

Sweet Potato Fritters

SERVES 4–6; MAKES 22–24 FRITTERS.

2 large sweet potatoes, or 1 red yam and 1 sweet potato, 1½ lb. altogether

2 eggs

¼ cup fine cornmeal

1 tsp. brown sugar

½ tsp. minced fresh ginger

⅛ tsp. orange flower water or ½ tsp. orange juice

¼ tsp. ground cardamom

¼ tsp. ground nutmeg

1 tsp. salt

⅓ cup pecans, chopped and lightly toasted

¼ cup dark raisins

30 oz. peanut oil or corn oil or half of each

▶ Peel the sweet potatoes. Cut them into chunks and divide into three piles.

▶ Put two thirds of the potatoes in a small saucepan, cover with water, and boil about 20 minutes until potatoes are soft. Grate the remaining potatoes.

▶ Drain cooked sweet potatoes and put them in a food processor or blender with eggs, cornmeal, brown sugar, ginger, orange liquid, cardamom, nutmeg, and salt. Puree, trying to keep it thick.

▶ Pour into a large bowl and stir in pecans, raisins, and grated potato.

▶ In a very deep saucepan, or whatever you use for deep-frying, heat oil over high heat to sizzling. Scoop up the batter with a soupspoon and use another spoon to tamp it, lightly flattening, so it holds together. Drop into the oil. Add as many as the pot will hold before fritters touch each other. Fry for 3–5 minutes, until the fritters are a rich dark brown. They will pop up to the top when cooked. Remove with a slotted spoon and drain on paper towels.

▶ You can put them on a cookie sheet and keep them warm in a 250°F oven while you continue frying.

▶ Serve plain or with maple syrup or yogurt spiced with cinnamon and honey and maybe ginger. Great for brunch with scrambled eggs.

Why the Cow Is Sacred

THE PRINCE Gautama Siddhartha who became Shakyamuni Buddha was born in the Iron Age, which introduced not only wheels and plows, but knives, swords, and other weapons of crass destruction. The steely implements escalated the potential for war and murder, and perhaps more significantly, increased the opportunity to kill for meat. The new technology transformed the occasional hands-on, throat-wringing goat or chicken sacrifice to placate or please a wrathful Hindu god into the daily throat-slashing butchery of any available animal. Tidbits of meat slaughtered by knives and swords continued to be tossed into devotional fires, but most of it—the proverbial lion's share—went into the stomachs of the priestly Brahman caste who presided over the "sacrifices."

The Brahmans had a particular fondness for beef and, with an arrogance that prefigured the much later "let them eat cake," they continually claimed cows by taxation, coercion, or any means of confiscation their priests could concoct in the guise of religious obligation. "The compulsive attention they paid to the size, shape and color of cattle suitable for a particular ritual occasion," anthropologist Marvin Harris said, trying to answer the riddle of the sacred cow, "bears a close resemblance to the detailed instructions found in the Book of Leviticus pertaining to similar ancient Israelite sacrificial feasting."

It was the Buddha, master of connecting cause and effect, who saw the beef on this caste's dinner plates as a major cause of the devastating famine that had begun to afflict the other classes. He recognized that the heedlessly slaughtered cows were the most valuable producers of food in all India. The native zebu, *Bos indicus*, was strong enough to pull a metal plow too heavy for humans. It gave dung to fertilize the fields and heat stoves, ably and freely providing fuel to a people bereft of any other source. Better yet, the zebu had the extraordinary ability to transform a few bites of scrubby weed into nutritional treasure: milk that could be consumed as it was or transformed into nutritious curds (yogurt and cheese), butter, or ghee. And despite all this giving, the docile creature asked for nothing. It subsisted on shockingly small amounts of scrub and no attention, even if it was half-starved. The cow was disease, pest, and heat resistant, and did not compete with human beings in any way. It was a great benefactor.

Many of the religions we recognize evolved as a reaction to wanton butchery like that of the Brahmans. The Bible begins with the story of Abraham wielding a knife and quickly moves to the commandment not to kill and urges the beating of swords into ploughshares. The Buddha essentially urged the same conversion. Instead of shouting blame at the Brahmans or laying down the gauntlet of an ultimatum, he skillfully emphasized how much more the cow was worth alive than as steak. The axiom was, as it still is: "The cow is a mother. She gives us milk and butter. Her male calves till the land and give us food." As we have rediscovered today in the loss of so much forest to feedlots, the dairy cow converts feed into calories and protein five to six times more efficiently than the beef steer, which means more people can be fed better on dairy, grains, and beans than on meat.

The Buddha's logical equation of the cows' survival with human liberation from suffering was a perfect example of interdependence, an ideal illustration of compassionate wisdom. Appreciation for Dharma spread rapidly across the land, in part because he rallied the oppressed masses to rise against the cow-oppressing Brahmans. Eventually the ever-widening and staunch embrace of the zebu's right to life became such an overwhelming threat to Brahman hegemony, to retain its prominence the priestly class had to resort to banning cow sacrifice. Craftily adapting the Buddha's teaching as Hindu truth, Brahmans declared themselves fervent adherents of *ahimsa*, Sanskrit for *nonharming*, and cow slaughter in India stopped forever. Widespread prosperity followed.

In Buddhist epistemology, the cow became one of the five sacred supports of human life, the others being water, earth, plants, and flowers from which honey can be made and seeds extracted. The animal is venerated for its extraordinary ability to transfer energy from green earth to human beings as protein, preventing us from having to kill for such a crucial nutrient. Its magical transformation of solar and plant energy into pure white food is the very essence of transformation and purification.

"Why the cow was selected for apotheosis is obvious to me," Mohandas Gandhi said, 2,500 years after the Buddha. "The cow was in India the best companion. She was the giver of plenty. Not only did she give milk but she made agriculture possible." When India became independent in 1947, the cow was still as important as ever, pulling plows through mud that would mire far more costly tractors. Thus, the new federal constitution included Article 48 in a section called Directive Principles of State Policy, to specifically prohibit "the slaughter of all cows and calves and other milk and draft animals." If this seems preposterous, consider that at the same time, the Illinois Department of Agriculture proudly issued an eye-catching poster of a cow draped in the laurel wreath of champions under the banner line: THE FOSTER MOTHER OF THE WORLD.

When Buddhism went to China, its missionaries naturally taught reverence for the cow. It didn't matter that the Chinese were mostly unable to digest dairy and consequently did not herd cattle. Zealously determined to be good Buddhists, they declared cow slaughter taboo. During the reign of the Tang emperors, many of whom embraced Buddhism, it actually became a punishable crime. The sacredness of the cow, and of the plow-pulling water buffalo that was conflated with it, became so embedded in Chinese culture, even the most vociferous adversaries of Buddhism in the ruling elite of the nineteenth century upheld the prohibition on killing any. "Everywhere we went in Fukien," a Dutch traveler wrote in 1893 in his diary, "we saw these admonitions against killing cows, often arranged pictorially as a buffalo, posted in cities and towns along the roads and on the bridges." In the mid-twentieth century when Western embassies in Shanghai tried to order steaks from local butcher shops, riots broke out. Even today you won't find much beef on a Han Chinese menu, except perhaps in entrees distinctly labeled "Mongolian" or sometimes "Szechuan," a Tibetan border region with an abundance of oxen.

Turkish Pumpkin Pancakes

These are lip-smacking tasty and, with all that beta-carotene and protein, more colorful and healthier than ordinary pancakes made from white flour.

SERVES 6 AS A MEAL, 15 AS AN HORS D'OEUVRE.

4 cups peeled, seeded, and grated sugar pumpkin or butternut squash

1 medium onion, peeled and finely diced

1 cup soft ricotta or a similar spreadable cheese

1 cup chickpea flour
(or regular white or fine-grain whole wheat)

½–⅔ cup chopped fresh dill

⅛ tsp. salt

⅛ tsp. ground cayenne

Freshly ground black pepper to taste

pinch nutmeg

2 eggs

1 cup corn oil for frying

▶ Combine all ingredients but the corn oil in a large bowl, breaking the eggs in last, and blend well to incorporate. Be sure the mix is reasonably dry, and add a tsp. of flour if it seems too drippy to mold into a pancake.

▶ Cover the bottom of a large frying pan or skillet with oil, a little more than ⅛ inch deep—not too skimpy and definitely not deeper than ¼ inch. Heat the oil over medium-high heat.

▶ To make small bite-sized cocktail fritters, take enough mixture to make a golf ball–sized ball, then flatten it with your hand into a small pancake. To make a meal-sized fritter, take twice that amount and flatten it into a pancake with a diameter of about 2½ inches.

▶ Fry the fritters in the hot oil in batches so they do not touch each other in the pan and you have room to flip them over with a flat spatula. Add oil as you need it. Fry about 2 minutes on each side, or until golden brown with crisp crust. Fry for a shorter time if they are starting to get burned. Drain on paper towels before serving.

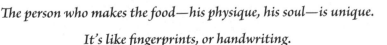

The person who makes the food—his physique, his soul—is unique.

It's like fingerprints, or handwriting.

—MUSA DAGDEVIREN, Turkish chef interviewed in *The New Yorker*

Volteados: Guatemalan-Style Black Beans

The most common menu offering in Guatemala is "plato tipico," which consists of a rice mound surrounded by fried plantains, guacamole, red tomato salsa, corn tortillas, and a slice of the unique *volteados*, often topped with a dollop of sour cream. It's cheap, colorful, nutritious, delicious, and wildly popular.

SERVES 6–8.

2 Tbs. corn oil, divided

1 small onion, minced

3 garlic cloves, peeled and minced

2 (15-oz.) cans black beans, not drained, or two cups cooked black beans plus 2 Tbs. water

1 tsp. salt

1 tsp. ground cumin

GARNISH

sour cream

chopped onion

chopped fresh cilantro

tomato wedges

▶ Heat 1 Tbs. oil in a large flat sauté or frying pan over medium heat. Add onion and garlic and sauté until onions are golden brown.

▶ Puree the black beans with their liquid and add to the pan, stirring. Stir in salt and cumin. Cook, stirring occasionally to prevent sticking to the pan, about 25–30 minutes, until beans lose all liquid and begin to pull away from the side of the pan and solidify into a paste.

▶ To make a loaf shape out of the beans, either use a flipping motion to get the bean paste to double over on itself, or form it by pushing and piling with a spatula or cooking spoon. Once the loaf is shaped, turn off the heat and let it sit to solidify further.

▶ To serve, slice into ½-inch pieces. Heat 1 Tbs. oil in a frying pan over medium heat and fry the pieces to get a crust on both sides, about 2–3 minutes each side.

▶ Garnish with any of the options, and serve one slice per person alongside eggs, with tortillas and salsa, or as part of your own "typical platter."

Out of the Oven

*I sometimes think that the act of bringing food is
one of the basic roots of all relationships.*

—THE DALAI LAMA, *Freedom in Exile*

Savory Bread Pudding with Asparagus

Bread puddings are an elegant way to recycle stale bread. They are most commonly made sweet for dessert and with the bread itself showing, but this one, where the bread is concealed as crumbs that dissolve in baking, is meant to be the heart of the meal. Asparagus offers vital nutrients—vitamin K, folic acid, and potassium—and in some cultures is thought to be a spring tonic.

SERVES 8–10.

1½ lb. fresh asparagus

1 tsp. olive oil

1 medium leek, cleaned

4 Tbs. unsalted butter, divided

1 tsp. dried thyme

1½ cups half-and-half

2 oz. Gruyère cheese

3 extra-large or jumbo eggs, separated

¼ tsp. salt

⅛ tsp. freshly ground black pepper, or more to taste

2 cups freshly made breadcrumbs (from 3–4 slices firm white bread ground in a food processor)

1 Tbs. grated lemon zest

▶ Preheat oven to 450°F.

▶ Trim the bottom inch off the asparagus stalks; cut the remaining stalks in 4 equal pieces. Line a shallow roasting dish, or large toaster pan tray, with foil and put the asparagus pieces on it. Coat with olive oil and a pinch of salt. Roast for 10 minutes at 450°F. Remove from oven.

▶ Reduce oven heat to 350°F. Grease an 8-inch square baking pan or round cake pan, whatever you have.

▶ Dice the leek. Melt 2 Tbs. butter in a small sauté pan over medium heat and add the leek and thyme. Sauté over medium-low heat until leeks are soft, 3–5 minutes.

▶ Pour half-and-half into a small saucepan and bring to a simmer (bubbles will rise along the pot edge). While waiting, put the cheese into a food processor bowl and chop it.

continued on next page

- Add the roasted asparagus to the food processor bowl. With the machine running, pour in the warm half-and-half, stopping as soon as it is absorbed. Add the remaining butter and 1 egg yolk at a time, processing with the pulse button to incorporate.

- Add the leeks from the sauté pan and salt and pepper. Add the breadcrumbs and quickly process just to combine.

- Beat the egg whites until stiff peaks form. Fold them and the lemon zest into the asparagus mixture.

- Pour into the baking pan. Optionally: sprinkle on top ⅛ tsp. smoked paprika and ⅛ tsp. ground nutmeg. Place the pan in a larger roasting pan and pour into that pan enough water to reach halfway up the sides of the pudding pan.

- Bake in the center of the oven at 350°F for 40–50 minutes, depending on whether you use convection or not, or until a cake tester comes out clean.

- Remove from heat and cool on a rack for 10 minutes. Invert onto a serving platter and serve warm.

Cabbage Crisp

I am not very adept at making or fond of eating pies, so during my dozens of summers in Maine, I always made the much-easier crisps, so famously that a friend who owned a restaurant "borrowed" my recipe and it became his most popular dessert. The crisps were merely fresh fruit cut up and cooked quickly under a very crunchy topping of nuts and oats. Then one midwinter day, I was asked to make lunch for a Dharma group and, not having much time or many ingredients on hand, I decided to see if I could make a vegetable crisp. This was it. The sour cream added to the cabbage was my tribute to all that vanilla ice cream people scooped over my peach and blueberry crisps. The Dharma group loved this so much, I've had to make it again and again for them.

SERVES 6–8.

4 Tbs. butter

1 tsp. caraway seeds

½ tsp. celery seeds

1 medium onion, finely diced

1 small red cabbage, cored and shredded

½ round green or white cabbage, cored and shredded (the goal is equal amounts of the two cabbage colors)

1 small celeriac bulb, peeled and grated (1 cup will do)

1 large granny smith or other very tart apple, peeled, cored, and finely diced

½ tsp. salt

juice of 1 large lemon

¼ tsp. balsamic or sherry vinegar

½ cup raisins, plumped for 10 minutes in water (you can add ¼ tsp. orange flower water, orange juice, or rose water to the water for added flavor) and drained

½ cup chopped fresh dill sprigs

¾ cup sour cream

TOPPING

8 Tbs. (1 stick) butter

1½ cups Kashi 7 Whole Grain Nuggets*

1 tsp. minced fresh ginger

⅓ cup almond meal, or roasted chickpea flour

1 Tbs. light brown sugar

½ cup slivered almonds

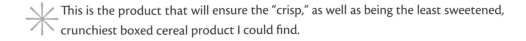 This is the product that will ensure the "crisp," as well as being the least sweetened, crunchiest boxed cereal product I could find.

- ▶ Preheat the oven to 350°F and get out a glass pie dish.

- ▶ Melt 4 Tbs. butter in a large sauté pan. Add caraway and celery seeds and stir into the butter. Add onion and sauté over medium-low heat until it is soft and translucent, but not brown. Add cabbages, celeriac, and apple, and carefully stir to blend all ingredients. Sauté 5 minutes over medium-low heat, until cabbage is soft. Turn up the heat and try to make any moisture in the pan evaporate. Remove from heat. Drain off any excess liquid. Add salt, lemon juice, vinegar, and the drained raisins.

- ▶ Let the cabbage cool 5 minutes. Add dill and sour cream. Blend well and put into the pie plate, smoothing the top evenly. Leave at least ⅓–½ inch at the top of the pan for the topping.

- ▶ To prepare the topping, cut butter into tablespoon-sized chunks and put it in a food processor with all other ingredients except for the slivered almonds. Use the pulse button 3 or 4 times until the butter and Kashi are clumped together.

- ▶ Transfer the mix into a bowl, add the almonds, and use your hands to blend them into the clumps. You will still have some loose and dry ingredients. Spread the clumps evenly over the top of the cabbage and fill in with the loose powder. Be careful to extend to the edges to seal the cabbage juices in underneath.

- ▶ Bake in the middle of the oven for 30–35 minutes, until the top is browned and the cabbage is boiling up the sides of the dish. Cool for 5–10 minutes before serving.

Pie in the Sky:
How Food Changed History

THE DREAM of food freely falling from the sky, which goes back at least to the Bible with its lyrical longings for manna from heaven, came true in the middle of the twentieth century. For fifteen months, tons of it steadily rained down over West Berlin during the spectacularly daring *Operation Vittles,* code name for a military campaign that never fired one bomb or bullet. "MILK," a proud Douglas Aircraft advertisement exclaimed, "new weapon of democracy!"

Actually flour, salt, yeast, dehydrated potatoes, and sugar also fell with that milk into the arms of the more than two million war-weary Germans stranded on the ground of West Berlin. Only three years before, in 1945, these same people now blessed with food from the sky had been enemy combatants. But, as the Buddha said, everything changes. When World War II ended with the four Allied victors carving up the defeated Germany into four quarters, the Americans, British, and French merged their zones into a seamless democratic West Germany. But their "award" also included part of the Reich's powerful capital city, Berlin, a noncontiguous piece of property that lay deep inside the section handed to the Soviets, and Stalin was quick to detect the opportunity in this geographical quirk. The imperative to eat makes human beings so obviously vulnerable that the oldest trick in the aggressors' handbook is a siege, which cuts off access to food. Heedful that Lenin had said, "Whoever has Germany has Europe," Stalin abruptly blocked supply routes into West Berlin, figuring the Germans stuck inside would have to surrender to Soviet Communism or starve to death. The collapse of West Berlin would provoke a domino effect in which all of West Germany, then all of Western Europe, country by war-weakened country, would yield to him.

Stalin had forgotten that the world he wanted to control had changed. There was a new avenue into West Berlin: a twenty-mile-wide corridor up in the air. Alarmed by the Soviets' startling siege and the ruthless calculation fueling it, the Western Allies nervously concluded the fall of Germany could only be prevented by a fall of food from that heavenly highway. On June 26, 1948, the United States Air Force and the British Royal Air Force, which three years earlier had been dropping firebombs on West Berliners, started bombing them with tins of coffee and corned beef.

The logistical triumph of the Berlin Airlift had no precedent nor has it ever had a replication. Just this once in time, 32,900 military personnel along with another 23,000 civilians devoted themselves to a mess call. The careful calibration of food rations, the agonized calculations of cargo carriage (including flour dust and salt corrosion), the grinding tedium of motor mechanics, and the excruciating alertness of tight precision flying—all combined into a campaign to forge an invincible food chain. Every few minutes around the clock for about a year, a cargo plane swooped through the narrow, often snow-filled or foggy airspace, and dropped tons of edibles into West Berlin. The choreography of the airlift was so tightly controlled that when, on a dark, bitterly snowy night, with planes in formation below and behind him, a young pilot named Sam Myers found himself losing altitude from ice building up on the wings and choking the carburetor, he had to send his copilot crawling through the cargo jettisoning sacks until the plane finally rose to its prescribed position and avoided deadly collisions with the other planes. "I've often wondered," Myers later said, "what people on the ground in Soviet controlled East Germany must have thought as 4,000 pounds of macaroni came raining out of the sky with all that snow." Ninety-two million miles covered, 277,000 flights flown, and all records broken in the "Easter Parade" of April 1949 when almost 13,000 tons of food and coal were dropped by planes landing every thirty seconds for twenty-four hours in a spirited show of can-do determination that finally provoked Stalin to stop the siege.

Although the first planes came clumsily and uncertainly down through bomb-shattered buildings, the commandant of America's section of Berlin later said, "they were the most beautiful things I had ever seen. As the planes touched down, and bags of flour began to spill out of their bellies, I realized this was the beginning of something wonderful.... I went back to my office almost breathless with elation, like a man who has made a great discovery and cannot hide his joy." The West Berliners couldn't hide theirs either, stalwartly refusing Stalin's invitation to move over to the city's well-larded east side, even though their raining rations were dismal: dehydrated potatoes, cereal, bread, and powdered milk with an occasional dollop of cheese and Spam. What truly heartened them and renewed their resolve, they later said, were the occasional square brown cartons packed with thirty pounds of gourmet goodies: varying combinations of bacon, jams, raisins, chocolates, macaroni, cornmeal, real coffee, peanut butter, canned tuna, cocoa, and more. Every box formulaically had enough for ten people for one day or one person for ten days, and was a "gift from an unknown stranger in America," someone who had compassionately shelled out ten to fifteen dollars for this CARE package, created by a charitable coalition that called itself Cooperative for American Remittances to Europe.

"Things really changed after the airlift started," one American pilot reported. "People said that before the airlift if an American soldier went into a café, the Germans would get up and leave. A week after the airlift started, it was altogether different." Hearts and minds had been won through stomachs. In a remarkable show of what the Buddha called interdependence, once the airlift got underway and West Berliners realized more runways would bring more food—that there was something they could do to help—17,000 of them rushed to outfit Tegel Airport in just 92 days, at which point it was inaugurated with a drop of 20,000 lbs. of cheese.

A young pilot from Utah, Gail Halvorsen, gained fame among the children of West Berlin when he began dropping parachuted candy bars to them as he passed by overhead. When a German reporter blew his cover, Halvorsen's superiors ordered him to quit the gimmick, but a commanding officer overheard and instead expanded the project into "Operation Little Vittles." Then, as Halvorsen later said, the floodgates opened. The American Confectioners' Association shipped tons of treats for the "Candy Bomber" to drop all over West Berlin in special parachutes made by children at schools in a Massachusetts textile town.

The outlandish Operation Vittles scored huge points for the wisdom of compassion. Offering food made trusted friends of bitter enemies, easing the vicious divisiveness of war. The successful cooperation that characterized the airlift gave birth to NATO, to the resounding prosperity of West Germany, and arguably to the fall of the Berlin Wall and the disintegration of the Iron Curtain.

The year after it was gone, in the harshness of winter, Russia ran out of food. With the tables turned, West Germans charitably stepped up to the plate, sending thousands of tons of dehydrated potatoes and millions of cans of tuna fish, supplies leftover from the airlift that had been stockpiled in Berlin, just in case the Russians ever tried a siege again.

Generosity is the virtue that produces peace.

—TIBETAN MEAL CHANT

Corn Tart with Peppers, Sunflower Seeds, and Pumpkin Seeds

Here are the flavors and foods of the American Southwest.

SERVES 6.

¼ cup ground sunflower seeds

6 ears of corn
(husked and kernels removed from the cob) or
2½ cups corn kernels

½ cup heavy cream

1 poblano pepper, seeded, roasted, skinned, and diced

6 Tbs. butter, softened

¼ cup sugar

3 large eggs, separated

3 Tbs. dark rum

1 tsp. baking powder

¼ tsp. salt

pinch chili powder

pinch cinnamon

½ roasted red pepper, diced
(from a jar is okay)

1 Tbs. pumpkin seeds

▶ Preheat oven to 350°F. Butter a 10-inch pie plate and sprinkle a scant Tbs. of ground sunflower seeds around the bottom.

▶ Puree 1½ cups of corn and all the cream in a food processor or blender. Stir in remaining corn kernels and diced poblano pepper and set aside.

▶ In a large mixing bowl, cream butter and sugar. Add egg yolks one at a time, beating as you do. Beat in rum. In a separate bowl, combine baking powder, salt, chili, cinnamon, and the remainder of the ground sunflower seeds. Add this to the mixing bowl, beating to blend. Stir in the creamed corn and chopped red pepper.

▶ In a separate bowl, beat egg whites with a pinch of salt until they form stiff peaks. Fold this into the corn mixture to leaven it and mix carefully.

▶ Pour mixture into the pie dish and shake it slightly to remove air and level the top. Sprinkle the pumpkin seeds around the top.

continued on next page

- ▶ Bake about 35 minutes, until the tart is brown and puffed. A cake tester should come out clean.

- ▶ Cool 10 minutes. Serve warm, either plain, with a tomatillo salsa to be savory, or with maple syrup and/or sour cream or thick yogurt to be sweet.

If we look at our body externally, it is an illusory body. It has no longevity, but in fact it is the body from which the body of the Buddha arises. Since it is the foundation from which the body of the Buddha arises, we shouldn't just see it as an ordinary body. We should meditate on it as the body of a deity. To see our body as the body of a deity is very important.

—RECHUNGPA

Curried Mushroom Frittata

In Italy and Spain, frittatas have evolved into picnic food from food originally carried by workers into the fields to have for lunchtime. Since the name means "fried" and is related to our word "fritter," they are usually made on top of the stove like a huge omelet, then at the last second slipped into the oven to brown the top and melt the cheese. But they can also be baked from start to finish in the oven, which is less traditional but much easier.

SERVES 6 AS A MAIN DISH, 8–10 AS A SIDE DISH.

3 Tbs. butter

1 Tbs. plus 1 tsp. olive oil

1-inch piece fresh ginger, peeled and minced

2 cups chopped leeks or red onion

1 lb. mushrooms—a mix of shiitake, button, and oyster works well—washed and sliced or chopped into bite-sized pieces

2 tsp. curry powder

½ tsp. salt, divided

8 extra-large eggs

¼ cup milk (skim is okay)

¼ cup chopped fresh cilantro

½ cup grated cheddar, jack, mozzarella, or Gruyère cheese

▶ Preheat oven to 375°F.

▶ In a large skillet, melt butter and 1 Tbs. olive oil over medium heat. Add ginger and sauté 30 seconds. Add leeks or onions and continue to sauté until they are soft. Add mushrooms and sauté for about 3 minutes. Stir in curry powder and ¼ tsp. salt. Continue to sauté another 2 minutes. Remove from heat.

▶ In a large bowl, beat or whip the eggs with milk and ¼ tsp. salt. Blend in chopped cilantro.

▶ Using 1 tsp. olive oil, grease a deep quiche or pie pan. Pour in the mushrooms and spread evenly around the pan. Pour the eggs over this and shake the pan slightly to distribute well.

▶ Bake in the center of the oven for 25 minutes, or until the frittata is only a little loose in its center. The edges should be brown and puffy. Spread the cheese around the center and continue to bake another 5 minutes. Do not remove from the oven unless a cake tester comes out clean.

▶ Remove from oven and let the frittata sit for 5 minutes before serving. Slice in wedges. Serve hot immediately or up to a day later at room temperature.

Grit Soufflé with *Piperade*

Piperade, the vividly colorful Basque staple, now has dozens of versions. It's served as a side or sauce for omelets, beef, and fish. *Lezco* in Hungary is a similar dish with the peppers stirred into rice, with or without spicy sausage added. It can also be served over penne pasta, baked potatoes, or cornbread. Here, in a marriage of new and old worlds, it's paired with old-fashioned Southern comfort food: a grit soufflé.

SERVES 4–6.

PIPERADE

1 large green bell pepper, washed and seeded

1 large red bell pepper, washed and seeded

1 yellow or orange bell pepper, washed and seeded

1 medium-large red onion, peeled

3–4 Tbs. olive oil

3 large garlic cloves, peeled and minced

¼ tsp. dried oregano

⅛ tsp. salt

Freshly ground black pepper to taste

OPTIONAL ADDITIONS

1 cup chopped tomatoes

1 small poblano pepper
(if you want some chili hotness),
treated like the bell peppers

GARNISH

¼ cup chopped fresh flat-leaf parsley

SOUFFLÉ

1 Tbs. finely grated Parmesan cheese

4 cups milk (can be skim)

1 cup grits (raw or quick cooking but not instant)

1 tsp. salt

½ tsp. chili powder

8 Tbs. (1 stick) unsalted butter, cut in 6–8 pieces

1 cup (2 oz.) grated cheddar cheese

⅛ tsp. ground cayenne

4 extra-large eggs, separated

TO MAKE THE *PIPERADE*

▶ Slice all bell peppers into long thin strips. Optionally, you can julienne them into short, thin matchsticks.

▶ Cut onion into thin rings, then in half, and break the rings apart into thin half-moon pieces. (Cut in half again if you are making matchsticks out of the peppers so everything is uniform size.)

- In a large sauté pan, heat oil (use enough Tbs. to thickly coat the entire bottom of the pan). Add garlic and oregano and stir-fry over medium heat for 30 seconds. Add onion and sauté for another 30 seconds.

- Add all peppers, trying to keep them in a uniform direction now and while cooking, so that they look attractive when served. Continue cooking over medium or medium-low heat until pepper strips are soft but haven't lost their bright colors. This will take 10–15 minutes. Add salt and pepper. Remove from heat. (If you are using tomatoes, add them here and continue to sauté over medium-low heat until they are mushy.)

- You can prepare the piperade a day ahead and reheat it either in a sauté pan or a microwave when ready to serve.

TO MAKE THE SOUFFLÉ

- Preheat oven to 375°F. Butter a 2-quart soufflé dish and sprinkle the grated Parmesan around the bottom and sides.

- Put the milk in a large saucepan and over medium heat bring to a slow boil. Just as it starts to boil, stir in the grits, salt, and chili powder. Continue stirring until the grits thicken into porridge. Remove from heat.

- Stir in butter, cheese, and cayenne. Carefully stir in the egg yolks, stirring constantly until they are incorporated. Let the mixture cool.

- Beat the egg whites into very stiff peaks. When the grits are warm but not hot, carefully fold in the egg whites.

- Pour the contents of the pot into the soufflé dish, being sure the top is level.

- Bake in the center of the oven at 375°F for 25–30 minutes or until a cake tester comes out clean. This will not rise as high as other soufflés.

- Serve immediately with *piperade*.

We are like the kernel that comes from the corn. With it we bring life, like the seed

of the corn. . . . Our lives, we must remember that they are holy. The corn is

sacred. We are sacred. We hold the seeds of the gods to the future.

—TAOS PUEBLO CORN-GRINDING SONG, translated by PAUL ENCISO

Pistachio and Pecan Pâté

This dazzling and delicious loaf can serve 10 as a meal entrée, 16 as an appetizer, and 24 as a party hors d'oeuvre. It's fabulous party food.

1 (14-oz.) can cannellini beans

½ lb. walnut pieces or halves, lightly toasted

½ pound pecan pieces or halves, lightly toasted

¼ lb. Gruyère cheese, shredded

1 cup shredded Parmesan, Asiago, or Grana Padano cheese

4 scallions, cleaned, with some green left on

5 parsley sprigs, stems off

3 garlic cloves, peeled

½ tsp. dried rosemary

½ tsp. ground cumin

1 tsp. dried thyme

1 tsp. dried marjoram

½ tsp. ground allspice

1½ tsp. salt

1 scant tsp. freshly ground black pepper

⅓ cup heavy cream

6 Tbs. butter

2 eggs

1 Tbs. brandy or calvados

¼ lb. shelled unsalted pistachios (lightly roasted or not)

4 pitted kalamata or similar black olives, coarsely chopped

GARNISH

cornichons

black olives

small cherry tomatoes

finely chopped parsley

slices of baguette

▶ Preheat oven to 350°F. Butter a large loaf pan (best size is 8" x 4" x3") or two small pans. Line the loaf pan or pans with parchment paper and very lightly butter the paper.

▶ Puree the beans in the bowl of a food processor. Add the walnuts and pecans and continue processing until the nuts are in tiny pieces. Add the cheeses, scallions, parsley, garlic, and spices (including the salt and pepper) and process into a smooth, solid paste. Add the cream, butter, eggs, brandy, and pistachios, and process to blend everything. Stir in the chopped olives. (These will end up looking like the truffles in liver pâté.)

▶ Fill the loaf pan or pans evenly to the top with the pâté, pressing down as you go to remove air holes. Smooth the top. Cover the loaf tightly with aluminum foil.

▶ Put the pâté into a large baking or roasting pan filled with 1 inch of hot water and bake for 1 hour at 350°F. (A good convection oven may reduce this cooking time but, in any event, a cake tester should come out clean when it is done.)

▶ Cool for 10–15 minutes before inverting the pâté onto a platter. Unmold it and carefully remove the parchment.

▶ Garnish with any of the options, and serve hot or at room temperature. This amazing pâté slices cleanly.

When eating, do not gobble noisily,

Nor stuff and cram your gaping mouth.

And do not sit with legs outstretched.

Nor rudely rub your hands together.

—SHANTIDEVA

The Buddha's Guide to Table Manners

MANY OF THE 250 monastic rules given by the Buddha," the late Chögyam Trungpa Rinpoche told his new Western students in 1979, "are connected with how to eat properly. When you eat properly, then you can walk properly, think properly and relate with other human beings properly. A lot of things are based on the idea of eating food properly, which is how to behave as a basically decent person."

Below, abridged and in twenty-first-century vernacular, is the Buddha's 2,500-year-old-guide to table manners. The rules were extracted from the Vinaya, his code of conduct for ordained monks and nuns, which actually has two chapters devoted to behavior around food. Vinaya rules still guide monastic activity today.

I vow to:
- receive food appreciatively.
- receive food with my eyes focused on the bowl.
- keep the richest element of my food in proper proportion to the rest.
- only take enough food to fill the one bowl.
- eat food with great appreciation for it.
- eat food with my attention focused on it.

- eat food methodically.
- eat food, not wanting more of what may be richer or fancier.
- not eat food by placing my mouth directly on a heap of it and gobbling.
- not cover up or hide the fancier food I get, pretending I don't have any because I want more.
- if I am not sick and weak, not speak up to request I be given richer food than I am offered.
- not look at another's bowl, intent on finding fault with it or my own.
- not take an extra-large mouthful.
- make a rounded mouthful.
- not open my mouth when the mouthful has yet to be brought to it.
- not speak with my mouth full of food.
- not throw food into my mouth.
- not nibble away at large mouthfuls of food.
- not eat in a way that stuffs out my cheeks.
- not shake food off my hand or fork back into the bowl or onto the ground.
- not scatter lumps of rice about.
- not eat sticking out my tongue.
- not smack my lips.
- not make a slurping noise.
- not lick my hands or fork.
- not lick the bowl.
- not lick my lips.
- not, in an inhabited area, throw away bowl-rinsing water that still has grains of rice in it.

And the Buddha's monks were required to confess to the community if ever they:

- eat more than one meal a day at a public soup kitchen or other charitable center.
- break a silent retreat to eat a group meal, except at the proper occasions.
- accept more than two or three bowlfuls of cakes or cooked cereal from a donor, unless they are immediately shared with others.
- turn down an offer of a particular food then eat something else.
- eat beyond appointed meal times.

- request finer foods if not physically ill and in need of them. (In the Buddha's time, fine food meant ghee, fresh butter, oil, honey, sugar/molasses, fish, meat, milk, and yogurt or cheese.)

- eat food that has deliberately been stored for the future.
- eat something that was not specifically offered.

Usually, excessive noise with spoons and chopsticks indicates your mind is wandering while you are eating.

—Sonoma Mountain Zen Center
Information Manual

Portobello Pizzas

1 PIZZA SERVES 1 PERSON AS A MAIN DISH.

FOR EACH PIZZA

1 large portobello mushroom, stem removed

2 tsp. high-quality olive oil

⅛ tsp. freshly ground or cracked black pepper, plus more to taste

1 tsp. fresh lemon juice

½ tsp. black olive paste or pitted black olives, lightly mashed

1 oz. herbed soft goat or feta cheese

5–6 capers

1 handful fresh arugula, chopped

▶ Preheat oven or toaster oven to 425°F.

▶ Coat the top and bottom of the mushroom each with 1 tsp. olive oil and place on a baking tray, with the stem side up.

▶ Sprinkle pepper and lemon juice on the mushroom. Fill the stem hole with olive paste.

▶ Spread goat cheese evenly on the stem side. Top with capers and arugula.

▶ Season with additional pepper and, optionally, a light splash of olive oil.

▶ Bake 10 minutes at 425°F. Serve warm.

Potato and Rutabaga Gratin

This is a toast to Alpine cooks for their love of cheese and milk, and for their ability to create simple, heartwarming dishes in snowy mountains.

SERVES 6–8.

1 Tbs. olive oil or butter

2 garlic cloves, peeled and minced

1 small onion, diced

½ tsp. salt

½ tsp. freshly ground or cracked black pepper

¼ tsp. ground nutmeg

2 cups heavy cream
(you can substitute 1 cup of evaporated milk for 1 cup of cream but the final dish will be soupy)

1 large leek, sliced into thin disks and washed

1¼ lb. baking potatoes, peeled and sliced into thin disks

¼ tsp. dried rosemary

½ lb. Gruyère cheese, grated

1 large rutabaga (1 lb.), peeled and sliced into thin disks

1 star anise, crushed (if you don't have star anise, substitute ½ tsp. dried tarragon or ⅛ tsp. ground cloves)

▶ Preheat oven to 375°F and get out an 11" x 7" or 9" x 9" baking pan.

▶ Heat oil in a small sauté pan. Add garlic and onion and sauté over medium heat for about 3 minutes, until the onion starts to soften. Remove from heat and add salt, pepper, and nutmeg. Stir in cream.

▶ Spread leeks evenly around the bottom of the baking dish. Don't worry if there are gaps, just be sure they are uniform. Cover leeks with half the potatoes as a layer. Sprinkle rosemary over the potatoes. Sprinkle ½ cup of cheese.

▶ Add a layer of rutabaga, using half. Sprinkle the crushed star anise on top and ½ cup cheese too. Repeat a layer of potatoes and cheese, then a layer of rutabaga.

▶ Pour the creamy onion mixture over everything as evenly as you can and bake for 30 minutes in a convection oven or 35 minutes in a regular oven. Sprinkle the remaining cheese over the top and continue to bake another 12–15 minutes, or until the rutabaga is tender and the cream seems to be solid. (It won't be if you used evaporated milk.)

▶ Remove from the oven and let it cool at least 5 minutes before serving. You can sparingly add chopped fresh flat-leaf parsley for color if you wish.

Spinach Pie

As a caterer, I made hundreds of spanakopitas, Greek spinach pies; I was often up to my elbows in spinach in huge washing vats. All those pies were dutifully wrapped in layers and layers of appropriate phyllo dough, all liberally brushed with butter. Then one day a friend asked me to make something special to take to her daughter's new apartment. The family was observing Passover so for that week they could eat no bread or wheat. I devilishly decided I would dare to make spanakopita without all that fattening, crumbly, and labor-intensive phyllo. It came out perfectly, was served in wedges, and everybody loved it. I've never bothered with phyllo since. Nobody misses it.

SERVES 8.

10–12 oz. fresh spinach leaves (2 bunches), stemmed, washed, and dried

½ lb. feta cheese

2 bunches scallions (12–14)

1 bunch dill, stems off

¼–½ tsp. salt

¼ tsp. freshly ground or cracked black pepper

6 extra large (or 7 large) eggs

1 tsp. olive oil

¼ tsp. flour or fine breadcrumbs

¼ tsp. ground nutmeg

▶ Preheat oven to 350°F.

▶ In a food processor, chop a mixture of spinach, feta, scallions, and dill into fine pieces. You will probably have to do this in batches. Combine all batches in a large mixing bowl.

▶ Add salt (less if the feta is already salty) and pepper. Add eggs, carefully stirring to blend. Everything should appear to be wet.

▶ Coat a 10-inch pie plate or other baking dish with olive oil. Sprinkle flour or breadcrumbs around the bottom to absorb any juices. Pour in the spinach mixture and spread evenly, leveling the top. This should be even with the top of the pan. If there is extra, pack it into a small (3½-inch diameter) Pyrex or other oven-safe bowl coated with olive oil.

▶ Sprinkle the top with nutmeg.

▶ Bake in the center of the oven at 350°F for 30–35 minutes, until the top is firm. (The leftovers in the small bowl will cook in 16–20 minutes.) Cool slightly before serving. You can also serve this at room temperature. Either way, cut in wedges.

Cutting Remarks

UNLIKE THEIR CHINESE COUSINS, Thai people set their tables with silverware. To the left of the plate is what we would call a soupspoon because it's long and large. To the right is the fork they use to push food onto that spoon. There are no knives anywhere on the table, for there is an unwritten rule in Thailand that food must be served bite-sized, ready to fit in a spoon. Theirs is the traditional Buddhist perspective that regards knives as essentially weapons of harm and aggression, small swords that should not be near people who gather to engage in the life-affirming practice that is eating a meal. The dinner table is thus regarded as a place of peace.

Much discussion about how to deal with the preparation of food emerged when the Dharma spread from India to China; a whole new code of Buddhist conduct had to be created. "A disciple of the Buddha," the *Fan Wang Ching*, a fifteenth-century sutra describing the practices in which a practitioner ought to engage, dictated, "should not store weapons such as knives, clubs, bows, arrows, spears, axes or any other weapons, nor may he keep nets, traps or any such devices used in destroying life." The Mahayana interpretation of this rule, appended in a commentary to the *Fan Wang Ching*, is that "a bodhisattva should not sell knives.... If one were to store knives and clubs to kill and maim, it would be against the spirit of compassion inherent in a buddha and therefore against the precepts. However, if knives are stored as kitchen utensils, such action does not go against the spirit of compassion, and therefore is not against the precepts." So the traditional Chinese Buddhist monasteries allowed only a cook to wield a knife, a distinctly shaped cleaver that could never be mistaken for a sword. As Dharma spread from China to Korea and Japan, and south to Vietnam and Thailand, the prohibition on knives beyond the kitchen door went as well. That's why Asian food is so distinctly served all cut up into bite-sized pieces, even Indian, Nepali, and Punjabi dishes.

No knives at the table is the Buddha's legacy.

True spirituality is to be aware that if we are
interdependent with everything and everyone else,
even our smallest, least significant thought,
word, and action have real consequences
throughout the universe.

—SOGYAL RINPOCHE

Swiss Chard Torte

This is an old, traditional southern Italian recipe that has variations in Greek cooking too.

SERVES 6–8.

1½ lb. Swiss chard (you can mix red and green, for you need two bunches)

¼ cup extra virgin olive oil

¼ tsp. salt

⅛ tsp. freshly ground or cracked black pepper

⅛–¼ tsp. (to taste) red pepper flakes

1 jumbo egg (or two small eggs)

1 cup grated pecorino, Parmesan, or Asiago cheese

¼ cup unbleached flour

2 Tbs. balsamic or Jerez (Spanish sherry) vinegar

pinch ground nutmeg

▶ Preheat oven to 400°F. Oil an 8-inch springform pan or quiche dish.

▶ Wash the chard and trim away all the thick stems, even up the back of the leaves. Chop the leaves into small ½-inch pieces.

▶ Heat the olive oil in a large sauté pan over medium-high heat. Add the chard, reduce heat to medium, and sauté, stirring until the chard has wilted. Add salt, pepper, and red pepper flakes. Remove from heat.

▶ In a medium bowl, whisk the egg. Blend in the cheese and flour. Stir in vinegar and nutmeg.

▶ Combine the cheese mixture with the greens, carefully mixing so everything is evenly distributed. Spoon everything into the oiled pan or dish, spreading it evenly, leveling the top.

▶ Bake 10 minutes at 400°F, until it is firm. (You might want to put a cookie sheet underneath to catch leaks.) Remove from the oven and cool 2 minutes before undoing the springform ring.

▶ To serve, cut into wedges and garnish with black olives.

Meraki . . . is a word modern Greeks often use to describe doing something with soul, creativity, or love—when you put 'something of yourself' into what you're doing, whatever it may be. Meraki is often used to describe cooking or preparing a meal . . . or setting an elegant table.

—CHRISTOPHER J. MOORE, *In Other Words*

Vegetable Strudel
with *Skordalia*

Skordalia is a primitive form of aioli, the Mediterranean garlic mayonnaise. It's beloved by Greeks and made from mashed potatoes instead of eggs, so it can be a valuable vegan substitute for mayonnaise.

SERVES 9–10 AS A MEAL, MORE AS AN APPETIZER OR TEA SNACK.

1 cup mashed potatoes
(to get that you will need to boil
2 medium potatoes, then mash them
with perhaps 1–2 Tbs. of the water
in the pot)

4 large garlic cloves, minced

¼ tsp. salt

¼ cup wine vinegar

1 cup olive oil, divided

1 bunch spinach, washed
and stemmed

1 large carrot, peeled and coarsely
chopped

1 bunch scallions, roots off and
cleaned

3 baby artichokes, outer leaves
and choke removed (canned is okay)

1 head bok choy, cored and cleaned
and leaves separated

2 medium zucchini, cut in large
chunks

1 small or ½ medium green bell
pepper, seeded and coarsely chopped

1 bunch broccolini, washed and
coarsely chopped

1 cup fresh or frozen shelled peas

2 tsp. dried oregano

1 tsp. dried marjoram

1 tsp. freshly ground or cracked black
pepper

pinch salt

1 pkg. phyllo dough, defrosted if
frozen

1 Tbs. black olive paste

2 Tbs. sesame seeds

▶ Preheat over to 350°F. Lightly oil or butter a large cookie sheet.

▶ To make *skordalia*, combine mashed potatoes, garlic, and salt in a blender or food processor. Combine vinegar with ½ cup olive oil and stream this into the potatoes, carefully blending to a smooth, thick sauce.

▶ Either by hand or in a food processor, finely dice all vegetables but peas. Combine in a large bowl. Add the peas, oregano, marjoram, black pepper, and salt. Stir in the *skordalia* and blend well.

- ▶ Open the package of phyllo; make sure the remaining ½ cup olive oil and a pastry brush, or a small piece of waxed paper if you don't have one, are nearby. Make sure the counter is very clean and dry and, working quickly, place one sheet of phyllo on it with the short side facing you. Brush or wipe the top with olive oil. Place another sheet on top and brush with oil. Do this two more times. After brushing the fourth sheet with olive oil, lightly spread some of the olive paste on it as well. Add two more sheets, brushing each lightly with oil.

- ▶ Leaving an inch clear from the end that is facing you, spread about ⅓ of the vegetable mix evenly over no more than ⅔ of the phyllo. Leave ½ inch clear along the sides to prevent the vegetables from oozing out when you roll it up. Starting with the short end nearest you, begin to roll the dough as tightly as you dare. As you do, dough that had been face-down on your work surface will roll up and face the ceiling. Brush this newly exposed surface lightly with oil after each revolution.

- ▶ Carefully lift the strudel onto the oiled or buttered cookie sheet, with the seam side facing down on the sheet. Brush the top with oil and sprinkle some sesame seeds on it. Using a large, sharp knife, cut 3 steam slits equidistant from each other on the top. They can be on the diagonal or parallel to the ends of the strudel.

- ▶ Repeat this process two more times, to make 3 strudels.

- ▶ Bake for 40–45 minutes or until the dough is very lightly browned or golden. Let the strudels rest for 5 minutes before slicing to serve. (You can also serve at room temperature.) Slice in thirds to have meal-sized portions or into 1-inch thick pieces to pass or serve as appetizers.

Winter Vegetable Timbale

Timbale is an old word for food that has been formed in a mold, a popular method of preparation in classical European cooking. (Italians call this *sformato*.) They are sometimes made single-serving size in ramekins. This large, pretty, golden one is heartwarming on a winter night.

SERVES 8.

1 parsnip, peeled and grated

1 large carrot, peeled and grated

1 small rutabaga, peeled and grated

1 small winter squash (e.g. red kuri, sugar pumpkin, or butternut), peeled and grated

4 Tbs. butter

1 red onion, peeled and diced

6 eggs

1 tsp. salt

⅓ cup grated cheddar cheese

⅔ cup grated Gruyère cheese

¾ cup breadcrumbs, matzo meal, or panko

2 Tbs. chopped fresh chives

2 Tbs. chopped fresh parsley

1 cup heavy cream

¼ tsp. smoked paprika (optional)

¼ tsp. ground nutmeg (optional)

▶ Preheat the oven to 325°F and butter a bundt pan, ring mold, or medium tube pan—any baking pan with a hole in the center.

▶ Mix the grated vegetables. You will need 5 cups.

▶ In a large sauté pan over medium heat, melt butter. Add onion and sauté until slightly soft. Add 5 cups of the mixed grated vegetables and blend. Sauté over medium heat until the vegetables are soft and start to cling together, 10–12 minutes. Remove from heat and cool.

▶ In a large bowl whip eggs. Add cooked vegetables, stirring well to coat. Add salt, then cheeses, breadcrumbs, chives, and parsley. Stir in cream, add optional smoked paprika and nutmeg, and combine everything well.

▶ Pour the mixture into the buttered pan or mold. Bake until a tester comes out clean. The cooking time will be between 35 and 45–50 minutes, faster in convection ovens, with the ring mold cooking faster than a bundt or tube pan, which have higher sides, making the timbale deeper and denser. Let it cool at least 5 minutes before unmolding.

▶ This looks very beautiful served on a bed of steamed dark leafy greens like Tuscan kale or spinach.

In the Soup

Harmony may be illustrated by soup. You have the water and the fire,
vinegar, pickle, salt and plums, with which to cook.... It is made
to boil by the firewood, and then the cook mixes the ingredients,
harmoniously equalizing the several flavors, so as to supply
whatever is deficient and carry off whatever is in excess.

—YEN TZU, an ancient Chinese
philosopher, circa 521 BCE.

Black Bean Chili

This becomes colorful when served with yellow rice underneath and a dollop of sour cream on top, perhaps crowned with a small cherry tomato.

SERVES 8–10 AS AN ENTRÉE.

¼ cup corn or olive oil

5 garlic cloves, peeled and minced

2 tsp. cumin seeds

2 large onions, peeled and diced

1 Tbs. dried oregano

3 tsp. ground cumin

1 poblano pepper, roasted, skinned, seeded, and diced

1 Anaheim chili pepper, seeded and diced

1 jalapeno pepper, seeded and diced

1 red bell pepper, roasted and chopped (from a jar is okay)

1 Tbs. red wine vinegar

1½ Tbs. chipotle chili powder

2 tsp. chili powder

¼ tsp. ground cayenne

1 lb. black beans, soaked overnight in hot water

1–1½ cups chopped tomatoes

¼ tsp. salt, or more to taste

GARNISH

⅓ cup chopped fresh cilantro

▶ In a heavy-gauge stockpot or large casserole, heat the oil. Add the garlic, cumin seeds, and onions, and sauté over medium heat until the onions are soft and golden. Stir in the oregano and ground cumin.

▶ Add chopped peppers and vinegar. Add chipotle, chili powder, and cayenne.

▶ Drain beans and rinse. Add to the pot. Add tomatoes and 6 cups of water. Stir to blend. Bring to a boil over medium-high heat, then cover and reduce heat to simmer. Simmer 3½ to 4 hours until the beans are tender. Test for salt and adjust.

▶ Serve with the chopped cilantro.

The man who is lazy and a glutton, who eats large meals and rolls in his sleep like a pig which is fed in the sty, is reborn again and again.

—*THE DHAMMAPADA*

Bonanza Borscht

This is a very hearty magenta-colored meal in a bowl. It's from Russia with love.

SERVES 4–6.

1 large onion, peeled

2 large carrots, peeled

3 large or 8 small fresh red beets, peeled

1 bunch of small beet greens, washed and dry

2 tsp. dill seeds

¼ cup olive oil

⅛ tsp. Szechuan pepper or Nepali timur or, for a slightly different taste, crushed juniper berries

1 tsp. celery seeds

⅛ tsp. ground allspice

1 Tbs. butter

¼ tsp. freshly ground or cracked black pepper

juice of 1 lemon, divided

¼ tsp. salt, divided

5 cups vegetable stock

¼ large white cabbage with outer leaves discarded, shredded as if for coleslaw

3 medium red or new potatoes, peeled and cut into bite-sized pieces

½ cup chopped fresh dill

Sour cream or thick yogurt

⅛ tsp. caraway seeds

1 Tbs. balsamic vinegar

▶ Finely chop onion, either by hand or in a food processor.

▶ Grate, shred, or finely chop carrots in a food processor. Do the same to beets and beet greens. Make sure not to puree but chop into small bits to get a thick soup.

▶ Grind dill seeds in a coffee grinder, small chopper, or mortar and pestle.

▶ Over medium-high heat, heat olive oil in a heavy-gauge soup pot or large casserole. When it is hot, add Szechuan pepper, ground dill seeds, celery seeds, and allspice, and stir to blend. Add onion and stir-fry for 1 minute. Add butter and, once it melts, add carrots and stir-fry for 2 more minutes. Add black pepper, beets, and beet greens. Stir to blend, lower heat to medium-low and cook for about 5 minutes, until vegetables are soft. Stir frequently to prevent burning.

▶ Add half the lemon juice and ⅛ tsp. of salt and stir to blend.

▶ Add vegetable broth, shredded cabbage, and diced potatoes. Bring to a boil, then lower heat to simmer. Cover the pot and simmer for 20 minutes.

- ▶ Stir in remaining lemon juice. Taste for salt and add to taste.

- ▶ Remove from heat. Toss in fresh chopped dill. Ladle into soup bowls and serve with a dollop of sour cream or yogurt in the middle of the bowl. Sprinkle caraway seeds over it and splash with balsamic vinegar.

Russian literature is rich in descriptions of food because to

a Russian cooking and eating are vital concerns.

—DARRA GOLDSTEIN, *Á La Russe*

Celery, Fennel, and White Bean Soup

SERVES 6.

5 Tbs. olive oil, divided

2 large garlic cloves, minced

1 red onion, peeled and coarsely diced or sliced

1 shallot, peeled and diced

1 leek, cut into ½-inch disks and washed

1 tsp. fennel seeds

4 large Roma tomatoes, diced, divided

4 cups vegetable broth, divided

2 cups cooked white beans (great northern, navy, cannellini—canned is okay), divided

1 bunch celery stalks with leaves, washed

1 large fennel bulb

1 Tbs. butter

1 red bell pepper, diced

1 tsp. dried thyme

1 tsp. dried marjoram

1 tsp. celery seeds

1 tsp. salt

½ tsp. freshly ground or cracked black pepper

1 bay leaf

juice of ½ large lemon

½ tsp. black olive paste

▶ Heat 4 Tbs. (¼ cup) of olive oil over medium heat in a stockpot or large casserole. Add garlic, onions, shallot, and leeks. Sauté over medium heat for 10 minutes, or until onions and leeks are soft. Add fennel seeds, half the tomatoes, and 1 cup of broth. Continue to cook over low heat for 10 minutes or until everything starts to look mushy. Remove from heat, stir in 1 cup of cooked beans, and put the pot contents through a food mill or food processor to make a chunky puree. Don't over-process to a silky texture.

▶ Cut leaves off the celery and set them aside. Wash the stalks and split the large ones down the center. Chop celery into bite-sized pieces. Save the leaves from the heart.

▶ Cut stems and fringe off the fennel. Strip the fringe and save it. Quarter the fennel, and slice it into thin strips.

▶ In the same pot, heat butter and 1 Tbs. olive oil over medium heat. Add celery, fennel, and red pepper and sauté 10 minutes or until they start to soften. Stir in thyme, marjoram, celery seeds, salt, and black pepper. Add remaining tomatoes and cook another 5 minutes.

▶ Add 3 cups of broth, bay leaf, lemon juice, and olive paste. Continue cooking over low heat for 15 minutes or until both the celery and fennel are soft and no longer chewy.

▶ Stir in the coarse puree and remaining cup of beans. Stir to blend everything, adjust seasonings to taste, cover, and simmer 5–10 minutes. Remove bay leaf.

▶ To serve, chop the celery leaves and fennel fringe for garnish.

Food tastes better when mother serves it .

—TIBETAN PROVERB

When this body hard to get that will so easily decay

Gets the nourishment it needs, it will flourish and be full of health.

— JETSUN MILAREPA

High Definition:
How *Hospital* Got into *Hospitality*

ALTHOUGH IT IS right there in the dictionary, seeing the word *hospital* as the core of the word *hospitality* can be startling. Supper doesn't seem like surgery, yet the dictionary assures us they are well connected. The chain starts with the Latin word for "guest." And thus, a *hoste* who took in *hospes* was committing *hospitare*, "receiving a guest," and did this in a *hospitale* or, if part of a religious sect, in a *hospice*—an inn that proffered *hospitium*, hospitality.

This illustrates the most fundamental and profound truth of human existence, one not changed a whit by our own evolution from cavemen to condo flippers: living requires eating. Almost two and a half millennia after the *Abhidharma* offered the ringing words "All beings exist on food," Jean Anthelme Brillat-Savarin opened his French meditations on gastronomy by declaring: "The universe is nothing without the things that live in it, and everything that lives eats." It's this never-ending realization that gave birth to extravagant traditions of hospitality, since anyone under your roof or your sway must be fed if you want them to get out alive.

When Brillat-Savarin went on to say, "To invite people to dine with us is to make ourselves responsible for their well-being for as long as they are under our roofs," his key word was *well-being*. It encapsulates the ancient and still widely held belief that being well comes from eating well. Faith in food came from observing how the body requires fuel to function and, since the body is in continual flux, how that fuel needs to be carefully and continually calibrated. The *Abhidharma* explains the metabolic process that breaks down every ingredient we ingest, how our digestive system rips food apart into various chemical elements that individually act in diverse ways, moving into the bloodstream, or kidneys, or intestines. If there is too much going one way, or not enough going another, or too much that is chilling or burning, the body slackens, weakens, ceases to function. Although the *Abhidharma* was codified long before x-rays and MRIs, its cause-and-effect analysis has yet to be discredited. In 1954, a local doctor told a Western scholar studying science in China: "Experts at curing diseases are inferior to specialists who warn against diseases. Experts in the use of medicine are inferior to those who recommend proper diet." In 1982, Madhur Jaffrey wrote in *Indian Cooking*: "There is something so very satisfying about Indian cookery.... It preserves our health and the proper chemistry balance of our bodies." In 1986 I watched a lieutenant of the macrobiotic guru Michio Kushi show an audience the correlation between the melanomas they'd survived and their stubborn consumption of chicken five to seven nights a week. "When you eat the same thing over and over, chemicals build up in a pool that becomes stagnant and toxic because the body can't process the overload fast enough," he said. This is a similar rationale to the explanation usually given for the twenty-first-century epidemic of diabetes: way too many carbs and sugars.

Although Ayurveda, which literally means "science of life," is thousands of years old, it is still the Indian subcontinent's main form of healthcare. Its modern practitioners are horrified by America's endless obsession with "diets": low-carb, no-carb, just juice, strictly protein, low fat, or whatever, for they believe a diet that deliberately excludes whole categories of food will destroy the possibility of body balance. Considering every individual a unique organism, Ayurvedic healers design individualized diets, based on factors such as age and gender, body tendencies, the strength of the tissues, and the level of toxins in the body. Geography and seasons also influence diet choices, along with foods that affect the non-physical aspects of the physiology: mental clarity, emotional serenity, and sensual balance. For instance, foods such as almonds, rice, honey, fresh sweet fruits, mung beans, seasonal vegetables, and leafy greens help coordinate body, mind, and heart.

Chinese medicine, with its emphasis on balancing *ch'i*, the life force, has a similar focus. Taoists associate intuitive wisdom, as well as harmony with the cycles of nature, with the stomach. They sort foodstuffs into *yin* (cold, dark, or thick) or *yang* (heat, light) in order to prescribe them as antidotes to imbalance. Healers, whether herbalists or doctors, might recommend Asian pears and lily buds for a winter cough, bone marrow soup for a broken toe, or tofu to get estrogen replacement. Medical knowledge of foodstuffs is passed down in families from cook to cook so that a hostess or mother who serves lotus root knows she is granting the boon of purifying the toxins that build up in blood. "The overriding idea about food in China," the scholar K. C. Chang explained in his pioneering work *Food in Chinese Culture*, "is that the kind and amount of food one takes is intimately relevant to one's health. Food not only affects health as a matter of general principle, the selection of the right food at any particular time must also be dependent on one's health condition at that time. Food therefore is also medicine."

The ancient Greeks had a similar belief—that the body was a puppet of variable temperaments (humors) continually subject to the vicissitudes of hot, cold, wet, and dry. Their oily, cold vegetable dishes like bean *plaki* (page 202) and *imam bayildi* (page 42) were intended to cool down a body afflicted by the hot, dry Mediterranean summer. The northern European tradition of spicing all the treats of Christmas time with cinnamon, ginger, and clove comes from awareness that these spices heat the body when the weather is chilly. On the far side of Asia, offering a dish stoked by chili peppers is offering a way to keep cool in the steamy heat, because chili peppers raise the body temperature enough to make it sweat, and sweating is the body's air conditioning mechanism.

If any of this kitchen aid seems surprising, it's because the wisdom was wiped off Western consciousness by the monopolizing machinations of the Holy Roman Empire. It was the Arabs who brought it to light from the Dark Ages. Food historian Reay Tannahill discovered, "The Arabs developed an interest in dietetic medicine which they studied largely from Greek sources and later helped transport back to the Western world which had forgotten it." The fall of Rome opened the floodgates that had dammed this scholarship. Almost immediately, a nonsectarian medical center sprang up in the protected harbor city of Salerno, in the southern tip of Italy. Scholars shuttling back and forth between Salerno and Alexandria translated the Arabic texts into Latin. "This," as Tannahill puts it, "restored Greek medicine to the West with Persian, Arabic, Hindu, and Chinese glosses, placing a more profound emphasis on diet...." The Salerno medical center developed treatments based on the ancient Chinese, Indian, and Greek theory of humors (sanguine, melancholic, choleric) and elements (fire, water, air) harmonized through food. The *hospitale*, or inns, of Salerno provided Crusaders *hospitium* that seemed to cure their ills, and this turned them into evangelists for faith in the medicinal power of food. Europe hungrily embraced their belief that a *hospitale* was the place for healing. We would've done that too, Tannahill says, for Salerno's regimen "was founded on the simple proposition, no less appealing then than now, that it was possible to look younger and live longer on the right diet."

The rising eighteenth-century faith in impersonal rationality with its emphasis on one-size-fits-all, and the zealous twentieth-century mass production that followed, nearly severed the connection between food and healing once again. Our age of pill-popping and drive-by fast food wants to trick us into thinking old-fashioned ideas like *hospitality* as *hospital* are superstitions disproved by high-tech equipment, but this one will not die. It lingers in "old wives' tales" that tell us to starve a fever and feed a cold, or eat a bowl of chicken soup. It's still in high definition in the dictionary. Webster's says *physician* comes from the Greek *phusike*, "knowledge of nature." Nature or what comes naturally is *physica*. A *physician* is therefore the same as a *physicist* who focuses on *physics*: study of the properties of matter and energy in nature. As the *Abhidharma* and the dictionary remind us, the works of nature through the properties of matter and energy are right in here in the human body. Physics is Ayurveda, the science of life. *Leib*, the old German word for body, gives us "life."

In perhaps the most revealing linguistic clue, the word we are most apt to use for a physician, *doctor*, is much the same as *docent*. Both grew from *doccere*, to teach. What doctors were meant to teach goes back to the beginning of our medical tradition, to Hippocrates who lived in classical Athens, only a century after the Buddha. He gave our doctors the Hippocratic oath, which includes this pledge: "I will apply dietetic measures for the benefit of the sick according to my ability and judgment…." Hippocrates also gave the following very concise advice: "Let your food be your medicine and your medicine be your food." We get this message in our common symbol or icon for a medical prescription, Rx—an abbreviation of the Latin verb "receive" in its command form: *recipe*.

*The Taoist believes the body, heart and mind must be
in harmony with nature's changes in order to be healthy.
Eating is a part of the cycle of yin and yang, day and night,
summer and winter, that nature follows….*

—Michael Saso, *A Taoist Cookbook*

Chickpea Soup from the Maghreb

This makes an excellent meal when served with crusty bread, cheese, and perhaps Raw Kale Salad (page 21).

SERVES 4.

3 Tbs. olive oil

1 medium red onion, peeled and diced

¼ tsp. caraway seeds

3 garlic cloves, peeled and minced

¼ tsp. ground turmeric

¼ tsp. ground ginger

¼ tsp. freshly ground or cracked black pepper

½ tsp. ground cumin

4 cups vegetable broth

1 Tbs. tomato paste

2 Tbs. chopped tomatoes in their juices

juice of ½ lemon

pinch saffron

2 small potatoes, peeled and cubed (about 1 cup when done)

1 (15-oz.) can chickpeas, rinsed and drained

¼ cup chopped fresh flat-leaf parsley

⅛–¼ tsp. salt to taste

▶ Heat oil in a medium casserole or soup pot over medium-high heat. Add onion and caraway seeds and sauté 5 minutes until onion is soft.

▶ Add garlic and all spices and continue to sauté 30 seconds.

▶ Add broth, stir in tomato paste, chopped tomatoes, lemon juice, and saffron. Bring to a boil. Add potatoes, chickpeas, and parsley. Reduce heat to low, cover and simmer 30 minutes.

▶ Stir in salt.

▶ Serve hot with lemon wedges and, optionally, a dollop of *harissa*, Tunisian chili sauce, or similar.

There are no such distinctions as delicacies or plain food, there is just one taste.

—DOGEN ZENJI, *Instructions to the Monastery Cook*

Corn Chowder
with Roasted Peppers and Tomatillos

Chowder is the English pronunciation of *chaudiere*, the French word for the cauldron used to boil soups and stews. It is thought to have come into colonial New England's kitchens from Newfoundland where Breton fishermen threw portions of their day's catch with whatever other food was available into a large *chaudiere*. This is my version of "East meets West": old fashioned New England corn chowder with Southwestern flourishes.

SERVES 6.

3 cups corn kernels (can be 4–5 fresh ears or frozen or canned corn), divided

2 Tbs. butter or ghee

1 large onion, peeled and diced

1 poblano pepper, roasted, skinned, and diced

1 serrano or other hot chili, seeded and diced

1 Tbs. dried sage

1 tsp. dried oregano

2 tsp. ground coriander

½ tsp. chipotle chili powder

1 tsp. freshly ground or cracked black pepper

3 celery stalks, cleaned and diced

2 cups vegetable broth, divided

3 medium potatoes (any color), peeled and cubed

1 tsp. salt

2 Tbs. diced pimento

2 tomatillos, peeled and coarsely chopped

12 oz. evaporated milk (not sweetened)

4 oz. heavy cream

GARNISH

chopped fresh chives

chopped fresh cilantro

shredded jack or cheddar cheese

toasted pumpkin seeds

▶ If you are using fresh corn on the cob, cut the corn off the cobs and put the cobs into a pot with 2 cups of water. Bring to a boil and simmer. This step yields a flavorful broth for the chowder.

▶ While the cobs simmer, melt butter in a medium soup pot or casserole. Add onions, poblano and chili peppers, sage, and oregano. Sauté over medium heat until onions are golden brown, about 6–8 minutes.

- ▶ Stir in coriander, chipotle, black pepper, and celery. Continue to sauté 2 minutes, stirring occasionally.

- ▶ Remove simmering cobs from heat. Remove and compost cobs. Save two cups of their broth, discarding the rest or saving for a later use.

- ▶ Puree one cup of corn with 1 Tbs. vegetable broth and add to the onion and pepper mixture in the pot, stirring to blend. Add potatoes, salt, and the rest of the vegetable broth. Stir to blend ingredients, cover and simmer for 10 minutes.

- ▶ Add remaining corn kernels, pimentos, and tomatillos. Add the two cups of reserved cob broth, or two cups plain water if you used canned or frozen corn. Continue to simmer covered over medium-low heat for 5–8 minutes. (You don't have to be exact.)

- ▶ Taste for salt and adjust to taste. Stir in evaporated milk and heavy cream. Cook over medium-low heat uncovered until the soup is warmed thoroughly. Do not bring to a boil once the milk and cream have been included. Stir once to blend all flavors.

- ▶ Ladle into large soup bowls and garnish with any or all of the ingredients listed above.

- ▶ Serve with blueberry pie for dessert!

For the [native American] Indians, food was more than just nourishment.
Food-gathering forays were social activities for groups of women who went
together to pick berries, dig roots, or collect seeds and greens. In Nevada,
the piñon harvest involved virtually the whole population of Paiute
villages in a period of intense activity.... Feasting was also
an essential part of many ceremonies.

—DR. CLARA SUE KIDWELL,

Spirit of the Harvest: North American Indian Cooking

Fragrant Split Pea Soup with Fresh Peas

The aromas of star anise and sage more than compensate for the lack of traditional smoked ham in this split pea soup. And it's just as hearty without that meat.

SERVES 4–6.

4 garlic cloves, minced

1¼-inch piece fresh ginger, peeled and minced

2 medium onions, peeled and halved

2 large carrots, peeled and coarsely chopped

2 stalks of fresh celery including tops, washed and coarsely chopped

2-inch piece fresh daikon, peeled and slit in half lengthwise

¼ cup olive oil

5–6 fenugreek seeds

½ tsp. freshly ground or cracked black pepper

½ tsp. Szechuan pepper or Nepali timur (optional, but do not substitute a different pepper if you can't find these)

1 tsp. ground turmeric

½ heaping tsp. ground cumin

¼ tsp. ground coriander

1 tsp. dried sage, minced

¼ tsp. ground allspice

⅛ tsp. ground cloves

1 lb. split green peas, cleaned

2 large star anise

½ tsp. salt

32 oz. vegetable stock

1 cup fresh or frozen shelled peas

GARNISH

4 snow peas, julienned

chopped fresh cilantro

▶ If desired, grind the garlic and ginger into a paste, Nepali style.

▶ Combine onion, carrots, celery, and daikon in a food processor and finely chop.

▶ Heat olive oil in a heavy-gauge soup pot or large casserole over medium heat. Add garlic, ginger, and fenugreek and stir-fry 30 seconds. Add black pepper, Szechuan pepper or timur, turmeric, cumin, coriander, sage, and allspice. Stir to blend and heat until fragrant, about 30 seconds.

▶ Add vegetable mixture and clove, stirring to blend. Cook over medium heat for 3–5 minutes, until mixture softens.

▶ Add split peas and star anise, carefully blending. Try not to break the anise. Cook 1–2 minutes or until peas are hot. Add salt. Add stock and 3 cups of water, stirring to blend. Bring to a boil.

▶ Reduce heat to low, cover, and cook 90 minutes, stirring occasionally. If you prefer a wetter soup, add more water ½ cup at a time at a minimum of a 10-minute intervals.

▶ Add fresh peas and taste for seasonings. Add salt if necessary. Continue cooking another 2 minutes. Turn off the heat. Remove star anise.

▶ Serve garnished with snow peas and/or chopped fresh cilantro.

Zen emphasizes attention to detail and taking care of things, being careful
and sincere and thorough in your effort, and that seems
as useful as anything in cooking.

—EDWARD ESPE BROWN

Kwati:
Newari Bean Soup

This very rich and nutritious soup is a beloved dish in Kathmandu, where it is served to new mothers, invalids, and others who need to gain strength quickly. It is also served on the midsummer full moon to everybody at the festival called *Kwati Purnima*. The traditional way to make it is to soak the beans and sprout them, which increases their nourishment. But this can take three days, so here is a "can opener" version for those who don't have that stretch of time. For those who do, soak and sprout all the beans, then follow this recipe using a pressure cooker. That's what today's Newari do.

SERVES 8–10.

¼ cup dried whole mung beans, soaked overnight

¼ cup soybeans, soaked overnight

2 Tbs. mustard, corn, sunflower, safflower, or olive oil

1 large onion, diced

4 garlic cloves, peeled and minced

1-inch piece fresh ginger, peeled and grated or minced

1 tsp. fenugreek seeds

2 bay leaves

1 (15-oz.) can of chickpeas (garbanzos), drained

1 (15-oz.) can of red kidney beans, drained

1 (15-oz.) can of black-eyed peas, drained

1 (15-oz.) can of cannellini or any white beans, drained

1 (15-oz.) can of black beans, drained

1 tsp. ground turmeric

2 tsp. ground cumin

1 tsp. ground coriander

1 tsp. arbol chili powder (or any chili powder that's fairly hot)

1 tsp. salt

3 cups vegetable broth

GARNISH

chopped fresh cilantro

1 tsp. caraway seeds, lightly fried in 1 tsp. butter/ghee (optional)

▶ Drain mung beans and soybeans. Put soybeans in a saucepan, cover well with water, bring to a boil, reduce heat, and cook 30 minutes. Add mung beans and cook another 20 minutes or until both beans are soft but not mushy. Drain.

- ▶ In a soup pot or large casserole, heat oil over medium heat. Add onion, garlic, and ginger. Sauté 4–5 minutes until onion is soft and golden. Stir in fenugreek and add bay leaves. Cook 30 seconds.

- ▶ Add all beans, spices, and salt. Carefully stir to blend. Add 1 cup water and the broth. Bring to a boil, cover, lower heat, and simmer 30 minutes.

- ▶ To serve: remove bay leaves. Garnish with chopped cilantro and, optionally, caraway seeds. Serve in soup bowls. Optionally, serve over aromatic rice.

Unless you live alone in a cave or hermitage, cooking and eating
are social activities: even hermit monks have one communal meal a month.
The sharing of food is the basis of social life.

—Laurie Colwin,

Home Cooking

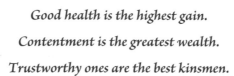

Good health is the highest gain.

Contentment is the greatest wealth.

Trustworthy ones are the best kinsmen.

—THE DHAMMAPADA

L'Chaim, Prosit, Salut!

THE UNSTOPPABLE NEED to feed has left us an enormous legacy of how to be hospitable. In the boondocks of history, food may have been the only status symbol nomads could flaunt, but the race to over-the-top generosity may also have been triggered by the realization that you really do need to do for others what you want them to do for you. Survival demands interdependence, the trading of good will. The Northwest coastal Indians' potlatch strategy, which survived up to modern times, was for a tribe to bestow food on other tribes while they had an abundance, knowing such hospitality also bestowed on guests an I.O.U. destined to come due when the beneficent tribe faced scarcity. More subtly perhaps, New Englanders have a tradition of not returning empty a pot, bowl, or dish somebody brought filled with food: to not refill it with food invites bad luck.

Hosting was (and is) the primordial photo op, an excellent way to look good and do good. It benefitted others, nurtured allies, established power, and exemplified the commandments to not kill and to love your neighbor as yourself. All in all, it served trust. From a Buddhist perspective, hospitality represents transcendent generosity, which, according to the Dzogchen Ponlop Rinpoche, means offering protection against fear: "giving some sense of protection from the fear of illness, disease, and the biggest fear, which is the fear of death. So all this is the generosity of giving life, helping beings prolong their life."

Our legacy of largesse continues in the place Jews set at their Seder table for Elijah, symbol of the stranger who may knock on the door, and on the plate of cookies Christian toddlers put out on Christmas Eve for a chimney-climbing Santa. It is the reason for the seven offering bowls spread in a row across the front of a Tibetan Buddhist shrine, for each represents what a perfect host 2,500 years ago would've offered a special guest like Shakyamuni Buddha: drinking water (*argham*), washing water (*padyam*), flowers (*pupé*), lights (*dhupé*), incense (*aloké*), perfume (*gendhe*), food (*newidye*), and music (*shabda*). Thus the practitioner invokes the Buddha or a bodhisattva with tangible reassurance that they are resplendently welcome.

"Each and every particle of my Kashmir is endowed with hospitality," the modern Himalayan poet Sir Mohammad Iqbal was moved to write, "even the rocks on the wayside offer me water to quench my thirst." The Persians are supposed to have sixty ways for saying "help yourself." The Russian word for hospitality is *khlebosol'stvo*, which means "bread," *khleb*, and "salt," *sol*. Ancient tradition renews itself with Greg Mortenson's three cups of Pakistani tea and in dirt-poor Tibetans competing with each other to fill both my water glass and tea cup every time I take a sip. It takes the form of Chinese banquets, catered wedding feasts, and White House state dinners. In *Couscous and Other Good Food from Morocco*, Paula Wolfert says the basic premise behind Arab hospitality is "No guest must go home hungry. And although this idea is often carried to the point of absurdity...after being served course after course...the guest will achieve *shaban* (total satisfaction) and know his host has held back nothing that would give him pleasure."

The enjoyment of good food draws people together in a way
that nothing else does. It is one of the few commonalities
shared by people the world over. Cultural, religious, even political
differences seem to be more readily set aside when sharing a meal.

—MARIA BAEZ KIJAC, *The South American Table*

Mirepoix Soup
with Beluga Lentils

Many societies start cooking with characteristic seasoning or ingredients. In the Himalayas, it's inevitably a paste of garlic and ginger. In Spain, it's *adobo*, which literally means "seasoning" or "marinade," and usually consists of at least garlic, paprika, and onion, though throughout Latin America and the Caribbean *adobo* varies with available spices and chilies and can be wet or dry. In France the basic beginning is *mirepoix*, a delicate blend of carrots, celery, and leek or onion. Here it is in a subtle, creamy soup highlighted by rich beluga lentils.

SERVES 8.

1 lb. carrots

1 large celeriac bulb

1 large onion or 1 medium leek

1 tsp. dried thyme

1 tsp. celery seeds

1 tsp. ground coriander

2 Tbs. fresh lemon juice

4 cups vegetable broth

1 tsp. salt, or more to taste

¼ tsp. smoked paprika

1 tsp. freshly ground or cracked black pepper

¼ tsp. ground cardamom

½ cup half and half
or light cream
or evaporated milk
for a thicker soup

1 cup cooked beluga lentils with ⅛ tsp. salt

½ cup chopped fresh dill

▶ Peel carrots and celeriac. Save celeriac leaves for garnish if you'd like. Slice carrots into thin disks and chop celeriac into bite-sized pieces. Put in a large casserole or soup pot.

▶ Peel the onion or wash the leek. Coarsely chop whichever you are using and add to the pot.

▶ Add thyme, celery seeds, coriander, lemon juice, vegetable broth, and 1½ cups water. Put over medium-high heat, cover, and bring to a boil. Lower heat to simmer and cook 25–30 minutes until vegetables are tender. Remove from heat and cool slightly.

▶ Puree contents of the soup pot and return to the pot. Stir in salt, smoked paprika, pepper, cardamom, and cream. Add the beluga lentils and taste for seasonings.

▶ Reheat uncovered on simmer for 8–10 minutes until it is just hot. Do not boil. Stir in chopped dill to serve.

▶ You can top each bowl with a hot garlic bread crouton and the chopped celeriac leaves.

It seems so simple, to be aware of what we are eating, but somehow
we have lost track of how to do it. Mindful eating is a way to reawaken
our pleasure in simply eating, simply drinking.

—JAN CHOZEN BAYS, *Mindful Eating*

Thick Mushroom Barley Soup

In the mid-1990s, I attended a Dharma retreat on the grounds of a farmhouse resort in the rolling countryside beyond Baltimore. At least half the 150 participants came, as I did, from afar, and were stuck for ten days within the confines of the property. Coffee, tea, and pastries with an occasional orange or banana were available at the start of the day, and lunch catered by a restaurant was incorporated into the scheduling. But no food was offered in the evening—not because the organizers were trying to adhere to Vinaya rules written for monks in the heat of ancient India, but because they felt it would break the budget. Unfortunately two evenings of no dinner broke the equanimity of a few practitioners, and four of them set off disruptive protests. Still, the organizers refused to relent and, being local, went home, probably to get something to eat. Although I had the mobility of my own car, it pained me to see so many so hungry with others so indifferent, so I got up the nerve to tell the unfed that if they'd each give me a dollar for ingredients, I'd cook dinner the next night. I easily collected $50 and the recipe that follows is what I made, my own favorite comfort food, because it seemed easily adaptable to the large crowd and small budget. I hoped it would teach the organizers a little lesson in how to do their duty, but I got a lesson too. Despite compulsory silence, more than a dozen people surprised me the next morning by saying thank you for making them feel "nourished," "so loved," and "genuinely cared for."

SERVES 4–6.

2–3 Tbs. olive oil

½ large onion, peeled and diced (red onion adds color)

1 small green bell pepper, coarsely chopped into bite-sized pieces

1 small poblano pepper, roasted, peeled, and coarsely chopped

1 cup pearl barley

2 tsp. dried thyme

¼ tsp. Szechuan peppercorns (don't fret if you don't have them, just use additional freshly ground black pepper)

1 tsp. dried oregano

3 celery stalks, washed and diced

½ tsp. dried rosemary

½ tsp. celery seeds

2 tsp. ground cumin

1 tsp. ground coriander

⅛ tsp. ground cloves

3 cups mushroom or vegetable broth

½ lb. mixed mushrooms
(shiitake, crimini, button, Portobello,
oyster), cleaned

½ Tbs. butter

¼ tsp. freshly ground or cracked
black pepper

½ tsp. curry powder or garam masala

½ roasted red pepper, diced, or a 2-oz.
jar of sliced pimentos, drained

2 Tbs. red lentils

1 tsp. salt

juice of 1 lemon

2–3 oz. baby spinach leaves

▶ Heat oil in a medium stockpot or large heavy-gauge casserole. Add onion and sauté over medium heat 3–5 minutes until it's lightly brown and glistening.

▶ Add green pepper, poblano pepper, barley, thyme, Szechuan peppercorns, and oregano. Continue sautéing for a minute, stirring so nothing sticks and the barley is hot. Add celery, rosemary, celery seeds, cumin, coriander, and clove, stirring to blend. Add broth and bring to a boil. Lower heat and cover the pot. Simmer 1 hour on low. (You don't have to worry about overcooking this; you can simmer it 10–20 minutes longer.)

▶ Slice and chop mushrooms into large bite-sized chunks. Melt the butter in a sauté pan over medium-low heat and, when it's bubbling, add the mushrooms. Add black pepper and curry powder (but not the garam masala if using that). Sauté 1 minute. Remove from heat.

▶ When the barley has been cooking for at least an hour and is starting to be soft to the teeth, add the contents of the mushroom sauté, the pimentos or roasted red pepper, red lentils, and salt. Blend into the barley. If the mixture looks too solid and you prefer it more soupy, add a cup or two of water and continue cooking at least 10 minutes or until the barley is tender.

▶ Stir in lemon juice. Top with spinach leaves, cover, and simmer 5 minutes to steam the spinach. Remove from heat. Add garam masala if you are using it.

▶ Serve in soup bowls. This goes very well with a side of any yogurt condiment.

Provençal Tomato Soup

This recipe was given to me by a French housewife who said her house was small, but if people wanted to come and eat, she could "push the walls."

Because this freezes very well, it's an excellent way to preserve summer's bounty.

SERVES 4–5.

3 Tbs. olive oil

1 Tbs. butter

2 Tbs. dried thyme

2 large onions, peeled and finely chopped

1 bay leaf

freshly ground black pepper to taste

2 lb. fresh tomatoes, skinned (optional) and chopped

¼ tsp. salt

1 mildly hot small pepper, whole

2 Tbs. minced fresh parsley (5–6 sprigs)

GARNISH

buttered garlic croutons (optional)

▶ In a medium heavy-gauge casserole, heat olive oil and butter together until butter melts. Stir in thyme and stir-fry 30 seconds. Add onions, bay leaf, and a pinch of black pepper. Stir to blend and sauté over medium-low heat until the onions are soft and glistening.

▶ Add the tomatoes and salt and mix well. Drop in the whole pepper. If the tomatoes aren't juicy, add ½ cup water to avoid burning. Cover and simmer on low for 20–25 minutes, until the tomatoes become soupy. (If the soup is too thick and pasty, add either another ¼ cup of water or dry sherry if you'd like.)

▶ Remove the bay leaf and whole pepper. Stir in the parsley. Remove from heat. Adjust salt and pepper to taste and serve with or without garlic croutons.

Red Bean Chili with Bulgur

This is my reach-for recipe for feeding a crowd. It is very flexible. You can double or triple it, and don't have to worry about exact proportions of vegetables. It usually all works out just fine.

SERVES 8.

⅓ cup olive oil

2 medium or 1 very large onion, peeled and diced

2 serrano or other green chili peppers, seeded and minced

4 garlic cloves, peeled and minced

1 small bell pepper, red or green, chopped

1 medium carrot, peeled and diced

1 large celery stalk, diced

1 small eggplant, finely chopped (about 1 cup)

¼ lb. button mushrooms, cleaned and finely chopped

1 Tbs. ground cumin

1 tsp. dried oregano

2 Tbs. chili powder

½ tsp. chipotle chili powder

2 tsp. salt

¼ tsp. freshly ground black pepper

1 bay leaf

2 cups chopped tomatoes in their juices

1 Tbs. Worcestershire sauce

juice of ½ lemon (about 2 Tbs.)

¼ tsp. balsamic or Jerez (Spanish sherry) vinegar

¼ cup cooking wine (can be Chinese) or dry red drinking wine

splash of hot sauce

2 (15-oz.) cans red kidney beans, not drained

¾ cup bulgur

1 cup vegetable or tomato juice

GARNISH

chopped fresh cilantro
sour cream

▶ Over high heat, warm oil in a medium casserole or soup pot. Add onions, chili peppers, garlic, and bell pepper. Sauté until onions and pepper soften, 3–5 minutes.

▶ Stir in carrots, celery, eggplant, mushrooms, spices, salt, and pepper. Sauté 2 minutes, stirring so nothing burns.

▶ Add next 9 ingredients and 1 cup water; stir to blend and bring to a boil. Reduce heat and simmer for 30 minutes uncovered, stirring from time to time so nothing sticks to the

continued on next page

bottom. If the chili is getting too thick, thin with ¼ cup tomato or vegetable juice, or water, at a time.

▶ Taste for seasoning and add salt if necessary. To make the chili hotter, add another ¼ tsp. hot sauce, or 1 tsp. red pepper flakes.

▶ Garnish with chopped cilantro. Serve with a dollop of sour cream on top and tortillas or tortilla chips on the side.

Whole Nine Yards Vegetable Soup

Probably the most difficult time I have spent in a kitchen was ten days of cooking three daily meals for the masters and monks teaching two hundred Americans in a remote hamlet in the high desert of Colorado. The challenges were nonstop. One monk could have no salt, no sugar, and limited fats. Another was on blood thinners and could have no tomatoes and no greens, not even parsley. And the nearest store was seventy-five miles away. The pinnacle of stress was being told to serve a vegetarian soup. With excruciating effort, I crafted a soup with none of the medically prohibited ingredients. The lamas and monks all sent their bowls back clean, a big *phew*!

Later, I heard loud knocking on the door. It was my teacher's vigilant attendant, the fierce-looking monk Lobsang Dorje. "Are you looking for food?" I said lamely.

He didn't respond at first. Finally, he said very solemnly, "Sandy, why you feed Rinpoche like a pig?" I felt my legs wobble and had to sit down.

"What is wrong with vegetable soup? You eat noodle soup. You eat a lot of noodle soup!"

"Sandy, you need to remember something important. When Tibetans eat, they have their meat here," he pointed to one side, "their rice here," he pointed to a center, "and a vegetable over here. We enjoy the meal and then when we're finished eating, we put everything that's left together and feed it to pigs. But you," Lobsang exhaled with feigned disgust, "no. First you put everything together in one bowl and then you offered it to Rinpoche. So you fed Rinpoche like he was a pig."

SERVES 4–6.

---

8 cups vegetable broth or water

⅓ cup split peas
(green or yellow or both)

⅓ cup pearl barley

¼ cup dried white beans
(lima or navy)

¼ cup dried mushrooms

1 Tbs. dried thyme

1 tsp. ground cumin

½ tsp. ground coriander

1 tsp. dried marjoram

2 tsp. salt, divided

1 Tbs. celery seeds

1 bay leaf

3 medium carrots, peeled and sliced
into thin disks

continued on next page

1 small onion, peeled and diced

2 Roma tomatoes, diced

¾ cup corn kernels
(frozen or canned is okay)

½ cup peas or green beans, cut into
small pieces

3–4 Swiss chard leaves,
stems removed and chopped

2 Tbs. orzo

6 Tbs. (⅓ cup) mashed pumpkin

⅛ tsp. smoked paprika or chipotle
chili powder

½ tsp. freshly ground or cracked
black pepper

¼ cup chopped fresh parsley

1 tsp. prepared horseradish (optional)

▶ In a small stockpot or large casserole, combine the water or broth, split peas, barley, white beans, dried mushrooms, thyme, cumin, coriander, marjoram, 1 tsp. salt, celery seeds, and bay leaf. Bring to a boil over high heat, reduce heat to low, cover, and cook for 90 minutes.

▶ Add carrots, onion, and tomatoes. Continue cooking, covered, over low heat for 15 minutes.

▶ Add the corn, green peas or beans, chard, orzo, and remaining 1 tsp. salt. Cook over low heat for 10 minutes. Remove the bay leaf.

▶ Stir in the mashed pumpkin, smoked paprika or chipotle, and black pepper. Heat on low for 5 minutes. Stir in the parsley and optional horseradish, and remove from heat.

▶ Serve with a grilled cheese sandwich or cornbread. And eat like a pig!

In Hot Water:
Noodles and Rice

*Food is our common property . . . our treasure of change
and transformation, sustenance and continuation.
It is the essence of all the Buddha's mind and practice,
the unfathomable effort of all beings who have
bought us this time to eat from most ancient times,
from every world past and present.*

—ZENTATSU RICHARD BAKER,
Tassajara Cooking

Everything you see I owe to spaghetti.

—SOPHIA LOREN

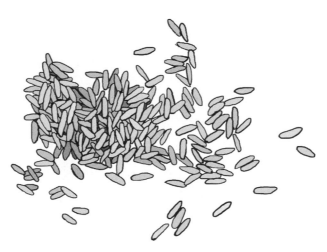

Noodles: "Boiled Bread"

AFTER LIBERATING NAPLES from foreign monarchy in 1860, Giuseppe Garibaldi supposedly turned to his aides planning *Il Risorgimento* and said: "It is macaroni, I swear to you, that will finally unite Italy." He was not joking. For more than two thousand years, with remarkable consistency even in the guises of diverse names in divergent languages, the Arabic *al-fidawsh* ("burst open like a bud"), Italian *vermicelli* ("little snakes"), and Hindi *lakhshah* ("slippery"), noodles have transcended cultural, geographical, and political boundaries, uniquely bringing far-flung, sometimes feuding residents of the planet to the table in absolute agreement on at least one important point: *mmm...good!*

Perhaps the greatest testament to the universal adoration of noodles is not how wide they're spread over the map, but the ongoing competition for the honor of being their creator (China, Italy, the Arabs?), even though the most likely parents of the whole caboodle lived around the Tarim Basin. The Central Asian steppes have historically been a perfect place to grow wheat, with plenty of rivers to add water. Auspiciously, for millennia they also happened to be the bustling intersection of crisscrossing civilizations always on the lookout for something tasty.

The union of flour and water was momentous. Mother Nature's handout, wheat berries, had originally been boiled into porridge, fermented for beer, cracked, or eventually cooked until they burst, at which point they were dried to create *bulgur*. Then the Iron Age brought the grindstone and suddenly the world was filled with flours. The inspired combination of ground wheat and water to make a paste (hence the word *pasta*) was such a *succes fou* that caravans and nomads carried their own grindstones, even though oases on the Silk Road proudly featured them. Where there was fuel to heat ovens, a ball of paste or dough was flattened and slapped on the inside wall to make thin bread like naan, roti, lavash, or pita. On the steppes, where there were no trees and thus no fuel, flattened balls of dough were cleverly stretched and sliced into thin strips that could be dunked into hot broth or water. It was thought of as "boiled bread." *Lagman*, fettuccini-like noodles in hot lamb broth with a name redolent of both lasagna and *lo mein*, has been a dietary staple of the chilly Central Asian region since at least 300 BCE when a Han Chinese intellectual mentioned it in his ode to pasta. *Lagman* is still served by Uighers, while the rest of us have a world of wannabes: Vietnamese *pho*, Indonesian *bakso*, Thai *khao soi*, Tibetan *thukpa*, Korean *ramyeon*, ramen (originally imported to Japan from China in soup), Malaysian *laksa*, Burmese *mohinga*, Hawaiian *saimin*, and chicken noodle in a can. In *Asian Noodles*, Nina Simonds says a bowl of noodle soup has become the world's premier comfort food. In his autobiography *Freedom in Exile*, the only event the Dalai Lama fondly recounts from the precarious days of his first escape to India is the journey "by train with my small entourage to Calcutta. On the way, I remember that my mother, unaware of any restrictions and feeling totally unrestrained, brought out a small stove and cooked a most delicious noodle soup."

While the Chinese are indeed responsible for the geographic spread of noodles, they could not have invented them because wheat is not native to their land. After offloading threads of silk in Persia, Pakistan, or Perugia, Chinese traders on their way home through the Tarim Basin most likely filled their emptied saddlebags with the makings of wheat. Han China was as short of trees as the steppes, so planting wheat solved a critical economic and cultural problem. In the cool, treeless north, it provided "boiled bread" and later the valuable gluten known as *seitan*. In the south where it did not thrive, the Chinese substituted flour ground from rice. Both kinds of noodles turned out to be ideal for Buddhist monks with their restrictive diets and commitment to a simple course between austerity and extravagance. Monks in fact may have inadvertently propelled their popularity, since for centuries their monasteries provided the only public food available to people away from home. With no other precedent to build on, the first entrepreneurs to open public restaurants in China could only emulate monastery dining rooms, and more often than not, they started noodle houses.

CHINESE NOODLES went south to Thailand, Vietnam, and Malaysia in the mass emigration of eighth-century merchants fleeing an onslaught of profit-crushing, antibusiness edicts issued by T'ang emperors converted to Buddhism.

Fury at these antimaterialistic Buddhists was compelling enough to uproot and drive the business class into exile, but its attachment to noodles turned out to be as strong as its commitment to capitalism. The diaspora brought noodle eating to the countries it found refuge in, and created Indochina's seemingly "indigenous" signature dishes: *pad Thai* and Vietnamese *pho*. In Malaysia and Singapore, its noodles encountered curry spice carried from India by monks, and the ironic comingling of Buddhism's devout with its defectors gave birth to the region's iconic *laksa*, curried Chinese noodles named after the Hindu word for "slippery."

Geopolitics also played a part in the globalization of the modern Thai favorite, *khao soi*. This spicy noodle soup, much favored by Genghis Khan, was originally created by Tarim-area Muslims who took the recipe with them when they were swept into the thirteenth-century Mongol invasion of China. The Muslims settled as farmers in the western mountains that border Tibet, and with the passing of centuries became indistinguishable from their neighbors. Their chili noodle soup might still be a subtle specialty of their hillsides if in 1865 the emperor's government hadn't responded brutally to an uprising in the region, forcing them to flee. They headed south into Burma and Laos, then across the borders into northern Thailand where they settled in Chiang Mai and continued cooking their noodle soup. Chiang Mai is now revered by gourmets as the epicenter of "traditional Thai" *khao soi*.

WHEN BUDDHIST MONKS imported Dharma from China to Japan, they took monastery noodles with it. They had no idea this seemingly innocuous import would touch off a craze that upended their country's eating habits, but *chukka soba*, Chinese noodles, filled stomachs on islands historically challenged to produce enough food for all inhabitants. This encouraged noodle houses and noodle carts to sprout wildly. By the time nineteenth-century religious refugees from China fled to Japan and set up shops selling their beloved yellow noodle soup, *ra-mian*, noodles were an ordinary staple of the Japanese diet. But as soon as those three little words *udon*, *somen*, and *soba* were joined by the word *ramen*, something happened. Chefs began to compete furiously to concoct the ultimate Japanese version, with a samurai fanaticism cheekily mocked in the hilarious 1980s hit movie *Tampopo*, a "spaghetti western" depicting the bloodthirsty, "high spoon" quest of gun-slinging noodle house proprietors for lone-range ramen glory. The passion hasn't abated. "Combine New Yorkers' love of pizza, hot dogs, and hamburgers, throw in some Southern barbeque mania, and you've still only begun to approximate Tokyo's obsession with ramen," Matt Gross reported in 2010 in the *New York Times*. "Tokyo is a city that can seem closed off yet all I had to do was mention my quest to find a perfect bowl of ramen, and I was besieged with recommendations, reminiscences, and requests to join strangers for meals."

During the difficult postwar years, a man named Momofuku Ando reinvented his beloved Japanese noodle soup as everyman's portable fast food. His cheery little packages of instant ramen invaded the kitchens in Japan, then so quickly and completely conquered the rest of the Earth that, by the century's end, Microsoft Word didn't even redline the word *ramen* as questionable. Yokohama now has a ramen museum. The Japanese are in fact so proud of this creation—this one product of all the goods they exported during their astonishing business boom, which included Walkmans, miso, cameras, copiers, and cars—that they voted instant ramen their nation's greatest contribution to the world.

Silk Road Noodles

This simple noodle dish comes from the Uighur people who live at what was the main Silk Road intersection and still refer to fresh noodles as "boiled bread." The flavor of cumin, not normally used with noodles, makes it distinct.

SERVES 6.

1½ large green bell peppers, seeded

1 large onion, peeled

1¼ lb. fresh wheat noodles

4 Tbs. corn, safflower, or other vegetable oil, divided

1 Tbs. very fresh cumin seeds

5 garlic cloves, peeled and very thinly sliced

2 serrano or other hot green chili peppers, seeded and thinly sliced

bottom half of a head of Napa or Chinese cabbage, cored

1 liquid cup chopped tomatoes or 4 fresh tomatoes, diced

2 tsp. salt

GARNISH

chopped fresh cilantro or Chinese chives

▶ Slice green peppers from top to bottom into thin strips. Slice the onion into thin disks, then chop disks into thin pieces.

▶ Bring a large pot of heavily salted water to a boil and cook noodles according to package instructions. Do not overcook. Drain immediately and coat with 1 Tbs. oil.

▶ While noodles are cooking, heat a large wok or sauté pan on high heat, and once it's hot, add 3 Tbs. oil. When oil is hot, lower heat to medium low and add cumin seeds. Cook 30 seconds.

▶ Add green peppers, onion, garlic, and chilies. Sauté with cumin seeds 5 minutes, or until soft.

▶ Add cabbage, tomatoes, and salt, stirring to blend. Simmer over medium-low heat 2–3 minutes to warm.

▶ Stir in the hot noodles and mix with vegetables. Stir-fry for 2–3 minutes.

▶ Garnish with cilantro or chives, if desired, and serve hot.

Szechuan Peanut Butter Noodles

SERVES 6–8.

1 lb. fresh Chinese egg noodles
(sold refrigerated, often near produce)

2 Tbs. olive, corn, or canola oil
(don't use fruity olive oil)

3 garlic cloves, peeled and minced

1-inch piece fresh ginger, peeled and
grated or minced finely

1 Tbs. rice vinegar
(or wine vinegar if you don't have any)

¼ cup soy sauce
(heavier is better but not mandatory)

½ cup Chinese sesame oil

⅛ tsp. hot chili paste or Tabasco or
habanero sauce

⅓ cup crunchy peanut butter

1 cup chopped fresh chives
(the thick Chinese chive works best)

1 Tbs. sesame seeds, lightly toasted

¼ lb. fresh snow peas, cleaned

► Cook fresh noodles in boiling water according to package instructions or for 2 minutes. Drain and refresh under cold water. Mix olive or other oil into the noodles to keep them from sticking and set aside to cool.

► In a large bowl, blend garlic, ginger, vinegar, soy sauce, sesame oil, and chili. Stir in peanut butter and keep stirring to make a smooth sauce.

► Put the noodles in a large serving bowl and pour the sauce over them. Use a fork to blend. Mix in chopped chives (you may have to use your hands). Sprinkle sesame seeds all over the top. Optionally, if you like chili, you can now sprinkle some red pepper flakes on.

► To garnish with snow peas, line the edge of the bowl by placing each snow pea upright next to another. You can also chop the snow peas and mix them into the noodles.

► Serve at room temperature.

Vietnamese Garlic Noodles with Greens

Chowhounds are still trying to sniff out the true origin and authentic composition of this addictively tasty dish. It appears to have been created in San Francisco by the An family at their Vietnamese restaurant, which so closely guards the recipe it's made in a closed kitchen. But some native Vietnamese recall eating a similar dish back in Indochina where, because of French colonization, noodles and butter were available in cities like Hanoi and Saigon, and the spaghetti-like noodles in it were called *nui* after their French name, *nouille*. For now everyone seems to agree that what's called "garlic noodles" is a crossover dish, Vietnamese-American, and unstoppably popular. There are probably almost as many variations as there are chowhounds trying to recreate what they first tasted either in Vietnam or at the An family's restaurant. This one, with the greens, is mine because, until I fell for garlic noodles (in a different Vietnamese restaurant), I regularly made and recommended a similar pasta dish with kale, garlic, and lemon juice—a rich dish in itself.

SERVES 4 AS A SIDE (IT'S TOO RICH TO BE THE MAIN COURSE).

½ lb. spaghetti, linguine, or bucatini	¼ tsp. freshly ground black pepper
4 cups coarsely chopped fresh kale or Asian mustard green leaves (no stems)	1 Tbs. finely grated Parmesan or Asiago cheese
1 Tbs. rice wine or dry sherry	⅛ tsp. salt
6 garlic cloves, peeled and minced	1 Tbs. fresh lemon juice
5 Tbs. butter	

▶ Cook spaghetti according to package instructions, except cook it about 60 seconds past when it is *al dente* because it should be soft. Halfway through add kale or mustard greens to the pot. When pasta and greens are cooked, ladle ½ cup of the cooking water into a cup and add the vinegar or sherry to it. Drain the noodles and greens but do not rinse them.

▶ While the spaghetti cooks, mash the minced garlic with the back of a cleaver or wide knife and blend it with 1 tsp water. (This will keep it from browning in the pan.) In a large sauté

continued on next page

pan over low heat, melt 4 Tbs. butter. Add the mashed, wet garlic. Stirring continually, warm it for 60–90 seconds until it's soft and fragrant. Do not let it brown.

▶ Add the pepper and the reserved cooking liquid, stirring to blend. Bring the contents of the pan to a vigorous boil and then raise the heat to medium and add the noodles and cheese. Using two forks or tongs, mix them into the sauce and continue to stir, until all the sauce is clinging to the noodles and there's no extra floating in the pan. Remove from heat.

▶ Season with salt to taste. Stir in the remaining 1 Tbs. butter and the lemon juice. Divide into bowls and serve immediately.

Variation:
Garlic Noodles with Fried Kale on the Side

▶ Proceed as above except do not add kale to the boiling water and omit the lemon juice. Instead bring 30 oz. peanut oil to a sizzle in a deep saucepan or other deep frying device. Make sure the kale is very dry. Using tongs, drop 2 or 3 leaves at a time into the hot oil. Stand back. Remove from oil after 90 seconds, or as soon as the leaves are crunchy. Drain well on paper towels or the kale curls will be too oily. Salt and serve with lemon wedges on the side.

O Children of Adam! Don your adornment at every place of worship

and eat and drink what you want, but do not be excessive,

prodigal, or wasteful.

—THE QUR'AN

Noodles:
The Origins of Dried Pasta

DESPITE THEIR CENTRAL ROLE in pioneering East Asia's noodle obsession, the Chinese had no part in the Italian passion predicted by Garibaldi. The legend of Marco Polo toting ravioli home to Venice from Peking is a corporate marketing myth like Betty Crocker baking biscuits in the Midwest and Uncle Ben planting rice in North Carolina. The gimmick doesn't hold up any more than a wonton would, stuck in a suitcase for the many years it took the real Polo to get home. The story ignores how Silk Road travel out of the Tarim Basin went in more than one direction, and consequently how cooks from Persia to Portugal were already boiling "bread" before the birth of Jesus. Bread cut and boiled in some shape or other was popular enough for the fifth-century Jerusalem Talmud to include a debate about whether or not it was acceptable for Passover. A surviving ninth-century Syrian document refers to dried string-like shapes of semolina called *itriyah*. (Wheat in Greek or Aramaic was *itrion*, in Arabic *itriya*, and became *triticum* in Latin.) There are Greek references to *lasanon* and Latin mention of *lagana* as sheets of dough. A century before Polo started packing, recipes appeared in a Sicilian cookbook for *maccherruni*. A half-century later, "maccheroni" was recorded in Genoa as part of an estate. Even at Polo's moment of departure, a baker in Pisa was advertising for assistance in his *vermicelli* manufacture, while not that far afield in Spain, cookbooks were providing instructions for making three distinct forms of pasta: round like seeds, large thin sheets, and worm-like threads.

What the myth of Marco Polo disguises is that, while Crusaders were on the march to crash the gates of Jerusalem and claim the property, Muslims were on a crusade to cash in on the properties of what Arabs called *al-fidawsh* ("burst like a bud"). The hard wheat necessary to produce this revolutionary noodle did not grow in Asia, for Chinese travelers to the West recorded surprise at finding wheat there tough enough to be preserved. Durum wheat, sometimes called *semolina*, required the sort of hard-rock, dry terrain Islam's new army

had conquered in North Africa, Spain, and Sicily—precisely the places macaroni first appeared, in recipes whose inclusion of almond milk, dates, and sugar
bespeak Arabic origins. North Africa, Spain, and Sicily also had the low-to-no
humidity perfect for drying dough. Then too, hard wheat was not called *hard* or
durum for nothing. Before machinery intervened, the dough had to be kneaded
by feet. The elision of words that translate into "to knead dough with full force,"
is the most prominent among the myriad interpretations of *maccheroni*, a vari-
ant spelling of *maccherruni* and Sicily's original generic word for all pasta that
was dried.

The eminent Mediterranean food historian Clifford Wright says the inven-
tor of a hard wheat noodle that could be indefinitely preserved was most likely
an Arab responsible for feeding the huge armies of nascent Islam moving rapidly across both North Africa and the Middle East. Dried pasta seems to have
been created to replace barley products in the common commerce of Islam's
growing domain, and to provide more appealing food for those on the move
and in the money. In a region short on firewood and long on heat that spoils
food, macaroni was the perfect product. The original little balls easily carried
and quickly cooked are still made in Lebanon, Syria, Tunisia, and Algeria, while
in modern Italy the balls survive as gnocchi. Strips stretched and sliced into
slivers of vermicelli, called in Arabia "hairs," in Persia "threads," and in Tunisia
"inchworms" are now the sine qua non of Middle Eastern pilaf and the American version, Rice-a-Roni. They also come packaged in Spanish speaking countries as *fideus* or *fideos*, the Spanish pronunciation of the Arabic *al-fidawsh*.

In 1154, the Arab geographer Mohammed al-Idrisi reported to the king
of Sicily on the dried pasta manufactured and exported from his realm. He
described strings of dough made in Palermo. "West of Termini," al-Idrisi said
in his *A Diversion for the Man Longing to Travel to Far-Off Places*, "there is a
delightful settlement called Trabia. Its ever-flowing streams propel a number
of mills. Here there are huge buildings in the countryside where they make vast
quantities of *itriyya* which is exported everywhere: to Calabria, to Muslim and
Christian countries. Very many shiploads are sent."

By the sixteenth century, macaroni was important enough in mainland Italy
for the Florentine princess Catherine de Medici to include it in her dowry to
the King of France. By the nineteenth-century, the dramas of politics, holy
wars, and conquest turned Catholic Naples into the macaroni mecca of the

Mediterranean, and the Spaniard king of Naples, Ferdinand II, became so impatient with the painstaking, traditional production of dough by foot, he commissioned an engineer to design a kneading machine. The contraption was busily extruding strings of dough—the word for string, *spago*, was pluralized into *spaghetti*—when Garibaldi liberated Naples from that foreigner's autocratic rule and made his prophesy about pasta. Today Italy is indeed one nation, united by a stringent and unique law promulgated to protect the legitimacy of its defining product. Authentic pasta can only be crafted the traditional Arabic way: from durum wheat and water.

Macaroni may have been a more momentous invention than the noodle, for dried pasta's uniquely long shelf life made it an even more potent political and economic tool. It could be stockpiled to mitigate famines and natural disasters. It could sustain political stability by countering the problems agricultural shortages provoke. But more importantly perhaps, a plentiful supply of hard wheat kneaded with water and dried into macaroni made possible long sea voyages, launching the era of European exploration. The Nina, the Pinto, and the Santa Maria, which set out from Spain under the command of the Italian Christopher Columbus, were packed with pasta. The rest, as they say, is history.

The destiny of nations depends
on how they nourish themselves.

—Jean Anthelme Brillat-Savarin

Peas with Rosary-Bead Pasta

This is an antique southern Italian recipe made with tiny tubes of pasta meant to resemble rosary beads. They are reminiscent of the original little balls with which dried noodles were launched. I found the perfect pasta in an upcountry New England supermarket packaged as *ditali*. It can also be called *ditalini*.
In a pinch, use the shortest macaroni you can find, or else perhaps wheels. Just remember, this is peas with pasta and not the other way around: there should be twice as many peas as rosary beads. The final dish, which has neither sauce nor cheese, is surprisingly finger-licking, especially if the peas and parsley are fresh from a farmers' market or your garden.

SERVES 3.

1½ lb. fresh shelling peas in the pod

2 soft lettuce leaves
(red lettuce works great)

¼ tsp. coarse sea salt or other salt

1 bunch flat-leaf parsley (you will need a dozen sprigs)

1 cup rosary-bead pasta

3 Tbs. extra virgin olive oil

1 garlic clove, peeled and minced

¼ tsp. freshly ground or cracked black pepper

¼ tsp. sea salt

½ cup vegetable broth

► Wash pea pods carefully in cold water. Shell them, saving the pods. Put the pods in a large saucepan or small stockpot with lettuce and cover with 1 gallon of water. Bring to a boil and add coarse salt. Cook over medium-low heat for about 20 minutes. You are trying to get highly flavored cooking liquid.

► Meanwhile, rinse and dry the peas. Remove the leaves from the parsley sprigs and coarsely chop them. (A small food processor works as well as a cleaver.) Discard the stems.

► Remove and discard the peapods and lettuce from the boiling water, saving the water. Bring it back to a boil and add pasta. Cook according to package instructions, which should be about 12 minutes.

► Meanwhile, in a medium heavy-gauge saucepan or casserole, heat the olive oil over medium heat. Add chopped parsley and garlic. Sauté 1 minute. Add peas, black pepper, and salt. Cover the pot and cook 5 minutes.

- ▶ Add broth to the peas, cover the pot and cook over low heat about 15 minutes or until almost all the liquid has evaporated.
- ▶ Drain the cooked pasta and add it to the peas. Mix well. Cook 1 minute over low heat. Add more salt and/or pepper if you wish and serve immediately in shallow bowls.

When it comes to the cooking of food, we can apply these same principles of respect and consideration. Is the kitchen a clean and calm place? Is the meal artfully served? Do we care for our family and guests?

—DENG MING-DAO,

Zen: The Art of Modern Eastern Cooking

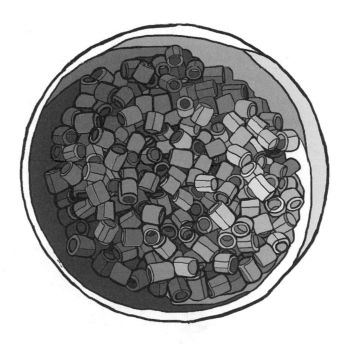

Shiitake Soba with Green Beans

SERVES 8.

¾ lb. soba noodles

3 Tbs. corn oil

2 Tbs. sesame oil, divided

3 large garlic cloves, peeled, smashed, and sliced into very thin strips

½ tsp. red pepper flakes

½ lb. Chinese long beans or any green bean like Blue Lake or Kentucky Wonder, cut uniformly into 2–2½ inch lengths

¼ cup vegetable broth or water

10 oz. shiitake mushrooms, stems off, washed, and sliced into thin strips

1 bunch scallions, cleaned and minced

3½ Tbs. Chinese rice wine or Japanese mirin

4 Tbs. soy sauce

GARNISH

chopped fresh cilantro

▶ Cook the soba noodles in boiling water according to package instructions. Drain, rinse, and shake dry. Coat with 1 Tbs. sesame oil.

▶ In a wok or other large sauté pan, heat corn oil and 1 Tbs. sesame oil over medium-high heat. Add garlic and red pepper flakes, lower heat to medium, and sauté 30 seconds.

▶ Add green beans and ¼ cup broth or water. Stir-fry over medium-low heat 1–2 minutes until the liquid has mostly evaporated.

▶ Add mushrooms, scallions, and rice wine, stirring to blend with other ingredients. Cover and cook 3 minutes or until mushrooms are soft and shiny. Remove cover.

▶ Add soba and soy sauce, carefully mixing. You will probably needs large forks or pasta implements to do this. Continue cooking over medium-low heat until noodles are hot, 1–2 minutes.

▶ Remove from heat. Garnish with chopped fresh cilantro to serve.

Rice

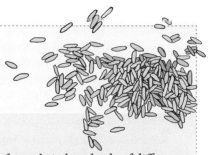

FOR AT LEAST eight millennia, millions of people in hundreds of differing climates and conditions have managed to subsist on a swamp grass now rooted on every continent but Antarctica. Rice has become Earth's foremost grain used exclusively for human food. Nobody seems to be allergic to it and almost nobody seems to tire of eating it. Persian cookbook author Linda Chirinian calls rice "the basic ingredient of most Middle Eastern and Persian cuisines.... In Iran, if one isn't served rice once a day, they feel they have not had a complete meal." It has been claimed that growing rice occupies the entire lives of over one billion people. Sixty percent of the planet's population relies on it to survive. The Burmese, whose ancestors probably domesticated the grass, are said to individually consume 500 pounds a year, which boils down to 1¼ pounds of rice a day. They are not wasting calories. Rice is high in complex carbohydrates, delivers both vitamins and minerals, and contains all eight essential amino acids. Although it is weak in the one known as lysine, the deficiency is smartly remedied by pairing it with beans or corn.

Even though they live in the pasta center of the Western world, northern Italians individually eat twenty pounds of rice every year, a hint that creative cooks have turned rice into a vast array of treasured dishes that go beyond the ubiquitous pilaf and pudding. There's the risotto of those northern Italians, the *arroz con pollo* of Central and South America, *moros y cristianos* in Cuba, Cajun *etouffée* and hoppin' john in the deep South, *mochi* and *onigiri* in Japan, *biryani* in northern India and *dosa* in the south, rice paper rolls in Vietnam, paella in Spain, Thai sticky rice with mango, *jook* and *zongzi* in China, Indonesian *nasi goreng*, the Dutch dish known as "Indonesian rice table," English kedgeree, and American Rice Krispies treats. Puffed rice, the American breakfast cereal that is the sine qua non of those eponymous sweets, is a popcorn-like street food in half of Asia.

In *The Joys of Nepalese Cooking*, retired professor Indra Majupuria emphasizes rice's importance to the Nepalese not only as food but as religious symbol. Rice is piled high in bowls on altars as an offering to deities. It's used in tantric diagrams, and it's thrown at the completion of rituals to symbolize health, wealth, and fertility. Rice is also the cause of celebration for babies. Because the Nepalese do not celebrate birthdays, the biggest fuss made over an infant is *Pasani*, or "first rice," when a baby is six months old. The feeding ceremony serves as official initiation into the family, and an enormous rice-based banquet is prepared for all friends and relatives invited to witness. Bengalis have the same ceremony, officially called *Annaprasan* but colloquially referred to as *bhat*, the Nepalese word for "cooked rice."

Like other Asian lexicons, the Bengali and Nepali provide many words for rice, to specify whether it is cooked, beaten, parched, pressed, or raw, this last having its own subset of names to differentiate quality. Most of the world's cultures also differentiate grains on the basis of fragrance (basmati, jasmine, and exquisite Bangladeshi *kalijira* or "prince of rice"), length, and starchiness ("sticky," dry, and even sweet). The endless quest for rice has now produced forty thousand different kinds, so that connoisseurs rarely speak generically of "rice," preferring names of special species like the highland grown basmati, which in Hindi means "queen of scents"; forbidden rice, the Chinese black rice only served to ancient emperors; Japanese *koshihikari*; Italy's carnaroli, arborio, and the fast-cooking Veronese *vialone nano*; the creamy, thick, short-grained *baldo* popular in Turkey and Vietnam; the unique Bhutanese short-grain red rice; *kuthari*, or *rose matta*, the red parboiled rice of South India; or Persia's *shahi*, a rice created for the ancient Shahs and now used for the dish *polow*, from which we get the word *pilaf*.

Each type is uniquely suited to a particular preparation such as braising or stewing, a desired cooking time, even a particular application such as stuffing or soaking up sauce. The Chinese rely almost entirely on long grains for steamed and fried rice. Spanish cooks claim they can't make proper paella without their local short-grain rice, which is neither the Japanese short grain used for sushi nor the renowned Italian arborio used in risotto, but a specific rice that came with the Moorish invaders. Medium-grain Greek rice is still harvested from descendants of plants brought back from India by Alexander the Great. Then there is the so-called "upland rice" or dry rice that survives far from traditional paddies, in mountains and rain forests, which should not be confused with the barley grass we call "wild rice."

"Rice eaters," Margaret Visser says in *Much Depends on Dinner*, "are intensely knowledgeable about varieties of flavor and aroma in their favorite food; they may be used to eating little but they care a great deal about whether that little is good." Most of the world's kitchens keep several varieties on hand, some for the purpose of grinding into flour or fermenting into drink. In Mexico, rice is the basis of the popular *horchata* drink and in Japan of the iconic sake. In the Himalayas, it is sometimes substituted for millet and fermented into the ceremonial *chang*. In America it's turned into a milk substitute.

In most of Asia, rice is routinely mounded high and alone in the center of a plate, subserviently surrounded by much smaller portions of everything else. I hadn't realized how sacrosanct this arrangement is until, in Bangkok in mid-November of 1990, my globe-trotting Thai hostess asked me to make her family a real Thanksgiving dinner. She managed to produce a turkey and I managed to produce severe anxiety by violating protocol, first by simply stepping inside the cookhouse, exclusively the servants' realm. Then, when I mixed their rice with my braised vegetables, they started gesticulating wildly. Finally, when I stuffed the mélange into the cavities of the turkey, they fled in panic. "You disrespected rice by mixing it with vegetables," my friend explained later. "Worse, because these are primitive rural people, they think you desecrated their rice by stuffing it into a dead animal. I guarantee you they won't even taste the turkey now."

Although rice comes in a coat of many colors—red, brown, black—it's frequently refined, sometimes polished, and sold as pure white. For joyful Buddhist rituals such as the consecration of a new monastery or a birthday celebration, Tibetans color white rice yellow with precious saffron to symbolize gold and all riches of the universe. Eating golden rice soaked in golden butter becomes a tangible way to share and internalize the blessings of the occasion.

In cultural myths, rice often takes a female form because it's equated with mother's milk, another white and nourishing food. In Burma, Thailand, and Malaysia, rice symbolizes ideal behavior: unassuming, gentle, and sensitive, as cooperative as its grains lying together in one bowl. In China, the Taoist goddess Tou Mu, protector of the standard rice measure, used to be routinely painted for protection on every Chinese junk. The rice measure itself, the *tou*, was invoked to mean the full measure of justice, mercy, and virtue that every living being was entitled to receive from every other—like motherly love. Many cultures still use rice to represent fertility and all the joy it is supposed to bring. Europeans and Americans throw rice at departing newlyweds—confetti was created in Italy as a substitute—and Hindus pour it over the couple's heads as they stand in a shallow basket.

Some people claim the Chinese character for the word *ch'i*, life force, is a pot of rice cooking. *Gung hay fat choy*, "may you get rich," is the best-known, most modern Chinese New Year greeting, but the old-fashioned, traditional one is "may your rice never burn!" And in Chinese the word for rice, *fan*, is used as the word for food itself, for all grains, even for agriculture. The phrase *chi fan*, to eat rice, means to have a meal. Similarly the Burmese expression for a meal, *htamin sar*, literally translates as *to eat rice*, and so does the Thai family call to the table, *jin kao*. In modern Chinese "an iron rice bowl" is a secure job, while "breaking the rice bowl" is to lose a job. For a common greeting like "how are you?" the Chinese say, *"Ni chi fan le ma?"* or "Have you eaten rice?" People in Bhutan and Bangladesh say something similar. A person in Madagascar, Robert Levine says in *A Geography of Time*, might describe a half hour as the time it takes to cook rice, as in "he was gone about the time of a rice-cooking." Filipinos say "one grain of rice equals one bead of sweat" and the Lao people metaphorically call great exertion "grains of rice." The Japanese word *yokomeshi*, a combination of the words for boiled rice (*meshi*) and horizontal (*yoko*), is intended to imply that the stress of speaking a foreign language is for the Japanese like trying to eat lying down.

Italians and Greeks share tiny pasta shaped to imitate rice and named *orzo* after the primary rice genus: *Oryza*. Our own word, *rice*, comes from the earlier Aramaic *ourouzza*, as does the Arabic word *arozz*. The Arabs sometimes refer to rice as *aish*, life, which is why they planted it prodigiously in what is now Spain, where the Arabic dish *pilao*, rice laced with meats, is called *paella*.

The Japanese consider rice to be so precious, their words for breakfast, lunch, and dinner—*asagohan*, *hirugohan*, and *bangohan*—translate as "morning rice," "afternoon rice," and "evening rice." It's even been said on the Internet that *Honda* means "main rice field." In his revered teaching, *Instructions to the Cook*, the great Japanese Zen teacher Dozen Zenji said: "Keep your eyes open. Do not allow even one grain of rice to be lost.... When you handle water, rice, or anything else, you must have the affectionate and caring attitude of a parent raising a child."

Maine Autumn Risotto

This is an earthy dish that warms the heart at the first sign of frost. It's my ode to the foods that linger in the ground after summer's gone.

SERVES 4.

1 qt. mushroom broth

2–2½ cups vegetable broth or water

8 Brussels sprouts

juice of 1 lemon

2 tsp. butter

24 baby shiitake mushrooms, cleaned, stems removed and saved, caps coarsely chopped

1 Tbs. plus one pinch dried sage

2 Tbs. sunflower seeds

⅛ tsp. plus one pinch salt

¼ cup olive oil

3 large garlic cloves, peeled and minced

⅛ tsp. freshly ground or cracked black pepper

1 tsp. celery seeds

1 tsp. dried thyme

1 tsp. dried oregano

1 tsp. ground cumin

½ tsp. ground coriander

1 large leek, washed and diced

1½ cups arborio rice

⅛ tsp. red pepper flakes or ground cayenne (optional)

¼ cup dry white wine

GARNISH

a small wedge of Parmesan cheese, grated

1 lemon, cut in wedges

½ cup chopped fresh flat-leaf parsley

▶ Bring mushroom broth and vegetable broth or water to a boil in a large saucepan; reduce heat to a simmer.

▶ Wash and quarter the Brussels sprouts, and put them in the lemon juice until you are ready to use them.

▶ Melt butter over medium heat in a medium or small sauté pan. Toss in mushroom caps and stems with a pinch of sage and the sunflower seeds. Brown to glistening. Turn off the heat. Stir in a pinch of salt.

▶ In a medium or large heavy-gauge casserole or Dutch oven, heat olive oil over medium-high heat. Add garlic, black pepper, celery seeds, thyme, oregano, cumin, coriander, and half of

continued on next page

the remaining sage; stir to blend, flavoring the oil. Add the leeks and stir-fry until they are soft and translucent, 5 minutes at most. Add the rice, half the Brussels sprouts (leaving the lemon juice), and the red pepper flakes or cayenne. Stir to coat the rice and sprouts with all the flavors in the pan. Add more olive oil if necessary to keep the rice from sticking and continue stirring until the rice is hot, maybe 3 minutes.

▶ Pour in the wine, stirring vigorously. Pour in 1 cup of the hot broth, and continue stirring vigorously to be sure it gets under the rice and sprouts.

▶ When almost of the broth has been absorbed by the rice, add more broth, 1 cup at a time, continually stirring. After the third cup, toss in the remaining Brussels sprouts, but not the lemon juice. After the fifth cup, add the lemon juice and remaining sage. Add mushrooms and sunflower seeds by turning the entire contents of the sauté pan into the risotto. Continue stirring.

▶ Add salt with the sixth cup. As the liquid evaporates, taste to see if the rice is soft and creamy yet and if the seasonings are to your taste. Adjust seasonings, especially salt, pepper, and sage. If more liquid is needed to finish the rice to a creamy texture, add another ½ cup of broth or water, still stirring. Cook until the liquid has evaporated and turn off the heat. The rice should have an earthy color and soft consistency. The cooking time to get here is around 45 minutes.

▶ Let the risotto sit on the stove and steam to a finish for a few minutes. Serve garnished with freshly grated Parmesan or any dry and salty cheese, lemon wedges, and chopped fresh flat-leaf parsley.

Willingness is also what enables the cook. Flavors are richer, aromas
are more enticing, the everyday burden becomes an adventure.
Discovery is possible once again.

—EDWARD ESPE BROWN, in the introduction to
Zen: The Art of Modern Eastern Cooking

Mexican Rice

This is a great master recipe to which you can add your favorite flavors or vegetables. For instance, try throwing in some chili relleños near the end and steam them in the rice.

The technique of placing a towel over the cooking rice is the same one that creates the unique, scrumptious crust on the Persian rice called *tadig*; it absorbs the steam at work inside the pot so it doesn't sink back into the rice and turn it to mush.

SERVES 6–8.

1½ cups long-grain white rice (for instance, Texas or basmati)

1 large tomato, peeled, seeded, and chopped—or a generous half-cup of canned chopped tomatoes

½ small onion, peeled

1 large garlic clove, peeled

⅓ cup sunflower, safflower, or olive oil

3½ cups vegetable broth

1 small carrot, scraped and thinly sliced

⅓ cup peas (about sixteen pods) or diced green pepper

2 tsp. salt

▶ Put the rice in a bowl and cover with hot water. Let sit for 15–20 minutes. Drain well and rinse in cold water. Shake the sieve and let it sit until rice is totally drained and dry.

▶ Combine tomato, onion, and garlic in a blender or small food processor and blend into a smooth puree.

▶ In a medium heavy-gauge casserole or saucepan, heat the oil until it is very hot. Stir in the rice, blending to coat all kernels with oil. Fry the rice over medium to medium-low heat until it's pale gold, about 10–12 minutes. Stir occasionally so nothing sticks to the pot.

▶ If there is a lot of oil still in the pot, push the rice aside and try to drain it off. If there is only a teaspoon or so, leave it. Add the tomato puree, blend, and continue to cook the rice, stirring continually until the puree has been absorbed.

▶ Add broth, carrot, and peas or peppers and blend. Cook over medium heat, uncovered until most of the broth has been absorbed, about 10–12 minutes. (It will boil wildly, and that's okay.)

continued on next page

▶ Reduce heat to simmer. Place a terry cloth towel over the top of the pot, cover with a tight-fitting lid, and cook 5 minutes.

▶ Turn off heat and let the rice sit, covered by the towel and lid, for 30 minutes. It will continue steaming.

Variation with Chili Relleños

▶ 4–6 small poblano chilies, roasted or charred, and peeled (put hot chilies in a brown paper bag for 10 minutes and they will start to peel)

▶ ⅔ lb. mild soft cheese like Monterey jack, cheddar, Muenster, or Havarti

▶ Carefully slit the chilies on one side and remove seeds. Slice the cheese and stuff it into the peppers.

▶ Add the chilies to the rice, slit side up, before covering the rice with the towel.

Nori Maki

When these vegetarian sushi rolls are cut, they look like flowers in a frame.

MAKES 40 PIECES.

2½ cups sushi rice, cooked according to package instructions

2½ tsp. plum vinegar (*umeboshi* in Japanese), or mirin (sweet Japanese cooking wine), or perhaps a fig or raspberry vinegar or, failing that, seasoned rice vinegar

2 carrots, peeled and sliced lengthwise into thin strips (it's easiest if you find carrots that are around 8 inches long)

⅛ tsp. sesame oil

1 tsp. wasabi paste

1 Japanese cucumber, peeled and sliced lengthwise into five strips

5 sheets nori (dried seaweed sheets available in packages at supermarkets, health food stores, Japanese and Chinese markets)

▶ Take the hot rice from the pot and immediately put into a large shallow bowl. Stir in plum vinegar. This will quickly cool it.

▶ Blanch the carrot strips in salted water for 1 minute. Drain and dry. Sprinkle sesame oil over them.

▶ Set up a clean counter area and put down either a real sushi mat or a thick napkin you don't mind using for the rolling process. Arrange wasabi, cucumber, carrot strips, and a small cup of water nearby.

▶ Lay out a seaweed sheet at the edge of the mat or napkin closest to you. If it has markings for cutting, be sure they run from the side closest to you to the side furthest away; in other words, up and down.

▶ Spread ½ cup of rice on the seaweed, leveling it with a spatula. Bring it out to the sides and to the edge closest to you, but leave a slight margin at the far end. This is to seal the roll.

▶ Spread a tiny dollop of wasabi along the edge closest to you. Then, about 1 inch further away, lay out a carrot strip, followed by a cucumber strip, and then a second carrot strip. They should be side-by-side but tight together. If the carrot is too short, cut a piece off another strip and add it.

continued on next page

- To roll, grab the end of the mat or napkin and seaweed. Begin to roll, pressing down as you go. As you approach the far end, using a finger, coat the exposed seaweed with water. Finish rolling and, with the seam underneath, press lightly to seal the roll.

- Once all rolls are made, put them on a cutting board and slice each one into 8 pieces. If you don't wish to serve immediately, wrap the whole uncut rolls tightly in clear wrap, twisting the ends, and store in the refrigerator. Bring to room temperature before serving.

- Serve with soy sauce and pickled ginger. For a full meal, add spinach *goma-ae* (see recipe on page 223) and edamame.

When you cook, you are not just cooking.

You are working on yourself.

You are working on others.

—SHUNRYU SUZUKI

Kashmiri Fried Rice

This is a tasty trick for leftover rice. Don't remove the whole cloves before serving—Kashmiris chew them after eating as a breath freshener.

SERVES 4.

4 Tbs. cooking oil (mustard, corn, sunflower, safflower, or canola)

½ tsp. cumin seeds

4–5 whole cloves

½ tsp. red chili powder
(most authentic would be arbol)
dissolved in 2 Tbs. water

½ tsp. ground ginger

3 cups cooked Basmati rice
(¾ cup when raw)

¼ tsp. salt

4 eggs
(1 per person to be served)

1 Tbs. chopped fresh cilantro

▶ Heat oil in a deep skillet over medium-high heat. Add cumin seeds and cloves. Sauté 30 seconds. This flavors the oil.

▶ Add ginger and chili-water solution and ginger, stirring as you do. The water will make the oil sizzle, so be careful. Immediately add rice, then salt, and stir to blend.

▶ Lower heat to lowest temperature and cook just until rice is hot, stirring so nothing sticks to the bottom of the pan. Add 1 Tbs. water if necessary.

▶ Arrange rice on serving platter and cover to keep warm.

▶ Fry 1 egg per person. Arrange the cooked eggs on top of the rice. Sprinkle lightly with salt and garnish with cilantro. Serve immediately.

Desi:
Tibetan Ceremonial Rice

This golden, jewel-studded and fragrant rice represents good fortune
and is traditionally offered by Tibetan Buddhist monasteries to guests at the start
of a celebration or consecration. Those who eat best-quality rice turned to gold
by precious saffron and melted butter, and sweetened by sugar, are receiving the
richness of grace and gaining the merit of participating in a beneficial occasion.
This generosity of inclusion is the essence of Tibetan hospitality.

As perhaps the only Westerner who'd learned from various Tibetans how
to make it, I was called upon so many times for the opening of Dharma centers,
start of retreats, or arrival of rinpoches that for a few years I was called the
Desi Dakini, *dakini* being a goddess in the Tibetan imagination. Frankly,
I didn't feel like a goddess standing 8,000 feet high on a Colorado mountain
on my tiptoes in the 4 A.M. dark, peering over an enormous stockpot as I
struggled to stir saffron into enough rice for 150 people. I was sleep-deprived
and worrying that my extravagant additions of flower water and cardamom
were going to disqualify my effort because they weren't traditional in Tibet.
So it was an enormous relief when two monks gave me thumbs up as they
took their first bite.

SERVES 12–16.

2 cups Basmati rice	¼ cup cashews, roasted
⅛ tsp. saffron, crushed, in 1 Tbs. hot water	½ tsp. ground cardamom
⅔ cup dark raisins	3–4 Tbs. unsalted butter
1 Tbs. orange juice or 1 tsp. orange flower water plus 1 Tbs. water	⅓ cup granulated sugar (Tibetans would use more)

▶ Rinse the rice well and cook according to package instructions.

▶ While it's cooking, plump the raisins in the orange juice or flower water for 5 minutes and
drain well.

- As soon as the rice has finished steaming, lift the lid and add saffron, stirring to blend.

- Pour rice into a large bowl and, while it is still hot, add raisins, cashews, cardamom, butter, and sugar. Mix all ingredients. Let cool before serving.

I had only the occasional visits of my mother to look forward to. When she came, she was accompanied by my elder sister, Tsering Dolma. I particularly enjoyed these visits as they would invariably bring presents of food.

—THE DALAI LAMA, *Freedom in Exile*

Thai Sticky Rice with Mango

SERVES 4–6.

1½ cups sweet or glutinous or sticky rice (no substitutes will work), soaked overnight

1½ cups thick coconut milk (a Thai brand in a 13–14 oz. can works best), divided

¼ cup granulated sugar

½ tsp. salt

2–3 ripe mangoes (the slim yellow-skinned mangoes are tastier than the bulbous red-skinned ones imported from Central and South America)

▶ Drain the rice and put it in a steamer. (A conical basket steamer would be the most authentic. Put muslin or cheesecloth under the rice if the steamer holes in your metal basket are larger than a grain of rice.) Steam the rice vigorously for 20 minutes.

▶ Meanwhile, combine 1 cup coconut milk, sugar, and salt in a small heavy-gauge saucepan and over medium heat. The mixture must get hot enough to dissolve the sugar, but should not boil.

▶ Put the cooked rice into a serving bowl and pour the hot coconut milk over it. Stir to blend. Let stand for 20–30 minutes.

▶ Peel mangoes and slice into serving portions.

▶ To serve: Pour the remaining coconut milk over the rice. Arrange the mangoes on top.

Tofu Made Tasty

Sentient beings possess the essence of buddhahood. . . . The actual way in which they possess it can be exemplified by the way silver is present in silver ore, the way sesame oil is present in sesame seeds or the way butter is present in milk. It is possible to obtain the silver that is in the ore. It is possible to obtain the oil that is in the sesame seeds. It is possible to obtain the butter that is in the milk and likewise it is possible to obtain the buddhahood that is in sentient beings.

—Je Gampopa, *Jewel Ornament of Liberation*

The Story of Tofu

NOBODY KNOWS for sure who was the first to actually realize that spoiled soybeans, the literal translation of the Chinese *doufu*, could provide extraordinary protein, but the story definitely starts in China. Soybeans are native to that part of the planet; peasants there were growing them at least four thousand years ago. The Chinese called them first *shu*, then *daodou*, or "great bean," revering them as a rotation cover crop, because the plants deposit in the soil the nitrogen necessary for vegetable plants to thrive. Yet despite this great agricultural benefit, the ancient Chinese didn't eat the beans because raw soy is toxic to humans. Then somebody figured out that boiling water leaches out the poison.

Stories that try to explain how soybeans went from being boiled to being spoiled all start by assuming the culinarily inventive Chinese eventually cooked them down or mashed them into a thin puree, "soy milk," which they drank like broth. There is no agreement on who figured out that a dash of sea salt could ferment and coagulate that "milk" into a profoundly nutritious curd. A likely candidate would be a Mongolian, for when early Mongolian tribes migrated into northern China, they brought with them the alchemy of fermenting cow's milk into yogurt—a coagulation process remarkably similar to the one that produces *doufu*. In what's known as the copycat hypothesis, historians presume the Chinese were curious enough to try curdling their "milk" the way Mongolians fermented theirs. But there are also "imported" postulations that point to India, where fermenting cow's milk into curd was in full swing at least one and maybe two millennia before soy was commonly curdled in China. These rest on the sixth-century evangelical spread of Buddhism from India to East Asia, and the fact that *doufu* first shows up in Chinese writing as *li ch'i*, or "morning prayer," hinting that the daily preparation of tofu may have been the matinal meditation of the newly converted Chinese monks.

It's quite possible that the first Chinese converts to Buddhism were as anxious as any of us would be to please a guru if he came to dinner, so they worried over what to serve visiting Indian masters who were accustomed to dairy-based protein not available in China. The acolytes' frantic search for the likes of yogurt and *paneer*—the common feta or ricotta-like cheese of India—supposedly led them to seize on the idea of fermenting Chinese soymilk in the monastery kitchen the way Indian monks fermented cow's milk in theirs. What makes this theory credible is how uncannily tofu can resemble yogurt and paneer, how easily it becomes a perfect recipe substitute, a "cheese" that could've fooled the Indians.

The Indian Buddhist connection is also bolstered by a charming allegory America's soy authority, William Shurtleff, found in a twelfth-century book. Its protagonist is the venerable Bodhidharma, the Indian monk credited with founding the Chan (Zen) sect in China. As Shurtleff decodes the tale, Bodhidharma becomes the teacher of a northern Chinese man of Mongolian extraction, a pious peasant whose complicated name, a pun on both tofu and soymilk, is reduced to simply "Fu," or "spoiled." Bodhidharma asks him: "Do you wish to become the heart and mind of the God of heaven, earth, and nature, rinse off all superficial knowledge, and follow me?" The tale is so replete with double entendres, this sentence can also mean: "Wash soybeans well and make them into *doufu*." Fu then goes home, washes his body, changes his clothes, and vows wholeheartedly to speak only truth. With more puns intended, Bodhidharma engages Fu in debate, and becomes very impressed with his humble, honest, straightforward nature. He tells Fu that his own teacher told him there is a subtle and wonderful essence that remains in curds when milk is curdled, and that the flavor of Fu's being is this most delicious essence. The Chinese word used, *dai gomi*, is supposedly the one used in Chinese to describe the dairy offering the Buddha accepted to end his decimating asceticism and launch his encounter with enlightenment. The word also refers to the Indian Buddhist teaching that enlightenment, sometimes called Buddha's essence, comes out of the mind like the rich, golden butter achieved from churning milk.

PERHAPS WHAT MATTERS MORE than how tofu got into monastery kitchens in China is that it stayed long after the Indians were gone, becoming the core of what was probably the first vegetarian diet in a notoriously omnivorous culture that happily consumed shark fins, swallows' nests, and bear gallbladders. China has been called the land where people eat anything with four legs except a table and anything that flies except a kite. So while meat had not been hard for Indian monks to renounce since it never was a major ingredient in their cooking, it was a big sacrifice for the Chinese. Because this proscription on eating meat set Buddhism in stark contrast to other Chinese traditions, tofu became not only crucial sustenance, but also a defining element of Chinese Buddhism.

For at least four centuries, monastery kitchens offered the only food available to travelers, essentially introducing wandering Chinese to the wholesomeness of vegetarian fare. Having no other precedents to follow, the first actual restaurants to spring up in the spirited urbanization of the tenth-century Sung Dynasty mimicked monks' cooking. The centerpiece of their menus, *louhan zhai*, which literally means "vegetarian meal of the accomplished ones," turned out to be so popular, it still shows up on Chinese menus a millennium later, a dish of tofu with vegetables listed in English as "Buddha's Delight." The monastery legacy is also evident in the way modern Chinese in Hong Kong, Singapore, and Taiwan as well as on the mainland still refer to all vegetarian dishes generically as *zhaicci*, Buddhist food. The diversity of their tofu dishes, often specially prepared in private homes on the Buddha's sacred first and fifteenth day of the month, is more telling, for it testifies not just to the impact of the monastery kitchen but the Buddha's teachings on China's culture. It was for at least a millennium a Buddhist nation.

Doufu became such a staple of the Chinese kitchen that the classic 1795 recipe book widely considered the Bible of Chinese cooking, *Suci-yuan Hintan*, includes it frequently as the key ingredient of many dishes. The Chinatowns of twenty-first-century America show how inventive the Chinese have been with it, for they sell *doufu ha* (tender blossoms), *nun doufu* (silken tofu), *ruan doufu* (soft tofu), *ying doufu* (firm tofu), *doufu gan* (pressed tofu), *wuxiang doufu* (pressed tofu with five-spice flavor), *doufu pi* (firm-skinned tofu), *gansi* (tofu threads), *bayie* (sheet tofu), *bayie jie* (knotted sheets of tofu), *doufu ru* (fermented tofu), *cho doufu* (stinky tofu), *yiu doufu* (tofu puffs), *za doufu* (fried tofu), *suji* (tofu resembling chicken or duck). Chinese poets lauded bean curd as the exemplary essence of equality, eaten easily by the emperor and by everyman, for while tofu is indispensable at glorious banquets in palaces, peasants in southern China think of it lovingly as comfort food. Bean curd even crept into everyday conversation as metaphor: "a tofu government official" is one who is honest, "tofu girl" indicates a rural peasant who's left home for the bright lights of a big city, and finding fault with somebody is thought to be like "finding a bone in your tofu."

There is absolutely no disagreement that bean curd went to Japan, where it was first pronounced *tofu*, as an integral ingredient of Buddhism. As in China, tofu provided protein to priests and monks in yet another ravenously carnivorous culture, immediately setting them apart from society at large. Japan's Buddhist monks also emulated their Chinese counterparts by opening their monastery dining rooms to the public, although not so much as a way station for travelers as a skillful means for spreading Dharma. One of these eateries appears to be the origin of the country's beloved tofu soup *kenchin-jiru*. The cooks at the Kenchoji temple in Kamakura, it's said, had planned to serve their everyday tofu dish at the end of a ceremony, but when a huge crowd unexpectedly showed up for the ritual, they hurriedly chopped the tofu cubes into tiny pieces which they combined with the available vegetables into a thick soup that wowed those who tasted it.

Apparently, all the monks' uniquely vegetarian food was that appealing, for it turned out that laymen went back to the temples not to learn about emptiness but about bean curd. In the early capital cities of Kamakura and Kyoto, sites of major monasteries, temple devotees opened tofu shops, lots of them. Influenced by the elite samurai class, which adopted Zen and patronized these businesses, ordinary people took up tofu with passion. By the eighteenth century it was the single focus of a bestselling cookbook. Today, most of the exquisite tofu cooking for which Japan remains acclaimed is done in or near its ancient Buddhist temples. Nanzenji Zen temple in eastern Kyoto is surrounded by tofu restaurants, among them one of Japan's oldest and most renowned, Okutan, which started as a teahouse inside the temple.

IT TOOK ABOUT FIVE HUNDRED YEARS for tofu to come into its own. Soybeans from China started as the staple of monastery cooking, advanced from curd to a paste fermented further by a Japanese fungus and called *miso*, and became the soul of *shojin ryori*, a classical cooking style. Whereas the Chinese, in their unswerving quest for tastiness, had ingeniously crafted *doufu* into a cornucopia of flavors and forms, the Japanese focused their curd efforts on achieving a silken blobby blandness whose absence of almost everything would somehow signify serenity. Tofu was the elegance of emptiness, the nothing that could be anything and everything. And in a bizarre way it turned out to be exactly that, for it was this very formless, flavorless tofu that came to the West in the 1960s as a vital ingredient of Zen Buddhism. It then rode the health food wave outward from the isolated communes of the flower children to common supermarket shelves coast to coast, packaged with Japanese branding. The product is so tightly associated with Japan that its premier English name is no longer *soy cheese* or *bean cake* or even *bean curd* but *tofu*. Perhaps this is because we got our own words *soy* or *soya*—for the bean, for the sauce, for the whole curdled shebang—by mispronouncing the Japanese word *shoyu,* soy sauce, that harkens back to the original Chinese word for the plant: *shu.* But that's a whole other soy story.

Kenchin Jiru:
Japan's Beloved Tofu Soup

I went all over San Francisco's Japantown searching the restaurant menus posted in their glass windows to find one that served this soup. It was a frustrating exercise in inexplicable futility, because every restaurant offered the same sushi and more sushi, tempura and soups with noodles. I was ready to cancel the quest when someone alerted me to a unique eatery that seemed to specialize more in home cooking than in all that yakisoba and sashimi. I found the modest place about a half hour before it was to open for dinner. The newspaper reviews taped to its windows were promising: they praised its home-style food, its country dishes.

Seeing someone setting tables, I knocked on the glass and eventually a very elegant, tall, and slender Japanese man with white hair emerged from the kitchen. As he opened the door, I rushed to ask: "Do you serve *kenchin jiru*?" The man froze. He stood stunned with one hand on the doorknob, the other holding a white towel. "*Kenchin jiru*? Did you ask me about *kenchin jiru*?"

"Yes."

A smile exploded across his face and his eyes took on the bright glow of youth. He let go of the doorknob. "My grandmother made that. We ate it at home. Japanese people eat it at home. Yes. We never serve it to Westerners in a restaurant. No, we don't serve *kenchin jiru*. And no other restaurant does either." He enjoyed a short reverie before remembering I was still there. "How...how would you know about *kenchin jiru*?" he asked in disbelief...

There are supposed to be as many recipes for this beloved soup as there are grandmothers in Japan to make it. Thus there is no definitive recipe. So feel free to vary this version, which was given to me by a young woman named Masumi who, having a hard time trying to codify what she did intuitively, said: "I hope you can imagine how to make it."

SERVES 6.

5 sheets of kombu
or nori, the seaweed packaged
for making sushi rolls

1 small daikon, peeled

1 medium Japanese sweet potato
or other small white sweet potato,
peeled

1 large carrot, peeled

1 small taro root, peeled

1 burdock root*

5 scallions, cleaned

2 Tbs. sesame oil

1-inch piece fresh ginger, peeled and
grated or minced

2 Tbs. tamari

¼ tsp. salt

½ lb. fried tofu, cut into
tiny bite-sized pieces

▶ To make the soup stock, soak kombu or nori sheets in 5 cups of water for at least 30 minutes. Carefully drain and discard seaweed. You should get more than 4 cups of strained brown water. Boil it 15 minutes, scraping foamy impurities off the top, for a clear broth.

▶ Cut daikon and sweet potato into thin disks. Cut the carrot on the diagonal to achieve a differing shape. Cut taro root in half, and then cut lengthwise. If the pieces are thick, cut them in half again lengthwise to make thin strips.

▶ Peel burdock and cut into 2–3-inch lengths, then cut each in half. Slice scallions on the diagonal at the bottom and then into thin disks at the green portion.

▶ In a medium soup pot or casserole, heat sesame oil over medium heat. Add ginger, daikon, sweet potato, carrot, and taro (and mushrooms). Sauté 2 minutes.

▶ Add burdock. Add seaweed broth and enough water to bring the liquid to 5 cups. Bring to a boil, lower heat, and cook 20 minutes.

▶ Stir in tamari and salt. Stir in tofu and cook 5 minutes. Remove from heat. Add scallions and serve.

✳ As its health benefits become better known, this is becoming more prevalent in markets. If you can't find it at an Asian grocery or health food store, omit it. For a totally different effect, try substituting 4 shiitake mushrooms, halved.

Cornmeal-Crusted Tofu over Broccoli Rabe with Red Pepper Coulis

This festival of color, texture, and tastes can brighten a winter heart. Make the coulis ahead of time and store overnight in the fridge to make pulling everything together easier.

SERVES 8.

RED PEPPER COULIS

2 Tbs. olive oil

3 large red bell peppers, sliced in thin strips

½ tsp. dried oregano

1 Tbs. red wine vinegar

4 large garlic cloves, peeled and sliced

1 bay leaf

1 mildly hot pepper like jalapeno or Portuguese hotshot, or half a serrano, peeled and seeded, diced

pinch salt

2 Tbs. chopped fresh cilantro

BROCCOLI RABE

2 bunches broccoli rabe, coarsely chopped

2 Tbs. olive oil

2 Tbs. minced fresh ginger

½ tsp. freshly ground black pepper

4 large garlic cloves, peeled and minced

1 Tbs. high-quality fruity olive oil

¼ tsp. salt

TOFU

12 oz. extra-firm tofu, drained

⅔ cup polenta or cornmeal

¼ cup chickpea flour or white flour or even almond meal

pinch chipotle chili powder

pinch salt

⅛ tsp. freshly ground black pepper

1 extra-large egg

12 oz. corn or peanut oil for frying

TO MAKE THE COULIS

▶ In a medium skillet, heat olive oil over medium heat. Add peppers and oregano and sauté 15 minutes. Stir in vinegar, garlic, bay leaf, hot pepper, and salt. Sauté 10 minutes.

▶ Stir in cilantro, lower heat, and cook 5 minutes.

▶ Puree the contents of the skillet. If you are making this a day ahead, store it in the refrigerator to reheat in the microwave or in a small saucepan over low heat when ready to use.

TO MAKE THE BROCCOLI RABE

▶ Blanch the chopped broccoli rabe in a large pot of heavily salted boiling water for 1 minute. Remove from heat and drain very well.

▶ In a large sauté pan, heat 2 Tbs. olive oil over medium-high heat. Add ginger and pepper and stir-fry 45–60 seconds. Toss in drained broccoli rabe and garlic. Sauté for 3–5 minutes, stirring once at the start, then occasionally so nothing sticks to the pan.

▶ Add 1 Tbs. fruity olive oil and salt, mixing them in. Sauté 1 minute. Remove from heat. Cover with foil to keep warm.

TO MAKE THE TOFU

▶ Cut the tofu into ¼-inch thin slices and cut each slice in half, to make squares. You should have 16 pieces, 2 per person.

▶ Combine the polenta, flour, chipotle, salt, and black pepper in a bowl.

▶ Break the egg into a small bowl.

▶ Heat the oil to sizzling in a small heavy-gauge saucepan or wok.

▶ Dip each square of tofu into the egg, turning to coat it well. Then coat with the flour mixture on both sides. When the oil is sizzling, put as many coated squares as will fit without touching and fry over medium-high heat for 2 minutes, until the crust is nicely browned. Remove from oil with slotted spatula and drain on paper towels.

TO ASSEMBLE

▶ If the components have gotten cold while you were working, you can reheat them in a microwave or in saucepans over low heat to serve.

▶ Cover a medium plate (one that has about 6 inches of flat serving space) with a thin but solid layer of broccoli rabe. Put two fried tofu cubes on top and spoon the pepper coulis across them as a thick ribbon.

Ram's Chili Tofu

My friend Ram is a computer technician in California who comes from a Newar family that still lives in the magnificent old quarter of Kathmandu called Patan, a cobblestone warren of astonishingly elegant houses and temples that gave Kathmandu its name, "wood-covered shelter." Ram's brother is a painter there of growing renown, carrying on the esteemed tradition of Newari artistry, for Newars are the venerated craftsmen of Tibetan Buddhist statues and thangkha paintings. What art curators refer to as the "Nepalese style" is essentially theirs. Ram is a passionate cook whose own artistry comes out in kitchen flourishes like this colorful dish he created when he married a vegetarian.

SERVES 4–6.

2 Tbs. cooking oil, divided

½ tsp. garam masala, divided

¼ tsp. chili powder, divided
(arbol chili is the most authentic
but it doesn't truly matter)

1 lb. firm tofu, drained

¼ tsp. salt, divided

4 large garlic cloves, minced

1 purple onion, diced

3 jalapeno chili peppers, seeded and
diced, divided

4 roma or other firm tomatoes,
coarsely chopped

1 bunch scallions, cleaned and
chopped

▶ Cut tofu into 1-inch squares about ⅛ inch thick.

▶ Coat bottom of a skillet or sauté pan with 1 Tbs. of the oil over medium heat. Sprinkle evenly with ⅛ tsp. each of garam masala and chili powder. When the oil is fragrant, add tofu and brown the squares. Make sure each one is flat in the bottom of the pan; you may have to do this in batches. Sprinkle an additional ⅛ tsp. garam masala on the top of the squares before turning them over. Once flipped, sprinkle lightly with salt. When evenly browned on both sides, remove tofu and drain on paper towels.

▶ Add the remaining 1 Tbs. oil to the pan. When hot, fry the garlic 30 seconds. Add onion, 2 of the peppers, and the remaining ¼ tsp. garam masala. Stir to blend and sauté 1 minute. (Ram says the onions should not get soft.)

▶ Add tomatoes and another pinch of salt. Cook over medium heat for 5 minutes or until, as Ram says, "it gives a good smell." Tomatoes should still be in chunks.

► Add tofu and remaining salt, stirring to combine all ingredients. Lower heat and cook until tofu is heated through.

► Slice remaining pepper into thin rings. Arrange the tofu in a serving bowl and garnish with the pepper rings and chopped scallions to serve.

The *Doufu* Dakini

I MET WEN XIAOHONG IN the early 1990s, when she was newly arrived on the coast of Maine. She'd come from the interior of China to teach Mandarin at a prestigious local college, accompanied by her husband Tiu, whom she'd met at a language institute in Beijing. She was maybe twenty-eight and had just given birth to her first child, Zhong Zhong, a boy she liked to call David as a way of emphasizing he was going to be American. Xiaohong was only five feet tall with a toothsome smile that seemed bigger than China, and she was a dynamo. Very quickly she earned a reputation among students, and awards from them, as a spectacular teacher who gave her all—even though she was simultaneously giving plenty to learning a lot herself: about life in the boondocks of a foreign culture, about being a new mother, and about getting by on her own because her husband had suddenly decided to commute to Boston to pursue a law degree. Since she lived next door, I tried to be helpful.

The easiest thing to do was to carry whatever I was cooking across the lawn to at least ensure the time-challenged Xiaohong had something to eat. Although it was not my intention, this generosity provoked her to reciprocate by inviting me very insistently for whatever meal she planned to cook on weekends when her husband returned. We went back and forth between kitchens, me showing her how to make spaghetti with tomato sauce and how to bake cookies, Xiaohong showing me how to use a chopstick as a cooking implement, to flavor fish with salted black beans. Then came her meal with tofu. "I hope you like this," she said as she gave her wok a shake. "It's one of my mother's favorites." I struggled not to grimace. I had eaten tofu at American Dharma centers, where it was sanctimoniously served every day, and was so mushy, tasteless, and squirmy in the mouth it made me want to demand meat.

Xiaohong saw my hesitation and frowned. I confessed I was not a fan. She turned the burner off, put down her chopstick stirrer, and looked up at me with her megawatt smile. "That is because you've never tasted it the Chinese way. Our way is very different from the way I see everywhere in America, so I am going to teach you. I promise you will like *doufu*," she said, carefully emphasizing the Chinese pronunciation.

True to her word, Xiaohong launched a campaign. For the next six weeks, she assigned her husband to return each weekend from Boston with whatever forms of *doufu* he could find in Chinatown, one or two at a time. She carefully constructed her Sunday meals to be tasting lessons: puffed balls, dried crumble, skins to make wonton, marinated, frozen, pressed, threaded into noodles… until she had very satisfactorily proved her point. I still make her *doufu gan* "salad"; the recipe is on the following page.

Not long after those kitchen lessons, I had a stopover in Hong Kong and decided to take the ferry to hilly Lantau Island where an old Buddhist monastery on the island's peak was famed for its cooking. I had been told eating lunch there was a "must-do" and evidently it was. The line of Chinese people waiting to get into the midday meal seemed to stretch for half a kilometer. I just got in under the count, maybe the only Westerner in the horde. I scrambled for space at the enormously long rectory table and watched in astonishment as nuns laid dish after sumptuous-looking dish down the center, steaming platters of bok choy with spinach and shredded carrots, mushrooms piled high on bamboo shoots, deep fried *doufu* puffs, bright green broccoli next to transparent noodles laced with marinated strips of bright yellow bean curd. I lost count of how many dishes they presented or how many I got my chopsticks into, because as soon as they touched the table, the plates seemed to be vacuumed clean. Every dish I managed to taste before the food vanished was more vivid and sublime than the one before. The monastics had created a truly magnificent feast for the eyes, stomach, and mind. Only later, waiting for the boat at the bottom of the island, did I realize the orgy of flavors, textures, and colors had been created entirely out of vegetables, noodles, and the various forms of *doufu* Xiaohong had shown me.

Chinese Dried Tofu with Glass Noodles

This is Wen Xiaohong's recipe.

SERVES 4–6.

6.5 oz. bean thread (cellophane) noodles

1 bunch scallions, roots cut off

3 (2-inch) squares Chinese dried tofu, known as *doufu gan* in Chinese, or soy beancurd cake

2 Tbs. soy sauce

2 Tbs. sesame oil

1 tsp. rice wine vinegar

GARNISH

chopped fresh cilantro

▶ Prepare the noodles according to package instructions or put them in boiling water for 1 minute and drain. Refresh with a spray of cold water and drain well.

▶ Put noodles in a serving bowl. Slice the scallions into thin disks and sprinkle over the noodles. Cut the tofu squares through their middle into 2 thinner squares, then cut each of those into thin strips. Put these on the noodles.

▶ In a small cup, combine soy sauce, sesame oil, and vinegar with a whisk and pour it over the salad to serve. Garnish with cilantro, if desired.

Beansprout Salad

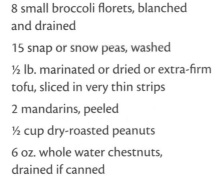

This is very colorful, very healthy, and so light you can have a rich dessert. The recipe can be doubled and whipped up quickly for crowds.

SERVES 6–8.

1 lb. fresh beansprouts

8 small broccoli florets, blanched and drained

15 snap or snow peas, washed

½ lb. marinated or dried or extra-firm tofu, sliced in very thin strips

2 mandarins, peeled

½ cup dry-roasted peanuts

6 oz. whole water chestnuts, drained if canned

1 large pickling cucumber, peeled

1 small red bell pepper, seeded

3 hard-boiled eggs, peeled

1 bunch scallions, roots off and washed

DRESSING

¼ cup soy sauce

¼ cup plus 2 Tbs. sesame oil

1 Tbs. corn oil

1 Tbs. rice wine vinegar

2 garlic cloves, peeled and minced

½-inch piece fresh ginger, peeled and grated or minced

GARNISH

finely chopped chives (optional)

▶ To make dressing: combine all ingredients in a large measuring cup or small bowl and let sit while assembling the salad.

▶ Put beansprouts in a very large serving bowl. Put broccoli florets, peas, and tofu on top. Break mandarins into sections and put on top. Add peanuts. Cut the water chestnuts into thirds and add to salad.

▶ Cut cucumber in half lengthwise and cut each half into thin strips. Cut each strip in half and add to the salad. Cut the pepper into long, thin strips and cut each strip in half. Add to the salad.

▶ Cut eggs in half, then cut each half into two or three pieces and add to the salad.

▶ Slit scallions in half lengthwise and slit each half again. Then cut the strips into thirds and add to the salad.

continued on next page

▶ Carefully toss the salad to blend all ingredients. Pour on dressing when ready to serve. Garnish with chopped chives, if desired.

The importance of food in understanding human culture lies precisely in its infinite variability—variability that is not essential for species survival.

—K. C. CHANG, *Food in Chinese Culture*

Dhal Bhat: Components for a Vegetarian Meal

THE DAILY MEAL of Nepal has always been an offering of rice (*bhat*) with beans (*dhal*) and a seasonal vegetable or two plus an *achar* (a condiment or chutney) to round out texture, color, and nutrition. These components add up to a surprisingly satisfying meal. Here are traditional as well as daring ways to prepare the components of a very soul- and budget-satisfying *dhal bhat* for two or 102, organized into three subsections of recipes from which you can mix and match to create—with the addition of rice—a hearty, tasty meal of beans, vegetables, and a flavorful condiment to enhance them all. You can also deploy the various dishes in other meal plans.

When the meditator eats or drinks,
having blessed his food as sacred,
his body a host of deities,
with an undistracted mind
he enjoys his meal.

—PATRUL RINPOCHE, *How to Bring*
the Four Kinds of Activities to the Path

Dhal:
Beans, Legumes,
Pulses, and Lentils

Those who follow me should eat the food that the sages themselves consume—
food that is productive of good qualities and is free of taint, the wholesome
foodstuffs of the wise of old. For my disciples, I prescribe a fitting
nourishment: rice and barley, wheat and peas, every kind of bean
and lentil, butter, oil, honey, treacle, fruits and sugar cane.

—from the *Lankavatara Sutra*

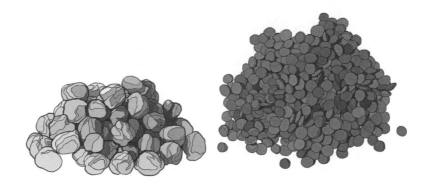

Chickpea Tagine

Because the ingredients are so universal and the flavors so recognizable, I have taught Nepali schoolchildren to cook this Moroccan dish—and they love it. It goes well with one of the yogurt chutneys in the condiments section.

SERVES 6.

2 (15-oz.) cans garbanzos (chickpeas), drained

2 tsp. fresh lemon juice

¼ cup olive oil

1 large onion, peeled and diced

3 garlic cloves, peeled and minced

½-inch piece fresh ginger, peeled and minced

1 green bell pepper, diced into bite-sized pieces

¼ tsp. ground cayenne

½ tsp. smoked paprika (or chipotle chili powder)

½ tsp. ground turmeric

1 heaping tsp. ground cumin

½ tsp. ground coriander

1 tsp. ground cinnamon

2 cups chopped tomatoes in their juices (canned or boxed is okay)

1 tsp. sugar

½ tsp. salt

1 Tbs. chopped fresh chives

¼ cup chopped fresh cilantro

2 Tbs. chopped fresh parsley

▶ Put drained chickpeas in a shallow bowl with lemon juice; shake the bowl so the juice touches all the beans.

▶ In a medium casserole or Dutch oven, heat olive oil over medium heat.

▶ Add onion and sauté until soft and golden.

▶ Add garlic, ginger, bell pepper, and spices, and cook a minute or two until they're warm. Add tomatoes and sugar. Cover the pot, reduce heat to simmer and cook about 15 minutes. Check periodically to see if the sauce is getting too thick; add ¼ cup water if needed.

▶ Drain chickpeas and add to the pot. Add salt. If the stew is too thick, add ¼ cup of water or tomato juice. Cover the pot and continue to simmer for 15–20 minutes. Adjust seasonings to taste and remove from heat.

▶ Stir in chives, cilantro, and parsley. Serve warm.

Egyptian *Fül Mudammas*

There are probably as many ways to make this satisfying breakfast, lunch, supper, and snack as there are Egyptians. It's also everyday food in Ethiopia and Somalia. Some people like the beans mashed, some like half mashed and half whole, some leave them all whole. People eat this in a bowl like soup or stuff it in a grilled or roasted pita to which they might even add falafel. Sometimes in Syria or in America where Egyptians can't find cans of *fül* (fava) beans, it's made with chickpeas. When I served this to Bhutanese monks, they kept asking for more!

SERVES 4.

1½ Tbs. olive oil

1 medium onion, peeled and diced

3 garlic cloves, peeled and minced

¼ tsp. freshly minced green chili or ⅛ tsp. chili powder

1 tsp. ground cumin

1 (15-oz.) can *fül* or *foul mudammas* (small fava beans) or ½ cup dried fava beans, soaked overnight and boiled in salted water until soft

1 tomato, chopped

2–3 Tbs. fresh lemon juice

½ tsp. salt

3 Tbs. high-quality fruity olive oil, divided

GARNISH

¼ cup chopped fresh parsley or cilantro

▶ Heat ordinary olive oil in a medium saucepan. Add onions, garlic, chili or chili powder, and cumin. Sauté over medium heat 5 minutes, until onions are soft.

▶ Add fava beans with the juice in the can. If you've made your own beans, add ½ cup of the water they boiled in. Add tomatoes, lemon juice, salt, and 2 Tbs. of the high-quality olive oil. Continue to cook over medium heat 10 minutes, stirring frequently as it bubbles and thickens. Some people mash some of the beans toward the end to make this a thick puree: your choice.

▶ To serve, add salt to taste. Garnish each portion with chopped parsley or cilantro and a splash of the high-quality olive oil. Add a splash of lemon juice if you like it slightly sour.

▶ Serve in a soup bowl or in a roasted/grilled pita.

The kernel of rice and so on

is obscured by its outer husk.

Likewise the vision of truth

is obscured by the husk of ignorance.

—THE UTTARATANTRA SHASTRA

Generosity:
Learning through Food

IN HIS TEACHINGS, the Buddha frequently used food as metaphor. The late Dilgo Khyentse Rinpoche taught using this example:

ONCE UPON A TIME, there was a very miserly person unable to give anything away. He went to see the Buddha. "It is impossible for me to be generous," he said, "what shall I do?"

"Imagine," the Buddha replied, "that your right hand is yourself and your left hand a poor unhappy person. Give from your right hand to your left hand some old food, which you don't like or need. Try hard to get used to this. Do it until you are no longer miserly."

The man began the practice but he was so tight-fisted that at first he could give away only a few leftovers or food he did not like. Gradually, however, he acquired the habit so that the day arrived when he did not feel so niggardly. Thereupon he went to see the Buddha and reported, "Now when I give food from my right hand to my left, I don't feel so miserly."

If we help others by providing them food …

it should not be with the expectation of some kind of recognition.

—DILGO KHYENTSE RINPOCHE, *Enlightened Courage*

Lentils
with Orange and Clove

I found this Egyptian recipe decades ago; it's an old favorite because it's an easy, tasty, healthy way to feed a crowd. You can make it a day ahead and you can serve it either hot or cold.

SERVES 8.

2 cups brown lentils, washed and picked over

2 bay leaves

3 garlic cloves, peeled

3 whole cloves

1 tsp. ground cumin

⅛ tsp. orange flower water (Use ¼ tsp. orange juice if you don't have it)

1 Tbs. grated fresh orange rind, divided

1 tsp. salt

¼ tsp. freshly ground or cracked black pepper

½ cup chopped fresh parsley

½ cup chopped fresh cilantro

1 large red onion, peeled and diced

2 Tbs. fresh lemon juice

1 Tbs. Jerez (Spanish sherry) or balsamic vinegar

1 cup olive oil

⅛ tsp. ground cloves

▶ Put lentils, bay leaves, garlic cloves, whole cloves, cumin, orange flower water, and half the orange rind in a large saucepan with 4 cups water. Bring to a boil over high heat, lower heat to simmer, and cook 25–30 minutes until lentils are tender. Do no overcook; lentils should not be mushy. Each one should remain distinct.

▶ Drain well and discard the bay leaves, garlic, and cloves if you can find them.

▶ Put the warm lentils in a large serving bowl. Add the salt, pepper, parsley, cilantro, onion, and the remaining orange rind. Carefully stir to blend.

▶ In a spouted cup, combine lemon juice, vinegar, olive oil, and ground cloves. Shake or whisk to blend. Pour over the warm lentils. Adjust salt to taste.

▶ Serve immediately or let cool and serve on lettuce leaves as a salad with chunks of fresh feta cheese and tomatoes on the side. This also goes well beside the parsley omelets on page 72.

Lima Bean *Plaki*

Plaki is a traditional eastern Mediterranean dish, one of many clever olive oil preparations designed to keep the body moist on sweaty summer days. This less oily version can be also served hot as a bean dish with rice.

SERVES 6–8.

2 cups dried lima beans or
2½ cups frozen cooked lima beans
(depending on the time you have)

½ cup olive oil

2 onions, peeled and finely chopped
(the food processor can do it)

3–4 garlic cloves, peeled and minced

1 carrot, peeled and diced

1 celery stick, diced

1 tsp. dried marjoram

1 tsp. dried oregano

1 tsp. dried rosemary

½ cup chopped fresh parsley

1½ cup chopped tomatoes
(canned or boxed is fine)

1–1½ tsp. salt, or more to taste

½ tsp. freshly ground or
cracked black pepper

1 Tbs. fresh lemon juice

GARNISH

extra virgin olive oil

chopped fresh parsley

▶ If you are using dried lima beans, put them in a medium pot, cover with water, and bring to a boil over medium-high heat. Reduce heat to low and boil 3 minutes. Remove from heat, cover, and let stand 1 hour. Drain and rinse.

▶ Check beans for tenderness. If they feel slightly tender, move to the next step. If they still feel hard, put them back in the pot, cover with water, and cook over medium heat for 15–20 minutes until they feel almost tender to a fork.

▶ In a medium-large casserole or large covered pot, heat the olive oil over medium heat. Add onions and garlic and sauté 4–5 minutes until onions are soft and golden.

▶ Add carrots, celery, marjoram, oregano, rosemary, parsley, and stir to blend. Continue to sauté 2–3 minutes.

▶ Add tomatoes, lima beans, salt, and pepper. Add 1 cup water. Cover and simmer over low heat for 15 minutes. Stir in lemon juice. Let sit covered for 3–5 minutes. Adjust salt and pepper to taste.

- ▸ Garnish with a splash of fruity olive oil and a handful of fresh chopped parsley.

- ▸ This can be served hot or cold the next day.

An empty stomach is not a good political advisor.

—ALBERT EINSTEIN

Moros y Cristianos

The name of this black bean and rice dish, Moors and Christians, slyly symbolizes the era when European Christians and the darker-skinned Moors of North Africa inhabited and fought over Andalusia. When the dish went with the Spanish to Cuba, where it remains one of the most beloved comfort foods, it came to symbolize the light-skinned Spanish conquistadors and the darker-skinned Caribbean natives. Cuban exiles have popularized myriad versions in the U.S.

SERVES 6–8.

1 cup dried black beans

1½ cups long-grain rice

3 Tbs. olive oil

1 large onion, peeled and diced

1 large green bell pepper, diced

3 garlic cloves, peeled, smashed, and minced

2 tsp. ground cumin

1 tsp. dried oregano

1 bay leaf

½ tsp. salt, or more to taste

½ tsp. freshly ground or cracked black pepper

2 Tbs. vinegar (red wine, Jerez, or white)

1 heaping Tbs. tomato paste

2¼ cups vegetable broth

GARNISH

high-quality olive oil

chopped fresh cilantro

▶ Put the beans in a medium saucepan with 2¼ cups of water. Bring to a boil. Boil for 3 minutes. Turn off heat and let stand covered for 1 hour.

▶ Drain and rinse beans. Put back in saucepan with another 2¼ cups of water. Bring to a boil and reduce heat to low. Cover and simmer until beans are tender, about 40 minutes. Drain.

▶ Rinse rice with cold water until water runs clear. Drain.

▶ In a medium casserole or stockpot, heat olive oil over medium-high heat. Add onion and green pepper and sauté over medium heat until soft, about 5 minutes.

▶ Add garlic and sauté another minute. Add cumin, oregano, bay leaf, salt, pepper, and vinegar. Sauté 30–40 seconds and add tomato paste. Stir to blend ingredients and sauté 1 minute. Add black beans and blend. Cook 1 more minute.

- Add rice and stir to blend. Add broth, blending. Bring to a boil, cover, and reduce heat to low. Simmer for 20–25 minutes until rice is fully cooked and all liquid is absorbed. Remove from heat and remove bay leaf.

- Taste for salt and add ¼ tsp. if you'd like more.

- Drizzle with high-quality olive oil and optionally garnish with chopped cilantro to serve.

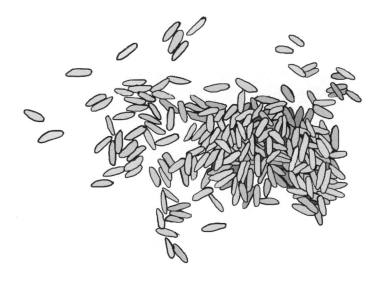

Pasang's *Masoor* Dhal

What makes this recipe special is that while most cooks simply boil lentils, my friend Pasang Doma, who grew up in both Kathmandu, Nepal, and Kalimpong, India, essentially braises them, cooking dhal like Italians cook risotto: continuously stirring while continually adding liquid in small streams. She believes this makes the final dish tastier and she has five siblings who agree.

SERVES 4.

1 cup salmon-colored or *masoor* dhal, rinsed, cleaned of stones, and soaked 1 hour

2 Tbs. butter or ghee or oil such as corn or mustard

1 large onion, peeled and chopped

3 garlic cloves, peeled and minced or blended into a paste with the ginger, as is common in Kathmandu and Kalimpong kitchens

1-inch piece fresh ginger, peeled and minced

½ tsp. ground turmeric

1¼ tsp. garam masala

1 tsp. salt

1 large tomato, cored and chopped

½ bunch cilantro, leaves only, washed and chopped

▶ Drain the dhal from its soaking water.

▶ In a small casserole or medium saucepan, heat the butter, ghee, or oil over medium heat. Add the onion and stir-fry until soft and golden. Add garlic and ginger and continue to stir-fry another minute.

▶ Lower the heat. Add the dhal, turmeric, garam masala, and salt, stirring to blend well. Continue to stir-fry a minute or two, adding butter or oil if necessary to prevent burning.

▶ Add the tomato and ½ cup water, stir to blend, and continue cooking. As the liquid dries up, add another ½ cup and continue stirring. As the lentils soak up the liquid and expand, add another cup of water, stir to blend, cover, and cook on low heat for 10 minutes, checking to be sure there's always enough water in the pot to keep the dhal from burning. Add a final ½ cup water, cover, and cook until the lentils burst. The process takes 40 minutes, and the salmon-colored lentils will turn yellow along the way.

▶ Adjust seasonings to taste. (I sometimes add a teaspoon of celery seeds.) Garnish with the cilantro and serve hot.

*On one occasion, when my mother did bring me a present of some meat
(sausages filled with rice and mince, our village specialty), I remember
eating it all at once, because I knew if I told any of my sweepers
about it, I would have to share it with them. The next day
I was extremely ill…so I was compelled to admit the
truth of the matter. It was a good lesson.*

—THE DALAI LAMA

Transcendence: Food and Politics

THE NEED TO EAT is so universal and indisputable that food finesses politics by uniting to conquer.

I had my own indelible experience in 1984 when the West German government invited me to their fortieth anniversary commemoration of a resistance attempt to assassinate Adolph Hitler. There were about eighteen of us in the press pool, and everybody but me was from the east or west side of a drastically divided Europe. It took only one day for the nine of us from Western democracies to realize that four of the nine from the Soviet Eastern Bloc countries, the ones in uniform dark gray who never spoke a word, were not journalists but KGB or Stasi agents sent to keep the Eastern reporters under tight control. So tight that at mealtimes they invariably stood, stone silent, marshaling the Eastern Bloc participants to a table of their own, quite separate from the rest of us. Our table carried on spirited conversations that often led to loud laughter that echoed over the heads of the easterners, who ate in spooky silence.

I eventually learned that one of the silent reporters was Hungarian. The next lunch time, I defiantly, or maybe it was disobediently, brushed past the KGB and rushed to sit at the Eastern Bloc table. The whole room was hushed in foreboding silence as plates of ham and potatoes were plunked down. Many eyes were on me. But I was on a mission. I turned toward the portly gray-haired man two seats away. "I'm so glad to finally meet a Hungarian," I said loudly, with a big smile. "For years, I've been trying to figure out whether you do or don't put sausage in *leszco*."

The man was so startled he froze, with his fork almost at his mouth. I saw his eyes start to move toward the KGB, but instead he put down his fork, let out a deep breath, and turned to me. "I haven't thought about that for years," he said. "But now that you ask, my mother always used to…" He went on to tell me how he had tried to find the right sausage in New York while studying philosophy at Columbia. That's how he discovered the Hungarian Upper East Side—where I myself had gone hunting for *leszco* ingredients not long after him. Yes! With animation and smiles, we tried to remember the various delis on Second Avenue. He told me everyone at Columbia wanted him to make chicken *paprikas,* because it was the best-known Hungarian dish, but he could never get it to taste right because our American chickens were so tasteless. How did we manage to make chickens with no chicken flavor? I talked about corporate consumerism with its emphasis on quantity and cash instead of quality. He went on to tell me what wines he served with *paprikas.* I told him I didn't know much about Hungarian wine beyond Tokay, so he gave me a short lesson. He dictated *paprikas* and *leszco* recipes, which I speedily recorded in my notebook, to the increasingly palpable consternation of KGB men absolutely powerless to thwart this togetherness. The Hungarian beamed at me for the rest of the tour.

If diversity and conflict must persist, I suggest it should be in the kitchen, not on the battlefield. Everywhere I read of Middle Eastern people vying for recognition as the very best hosts serving the very best foods. Oh, that such a feeling of friendly rivalry at the dinner table could be extended to the conference table of diplomats!

—Eva Zane, *Middle Eastern Cookery*

Punjabi-Style Black-Eyed Peas

You can prepare this rich and pungent dhal rather quickly by using canned, precooked black-eyed peas instead of dried ones, so here is the recipe both ways. SERVES 6.

Faster, Modern Way

4 Tbs. olive or canola oil

1 Tbs. butter or ghee

5 garlic cloves, peeled and minced

2½–3-inch piece fresh ginger, peeled and minced

1 large red onion, peeled and finely diced

2 tsp. ground cumin

1 tsp. ground coriander

1 tsp. chili powder

2 cups chopped tomatoes in their juices (canned or boxed is okay)

⅓ cup plain yogurt, thicker is better, at room temperature

2 (15-oz.) cans of cooked black-eyed peas

⅛ tsp. salt

¼ tsp. smoked paprika

½ bunch cilantro, leaves only, washed and chopped

▶ Heat the oil and butter or ghee in a large heavy-gauge saucepan or medium casserole over medium heat. Add the garlic, ginger, and onion, and stir-fry for 3–5 minutes to soften.

▶ Mix in the cumin, coriander, chili powder, and tomato. Lower to medium-low heat and continue to sauté another 2–3 minutes until the sauce is very warm. Stir in the yogurt very slowly (yogurt that is too cold in a sauce that is too hot can come apart) until the pot contents are a smooth sauce. Continue to heat for another 2 minutes.

▶ Add the black-eyed peas and salt. If there is not enough sauce to cover the beans, add ½ cup water or vegetable broth and blend in. Continue to simmer about 10–12 minutes, whatever it takes to get everything nice and hot without drying out the sauce. Test and adjust salt to taste. Stir in the paprika.

▶ Pour into a large serving bowl and garnish with the chopped cilantro.

Slower, Traditional Way

1½ cups dried black-eyed peas, soaked overnight and drained

¼ tsp. salt, divided

4 Tbs. olive, canola, or mustard oil

2 Tbs. ghee or butter

1 large red onion, peeled and minced

6–7 garlic cloves, peeled and minced

3½-inch piece fresh ginger, peeled and minced

3 tsp. ground cumin

1½ tsp. ground coriander

1½ tsp. chili powder

2 medium tomatoes, chopped

⅓ cup thick yogurt at room temperature

½ bunch cilantro, leaves only, washed and chopped

▶ Put the beans in a medium pot with 5 cups of water and ⅛ tsp. salt. Bring to a boil over high heat, reduce heat to simmer, cover, and cook 3 minutes. Remove from heat; do not drain.

▶ In another medium pot, heat the oil and ghee or butter over medium heat. Add onion and stir-fry 3–5 minutes until slightly browned. Stir in the garlic, ginger, cumin, coriander, and chili. Continue to cook over medium heat for 30 seconds. Add the chopped tomatoes and stir-fry until the tomatoes are soft.

▶ Lower heat and continue to stir for another minute. Slowly stir in the yogurt until it makes a smooth sauce. Continue to cook another 2–3 minutes.

▶ Pour in the black-eyed peas and their cooking water. Add remaining ⅛ tsp. salt and stir to blend all ingredients well. Cover and simmer until the black-eyed peas are tender, 40–50 minutes. The mixture should be thick.

▶ Pour into a serving bowl and garnish with the chopped cilantro.

Split Peas
with Kale and Cinnamon

This very fragrant, colorful, and flavorful dhal can be served the next day as a delicious and rich soup if you thin it with vegetable broth or water.

SERVES 6.

2 cups yellow split peas, cleaned

1 tsp. ground turmeric

1 large cinnamon stick

2 tsp. salt, divided

2 Tbs. olive oil or ghee

2 bay leaves

5 whole cloves

1 tsp. cumin seeds

1 medium red onion, diced

½-inch piece fresh ginger, peeled and minced

2 garlic cloves, minced

1 bunch Tuscan kale, chopped (thick stem removed)

½ tsp. ground cardamom

½ tsp. ground cumin

1 tsp. freshly ground black pepper

GARNISH

½ bunch cilantro, chopped

▶ Bring 5 cups of water to boil in a large saucepan or medium casserole.

▶ Add split peas, turmeric, cinnamon stick, and half the salt. Cook covered for 1 hour, checking that there is always some water in the pot.

▶ While the peas cook, heat the oil or ghee in a medium frying or sauté pan. Over medium heat, fry the bay leaves, cloves, and cumin seeds for 1 minute. Add the onion, ginger, and garlic and cook until the onions lightly brown, stirring to blend. Stir in the kale and remaining tsp. salt. Continue cooking until the kale is glistening and soft. Remove the bay leaves from the pot.

▶ Add the contents of the fry pan to the split peas. Add the ground cardamom, cumin, and black pepper, stirring to blend. Taste for seasonings and adjust to taste.

▶ Continue cooking until the peas are soft, adding water if necessary. Some people prefer this soupy and others on the dry side.

▶ Ladle into bowls and sprinkle with chopped cilantro.

The word species (for spice) was first employed as an umbrella term signifying

a great many high-value, readily transferable, and generally low-volume

goods, as distinct from the ordinary or bulk items of commerce.

Along with the implication of high cost, the word conveyed

a sense of extraordinariness, of special distinction.

—JACK TURNER, *Spice: A History of a Temptation*

Vegetables

Plant a carrot, get a carrot,
Not a Brussels sprout,
That's why I like vegetables,
You know what you're about!
—THE FANTASTICKS

Vegetables are remarkable. They give all; they provide
nourishment and purification for body and soul,
yet they ask nothing in return.
—TOSHIO TANAHASHI,
modern *shojin ryori* master in Kyoto, Japan

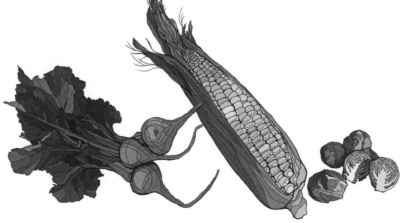

Bhutanese Asparagus
or Fiddleheads with Cheese

Asparagus and fiddlehead ferns, which are also a New England delicacy, are wild plants that sprout in Bhutan in late March as snow melts and the ground thaws. This is a typical way Himalayan people prepare their mountain vegetables and mushrooms.

SERVES 4–6.

1 small red onion, peeled

1 medium fresh green chili, stemmed and seeded

½ lb. asparagus, lower ends trimmed off, or ½ lb. fiddleheads, carefully rinsed clean of grit

4 Tbs. unsalted butter

1 cup (6 oz.) farmer's or feta cheese, crumbled

⅛ tsp. salt

freshly ground black pepper to taste

▶ Quarter the onion and chop finely. Slice the chili into thin julienne strips. Cut the asparagus into 2-inch pieces.

▶ Melt butter in a large saucepan. Add the onion and sauté until translucent and soft. Add asparagus or fiddleheads and ¾ cup water. Simmer over low heat until tender, about 10 minutes.

▶ Add the chili, cheese, and salt. Stir to blend. Continue to cook about 5 minutes until the cheese melts into a smooth sauce. Add black pepper to taste and serve hot.

French Ratatouille, Southwestern Style

After too many years of making this famous Provençal summer stew over and over, I got so bored I decided to play with the colors and tweak the flavors. Like many other cooks, I was moving away from the exclusive focus on European cooking to engage with the rest of the world. I substituted New World vegetables for some of the European favorites, a subtle shift that made this dish somehow look more vivid and taste more vibrant.

SERVES 6–8.

1 large poblano pepper

3 large tomatillos

1 lb. firm eggplant (any kind will work except the small Thai egg-like eggplant)

1 tsp. salt, divided

½ cup olive oil, divided

1 tsp. freshly ground or cracked black pepper

1 tsp. dried oregano, divided

pinch chipotle chili powder (optional, for smoky flavor)

1 bay leaf

1 large red onion, peeled and cut into thin disks

4 garlic cloves, peeled and minced

1 red bell pepper, seeded and sliced into thin strips

⅔ cup chopped fresh cilantro, divided

¼ tsp. ground coriander

¾ lb. yellow or crookneck squash, cut into ¼-inch thick disks

1¼ cup chopped tomatoes in their juices (canned or boxed is okay)

▶ Roast the poblano pepper and the tomatillos at 450°F for 5–8 minutes, until the skin cracks and starts to char. Let them cool.

▶ Wash the eggplant. Slice it into thin disks. If the disks are much larger in diameter than 1 inch, cut the disks in half. Place on a baking sheet, sprinkle lightly with ¼ tsp. salt and 2 Tbs. olive oil. Cover and roast at 425°F for 10 minutes.

▶ Peel the poblano pepper and the tomatillos. Seed the pepper and cut into thin strips no longer than 2 inches.

▶ In a medium heavy-gauge casserole or large saucepan, heat the remaining olive oil over medium heat. Add black pepper, ½ tsp. oregano, chipotle (if desired), and bay leaf. Sauté 30 seconds.

► Add onion disks in a layer and top with garlic, poblano, and red peppers. Do not stir. Continue to sauté 3–5 minutes until onions are soft. Sprinkle 1 Tbs. chopped cilantro on top.

► Lower heat to simmer. Add eggplant as a layer. (Pieces might be two deep if the pot is not wide.) Sprinkle on remaining ½ tsp. oregano, ground coriander, and ¼ tsp. salt. Add 2 Tbs. chopped cilantro. Cover pot and simmer 2–3 minutes.

► Add a layer of yellow squash and half the remaining chopped cilantro. Pour tomatoes into the pot. Sprinkle ¼ tsp. salt over the top layer. Cover and simmer for 10 minutes, or until the squash starts to soften.

► Slice roasted tomatillos into thin disks or any small pieces you can manage. Add to the pot as the top layer. Cover and simmer 3–5 minutes until the squash is soft (not mushy) and the juices are bubbling. Remove from heat. Remove bay leaf. Add remaining salt if desired.

► Serve hot, at room temperature, or cold, garnished with the remaining chopped cilantro. To make this into a full meal, serve over squares of fried polenta or with *arepas* (page 63).

Shojin Ryori

THE CONCEPT, ingredients, and recipes of the Japanese cooking style called *shojin ryori* were handed down by thirteenth-century monks who went to China to study Buddhism and brought them back as Dharma practice. *Sho* means "to concentrate," *jin* "to go forward" or "to progress along the path," and *ryori* is the mundane word for cooking, or the collection of dishes produced by it. The phrase is sometimes translated as "advancement of the mind through food," although a young Japanese woman recently explained to me, "If someone tells you to 'Shojin,' they mean that you should control and go above your self in spirit."

Shojin ryori was initially meant as a Zen meditation to purify body and mind, but with the aspiration to make Dharma teachings available to everybody, some major Buddhist monasteries opened restaurants inside their temples as a lure. The surprising popularity of these evangelical eateries demystified the monks' exotic vegetarian fare and encouraged commoners to set up shops to sell the key ingredients of this temple food to the general public. Their success was accelerated when the aristocratic and educated elite embraced Buddhism, making simplicity fashionable. Once the influential, much-imitated samurai wholeheartedly adopted Zen, making it "high class" to live on little, *shojin ryori*'s main ingredients—soybeans, seaweed, and sesame—became the sine qua non of Japanese food. Even now, no cook would be caught in the kitchen without at least tofu, miso, or *gomashio*, the indispensible seasoning of toasted sesame seeds ground up with salt. Temple food, as it's known, has been so assimilated into ordinary life, it is mandatory on ritual occasions. A family gathered for a funeral, for instance, will only eat food from a *shojin ryori* restaurant.

This cooking is not so elaborate as *kaiseki ryori*, the haute (and omnivorous) cuisine that also began in Buddhist monasteries where *kaiseki* referred to the heated stone kept by monks in their kimonos to stay warm and distract them from their hunger. *Ryori* in this case represented tiny dishes monastic cooks exquisitely crafted to accompany tea and appease that hunger. "Tea service" food so fascinated samurai society that they replicated it in ceremonial meals at public teahouses, where it slowly evolved into today's intensely complex, extravagant restaurant offerings of fish and meat in dramatic "bonsai" presentations.

The rigorous but elegantly manicured artifice of *kaiseki ryori* contrasts starkly with the modesty required by *shojin ryori*. Yet *shojin ryori* should not be mistaken for ordinary veganism or rigid macrobiotics, with which it is sometimes confused since the macrobiotic movement borrowed heavily from it. Its essence is still *sho*, Dharma practice, so that cooking requires years of training and continually disciplined focus. The cook's preliminary process of preparation is, for example, as important as the customer's denouement of digesting. *Shojin ryori* cooks cannot waste ingredients. Zen Buddhist master Fujii Sotetsu says, "We even sauté the greens and peelings of carrots and daikon radish, then simmer them in a little water, or we add them to soup.... This 'recycling' is easy if one minimizes seasoning, letting the natural flavor of the ingredients define the taste. The Zen aversion to waste extends to dishware, too. When Japanese people eat deep-fried *tempura*, they use extra dishes for the dipping sauce. Followers of Zen, on the other hand, feel that sauces are extravagant to prepare and tend to drip and make a mess anyway, so we forgo using dipping sauces altogether. In fact, sauces are unnecessary with a little salt in the batter, or if one simmers vegetables in *miso*-flavored water before deep-frying them."

A *shojin ryori* chef must master not only consideration for the pleasure of the diner, but also sincerity, cleanliness, and gratitude for the ingredients. Since the cooking represents Buddhist practice, there can never be any product of animal origin: meat, poultry, fish or eggs, butter, lard, or fish oil. There can never be pungent produce such as garlic and onion, definitely never strong spices that interfere with the delicate flavor of local, seasonal vegetables. Typically a chef must figure out how to forge a meal in which soybeans provide protein, seaweed furnishes minerals, seasonal vegetables offer vitamins, and sesame seeds supply critical calcium, iron, and folic acid.

"People ask me," the Zen priest Fujii Sotetsu said in *Zen Culinary Fundamentals*, "if I can maintain a balanced diet while eating only vegetables; the answer, of course, is yes. I have been following Buddhist training and eating only vegetarian meals for more than 50 years, yet I have never even caught a cold in all that time. Life at a Zen temple is strict and demands much physical labor, but I can take it in stride because I have the power of seasonal vegetables on my side. Of course, *shojin ryori* is part of the Buddhist temple regimen, yet it is also my way of maintaining a sound mind and body."

Composing a meal is a delicate exercise, much like assembling pieces of a jigsaw puzzle. Acceptable ingredients must be combined to reflect not only the place and season at that moment, but the nutritional palette's entire range—sweet, sour, salty, etc.—making the chef a true guru who leads the diner to a wider perception of possibility. Also every cooking method—stewing, boiling, frying, and grilling—must be employed, the dishes progressively presented to convey respect for the farmers, the soil, and especially Mother Nature whose generous bounty made it all possible. Done properly, the meal's choreography should prompt diners to be overwhelmed by gratitude, particularly for the cook as the skillful mediator between such heavenly food and the earth it came from. A *Financial Times* reporter once wrote that her first *shojin ryori* experience was so startlingly sumptuous that it left her feeling loved and content.

Spinach *Goma-ae*

This popular Japanese dish, which is also very good made with green beans, is an excellent example of "temple food." It will taste very different if made with Chinese cooking wine and soy sauce.

SERVES 4.

1 lb. spinach leaves, washed (or 12 oz. green beans, cut into 1-inch pieces)

4 Tbs. sesame seeds

2 Tbs. mirin (Japanese cooking wine) or Chinese cooking wine

1 Tbs. tamari (wheat-free Japanese soy sauce) or any soy sauce

½ tsp. rice wine vinegar

▶ Blanch the spinach leaves in heavily salted boiling water for 1 minute. Drain well. Form the wet leaves into a ball and squeeze out as much moisture as you can. Then put inside a towel and do the same. Once the spinach is dry, chop it coarsely.

▶ In a dry skillet or frying pan, toast the sesame seeds over medium heat for 2 minutes or until they start to become golden brown. This can happen very fast.

▶ Grind or smash the sesame seeds into a paste. Stir in the cooking wine, tamari, vinegar, and enough water to thin the paste into a dressing.

▶ Put the chopped spinach into a serving bowl and stir in the sesame dressing to serve. Serve at room temperature.

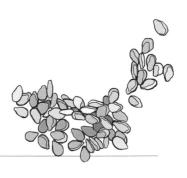

Nepali Braised Pumpkin

The Nepalis' skillful use of spices—lighter than the Indians—seems to make everything and anything very tasty, including pumpkin. Unlike North Americans, they recognize that it's actually a vegetable—a squash—and doesn't have to be relegated to a sugary dessert like pie. The schoolchildren use this basic recipe when the monastery harvests the pumpkins it grows under the cornstalks and delivers a pickup truck–load to them.

SERVES 4–6.

1 Tbs. corn, sunflower, or mustard oil (not olive)

1 tsp. cumin seeds

½ tsp. fenugreek seeds

¼ tsp. minced fresh ginger

4 cups (1 small) sugar pumpkin or butternut squash, peeled and chopped

1 tsp. ground turmeric

1 tsp. salt

1 tsp. garam masala

1 Tbs. toasted, salted pumpkin seeds

GARNISH

¼ cup chopped fresh cilantro

▶ In the bottom of a medium heavy-gauge saucepan or wok, heat the oil to very hot. Fry the cumin and fenugreek seeds until they turn brown/black. Add the minced ginger, pumpkin/squash, turmeric, and salt. Stir and sauté for 5 minutes over medium-high heat.

▶ Reduce heat to medium, add ½ cup water, and cook 15–20 minutes until pumpkin/squash is tender.

▶ Add garam masala and pumpkin seeds, and stir to blend. Remove from heat and drain off any liquid.

▶ Garnish with chopped cilantro to serve.

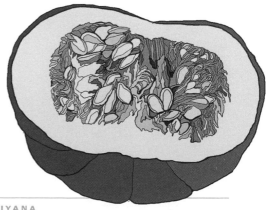

When asked by a farmer, "I hear you don't eat meat. Where do you get your strength?"

Thoreau, pointing to the husky team of horses drawing the farmer's wagon,

replied: "Where do they get their strength?"

—Philip Kapleau

Persian Celery Stew

If you think of celery as nothing more than filler in tuna salad, a dieter's must-chew, or snack sticks for kids, this simple, straightforward, and succulent stew will be an amazing revelation.

SERVES 6–8.

1½ bunches of celery with leaves, stalks separated and cleaned

4 Tbs. butter

1 large red onion, peeled and diced

¼ tsp. freshly ground or cracked black pepper

2 bunches flat-leaf parsley, cleaned and chopped (at least 3 cups), divided

¼ tsp. saffron

2 cups vegetable broth

2 Tbs. dried crushed mint

¼ tsp. salt

1 Tbs. fresh lemon juice

▶ Cut celery, including leaves, into 1-inch pieces.

▶ Melt butter in a large saucepan or medium casserole. Sauté onion over medium heat until soft and translucent. Add black pepper and celery and continue to sauté 5 minutes.

▶ Add half the parsley (1½ cups or 1 bunch), saffron, and vegetable broth. Stir to blend. Bring to a boil. Cover and reduce heat to low. Simmer 30 minutes.

▶ Add remainder of parsley except for 1 Tbs. Add mint, salt, and lemon juice, stirring to blend. Continue cooking for 10–12 minutes or until celery is soft.

▶ Adjust for salt and pepper. Garnish with remaining chopped parsley to serve.

Handle even a single leaf of a green in such a way that it manifests

the body of the Buddha. This in turn allows the Buddha

to manifest through the leaf.

—DOGEN ZENJI, *Instructions to the Monastery Cook*

Feeding Your Face

THE MAGICAL PROPERTIES of what we eat have never been much of a secret. Salt quenches fire without all the smoke water causes; limes that are acidic enough to "cook" fish can also in ten to twelve minutes wipe bacteria off raw greens and vegetables. A perimeter of cinnamon will keep ants out of your house. A poultice of baking soda and water can suck the itchy swelling from an insect bite. A British physician discovered in desperation in the killing fields of World War I that honey smeared on wounds becomes a dependable antibiotic. Indians chew cloves as breath freshener and to calm a toothache. The best revenge for "Montezuma's revenge" is bananas, rice, yogurt, or chocolate. The Nepalese rub turmeric over their chicken before making curry because they're sure it kills bacteria on the skin and they don't dare make dhal without it, believing the root relieves beans of their gas. They feed new mothers lots of fenugreek because it makes breast milk flow. The Chinese know ginger quells nausea and burdock root cleans the blood. I know cranberries prevent and kill urinary tract infections because as a child I constantly carried glasses of cranberry juice to the room of my ailing great uncle.

Modern marketers keep pelting us with bravado claims for antioxidants, omega oils, beta-carotene, and vitamin C—and bombard us with artificial phar-macological products to match. The last time I had to wait for a prescription to be filled, I noticed the "supplement" shelf at my local pharmacy was brimming with sealed bottles full of pills and capsules of stuff that should ordinarily be in the kitchen: cayenne, cinnamon, ginger, garlic, turmeric, fenugreek, cranberry, pomegranate, papaya, elderberry, bilberry, acai berry, "superfruits plus," soy, fish oil, artichoke extract, black cherry extract, green tea, and seaweed. They are a sad sign of how much we've neglected our wisdom inheritance.

So are superstore shelves now proudly filled with apricot exfoliate, mango-mandarin body cream, pineapple facial cleanser, raspberry pomegranate scrub, Asian pear deodorant, grapefruit soap, peppermint conditioner, and coconut body wash. People not suckered into the great maw of modern marketing have always known that food good for the inside of your body also works wonders on the outside as a cosmetic. The ancients were so wild about anointing their skin and hair with olive oil that they called it "holy oil." It still nicely remedies a dry, flaky scalp. Asians trust coconut oil to make their scalp moist and their hair shine in much the same way. In the 1940s, hair detangler in America was fresh lemon juice and conditioner could be beer. Not long ago my goddaughter showed up smelling just like the vanilla essential oils I use for baking—apparently this had become the rage in Hollywood. She brought me a jar of orange essence.

About once a month, while cutting an avocado, I save a piece of skin whose interior I rub all over my face, smearing bright green bits of avocado on it. After about five minutes of looking like a Dada painting, or perhaps E.T., I feel the astringent avocado oil pull the skin. In another five minutes I wash it off, apply aloe, and the frugal facial is complete. Sometimes I lay down and put used black tea bags over closed eyes for five to eight minutes so their tannin can remove puffiness. I learned those tricks from my friend Simone's mother, a refugee Hungarian countess who ended up in Greenwich Village after World War II. She had grown up with the traditional Eastern European beauty regimen being lucratively bottled and sold by her compatriot émigrés Estee Lauder, the sisters Gabor, and the Polish Helena Rubinstein. She told me I didn't need their pricey products, just a corner grocery.

Cucumbers work as an astringent on the skin and eyes, although they are much stronger and their application requires more skill than avocados and used tea bags. An egg beaten with a teaspoon of olive oil and applied to brittle, lifeless hair for an hour (just leave it there with a towel around your neck to catch any drips) can perk it up with the protein it lacks. Almond milk can blanch the redness of facial skin. I recently watched a Tibetan woman boil raw milk, skim the cream off the top and refrigerate it overnight so it gelled, then smear that "cold cream" on her face to make her skin soft and radiant. Rub butter on your hands to soften the skin. Pour a quart of milk into your bath to pamper the body. And don't forget from time to time to cut an onion and cry your eyes out—cleaning them so they sparkle.

So the best medicine is to eat your food properly and drink your drink properly. When you do that, everything becomes homogeneous and nothing is poisonous. The poisonous aspect always comes from your speed, your aggression, your desire, your wantingness.

—CHÖGYAM TRUNGPA RINPOCHE

Sesame Snap Peas

Snap peas are a cross between the flatter Chinese snow pea and the plumper English garden pea. Peas are legumes and thus full of vitamins, minerals (even iron), and protein. Ditto for sesame. So this colorful, crunchy Chinese preparation is the picture of health.

SERVES 6.

1 Tbs. corn oil

½-inch piece fresh ginger, peeled and grated to get the juices

1 garlic clove, peeled and minced

1 lb. snap peas, cleaned

1 Tbs. sesame seeds

1 tsp. soy sauce

2 tsp. sesame oil

▶ In a wok or similar pot, heat the corn oil over medium-high heat. Add ginger and garlic and stir-fry 30 seconds.

▶ Add peas. Stir-fry 1 minute, carefully coating them in the oil. Add sesame seeds and soy sauce and continue to stir-fry over medium heat for 3 minutes. Add sesame oil and continue to stir-fry another minute.

▶ Serve warm.

English Smashed Peas

This cheery, bright green comfort food is healthy, tasty, and nursery food perfect for kids.

SERVES 6–8.

¼ tsp. salt, divided

1 lb. shelled peas
(probably 3 lbs. in the pod)

½ cup chopped fresh mint

2 Tbs. butter
(3 Tbs. if you want full butter flavor)

¼ tsp. freshly ground or cracked black pepper

▶ Bring ½ cup water and half the salt (⅛ tsp.) to a boil on high heat.

▶ Add the peas, reduce heat to medium high, and cook for 2–3 minutes or until peas are tender.

▶ Pour the contents of the pot into the bowl of a food processor. Add mint, butter, pepper, and remaining salt. Process until you have a coarse puree in which you can still see the shape of some peas.

▶ Serve immediately.

Piro Aloo: Spicy Potatoes

At the incredibly busy Garden Restaurant in the Boudha quarter of Kathmandu, the waiters always recognize me with a wry smile as soon as I step in, for I am "the *piro aloo* lady." I truly had no idea when two Bhutanese monks first took me there and ordered their favorite "snack," that when I accepted their entreaties to "please taste" I would end up so addicted I eat them every day I am in Boudha. But I have to confess: that's how it is. And to make me seem even more bizarre, although *piro aloo* is on the snack menu, the waiters know I am going to ask the cook to make it for me for breakfast. These potatoes with scrambled eggs and a side of plain, fresh yogurt is my standard start to a Kathmandu day—along with a wave from the cook who knows it's me when the order comes in. He knows because I actually went into the kitchen to watch him make this. I don't think anybody, let alone a Westerner, had ever done that, and he has never forgotten. And I have his recipe!

SERVES 4 AS A MEAL, 6 AS A SNACK.

1 lb. medium boiling potatoes

3 Tbs. corn, sunflower, mustard, or safflower oil

1 hot green chili, seeded and minced

3 garlic cloves, peeled and minced

½ tsp. ground cumin

1 tsp. arbol chili powder, or similar chili powder

¼ tsp. ground turmeric

½ tsp. salt

GARNISH

chopped fresh cilantro

▶ Boil potatoes in their skins in salted water until tender. Do not overcook; potatoes should not be mushy. Drain, cool, and peel. Chop into large bite-sized pieces.

▶ Heat the oil in a medium or large skillet over medium-high heat. Add chili, garlic, cumin, chili powder, and turmeric and stir to blend. Lower heat to medium and fry for 1 minute.

▶ Add potatoes. (For best results, the frying pan or skillet should be big enough to hold them in 1 layer.) Add salt onto the potatoes and stir to blend them into the spicy oil.

▶ Sauté for 3–4 minutes, until potatoes are lightly crisp, shaking the pan so nothing sticks and potatoes stay coated. Remove from heat, add salt to taste, and garnish with a handful of chopped cilantro.

▶ Serve as a side dish or snack (offer toothpicks), with a dish of cooling yogurt.

Achar: Chutneys, Condiments, and Pickles

*Do not be negligent and careless just because the materials seem plain,
and hesitate to work more diligently with materials of superior quality.
Your attitude towards things should not be contingent upon their quality.*

—DOGEN ZENJI, *Instructions to the Monastery Cook*

Daikon "Achar" Salad

Although this is served in Nepal as an *achar*, it's so hearty, we'd call it a salad. It is a family recipe from a beautiful climate scientist named Rakita Singh, a Newar from Kathmandu who now lives in San Francisco.

SERVES 6–8.

1 large daikon, peeled and grated

½ cup sesame seeds, toasted and ground

½ tsp. ground cumin

½ tsp. salt

juice of 1½ lemons

2 Tbs. canola oil

1 green chili

½ tsp. ground turmeric

⅓ cup chopped fresh cilantro

▶ Rinse the grated daikon in warm water and squeeze out all moisture with your hand; this will remove bitterness. Put drained daikon in a serving bowl. Stir in the sesame seeds, cumin, salt, and lemon juice. Mix.

▶ Heat oil in a small frying or sauté pan. Chop the chili into thin disks and quickly stir-fry in the hot oil 60 seconds. Add turmeric, stir to blend, and turn the heat off.

▶ Pour the contents of the frying pan over the daikon and mix. Add the chopped cilantro and serve.

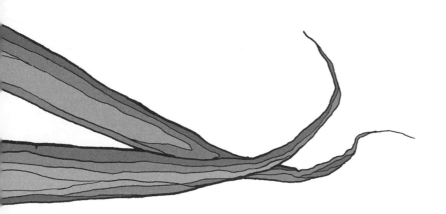

Rhubarb Ginger Chutney

Rhubarb is an ancient food, and a favorite of Mongolians, who probably get the credit for figuring out that, while the leaves are poisonous, the roots are a potent purgative and the stems are a miraculous tonic that can purify the body of toxins. They are full of vitamin C and potassium. Thanks to the Mongolians, rhubarb is a revered medicinal plant in China.

Serve this with an omelet, corn cake, or bean stew. Slather it along with mascarpone or cream cheese on a scone or biscuit. Enjoy it with yogurt.

SERVES 10–12.

1 Tbs. corn oil

1 serrano chili, seeded and diced

1 small red onion, diced

1½-inch piece fresh ginger, peeled and grated or minced

1 lb. rhubarb, coarsely chopped

½ cup currants

½ cup cashew halves or pieces, lightly toasted

¼ tsp. ground cloves

⅛ tsp. ground cardamom

⅛ tsp. ground nutmeg

⅔ cup brown sugar (don't pack it tightly)

juice of 1 lemon

juice of 1 lime

▶ Heat oil in a large heavy-gauge saucepan over medium heat. Add chili, onion, and ginger. Sauté until onion is soft and translucent, stirring occasionally.

▶ Add rhubarb, currants, and cashews without stirring, and cook over medium-low heat for 2 minutes.

▶ Add spices, sugar, and citrus juices. Stir to blend and cook over medium heat 10–15 minutes until the chutney thickens. It may spatter as it gets hot, so to protect your clothing, cover the pot with a spatter guard.

▶ Cool to serve.

▶ To save for another day, put it in a large tightly lidded jar while hot and store in the refrigerator for 3–4 days.

Bhutanese *Emadhasi*

This condiment is the unofficial national dish of Bhutan: chilies and cheese combined in myriad ways and slathered over everything. Here are two different versions: the first from a former monk, a Tibetan named Senge who learned it from Bhutanese monks at his monastery outside Darjeeling; the other from my friend Damtsik who made it at home in Sikkim and now famously makes it for Bhutanese visiting the San Francisco Bay Area.

Senge's Bhutanese Version

Senge says adding salt to chilies helps put out their fire and says he never adds tomatoes because tomatoes make *emadhasi* spoil faster and Bhutanese people like to keep this around.

SERVES 6.

16 fresh chilies (jalapeno will provide less heat than serrano or arbol)

1 tsp. salt, divided

1 medium onion

4 large garlic cloves, peeled

1 Tbs. ghee or butter or 2 Tbs. oil (corn, safflower, canola—not olive!)

½ lb. blue cheese (it can be whole or crumbled)

▶ Wash the chilies and split them. If you want to diminish their heat, remove the seeds.

▶ Put split chilies in a small saucepan with a lid and amply cover with water (at least one knuckle of your forefinger over the top of the chilies). Add ½ tsp. salt. Cover the pot and bring to a boil over high heat. (The steam from these chilies can cause you to choke; make sure to keep the lid closed and a fan on.) Reduce heat to simmer and continue to boil 10 minutes or until chilies are soft.

▶ Meanwhile, dice the onion and mince the garlic.

▶ In a medium frying or sauté pan, melt ghee or butter, or heat the oil over medium heat.

▶ Fry onions and garlic until soft.

continued on next page

- Drain chilies and add, still wet, to the onions, stirring to blend. Add the remaining salt and the cheese. Lower heat and stir rapidly as cheese melts. If it threatens to burn, add 1 Tbs. water. Continue stirring until cheese is thoroughly melted and everything is blended.

- Serve hot or warm. Store in a jar in the refrigerator up to 3 days.

Damtsik's Sikkimese Version

Damtsik makes the cheese from buttermilk because, unlike the Bhutanese, the Sikkimese would never use "stinky" cheese, only fresh cheese. Some people, she adds, use a tsp. of lemon juice to sour the cheese because they prefer that taste. The other departure in her method is that she sautés rather than boils the *emadhasi*; according to Damtsik, the Bhutanese always boil everything and never sauté but the Sikkimese always sauté, especially this.

SERVES AT LEAST 4.

3 cups buttermilk

6 jalapeno or serrano or
3 Thai chilies, stemmed

4 scallions

¼ bunch cilantro

1½ Tbs. ghee or unsalted butter

1 medium onion, peeled and diced

2 large garlic cloves, peeled and minced

3-inch piece fresh ginger, peeled and minced

2 tomatoes, finely chopped

2 tsp. salt

- In a heavy saucepan over high heat, bring buttermilk to a boil and boil 10–15 minutes until the solids form a soft cheese mass in the center of the pot. Remove from heat, cool, and drain off liquid.

- Cut the hot peppers into thin strips. Slice the white part of the scallions into thin disks and chop the greens finely. Chop the cilantro.

- In a small or medium pot with a lid, melt ghee or butter over medium heat. Add onion and sauté until it softens. Add garlic and stir to blend. Sauté 30 seconds. Stir in chilies, ginger, and chopped tomatoes. Cover and cook until tomatoes have released all their juice and are mushy, maybe 5 minutes at most.

- Stir in scallion disks and salt. Continue to sauté for 60–90 seconds.

- Remove from heat. Stir in the buttermilk cheese. It should melt right in.

- Garnish with chopped cilantro and scallion greens to serve.

Whatever joy there is in this world,

all comes from wanting others to be happy.

—SHANTIDEVA

Yogurt

Yogurt was created somewhere between 7,500 and 5,000 years ago. Whether it emerged from mare's milk shaken in the saddlebags of Mongolians on horseback or goat's milk left in the hot sun of Mesopotamia, nobody knows for sure. In the first Christian century, Pliny the Elder talked about nomadic tribes who knew how "to thicken milk into a substance with an agreeable acidity." We know that the English word for this achievement, *yogurt* or *yoghurt*, comes from the Turkish *yogun* meaning "dense" or "thick," or *yoghurmak*, which means "to thicken." But that doesn't provide a useful clue about who accomplished it, for Turkish-speaking tribes stretched from Ottoman Istanbul to Mongolian Ulan Bator, and all of them were avid fans of this preserved milk.

Whether called *dadiah, dahi, dudh, doogh, zabady, kefir, kiselo mlyako, rahm-joghurt, jameed*, or just plain *curd*, yogurt is everywhere the same tart, long-lived, richly nutritious pudding that bacteria make out of milk by "cooking" its sugary lactose into lactic acid. The specific bacteria used for this ferment, *Lactobacillus bulgaricus* and *Streptococcus thermophilus*, convey powerful therapeutic qualities that make yogurt seem magical. Francis I, who ruled France at the start of the sixteenth century, supposedly suffered from severe diarrhea no French doctor could cure, so his Ottoman ally Suleiman the Magnificent sent a doctor who cured it by making the king eat yogurt. Although the grateful monarch then tried to popularize it, yogurt remained relatively rare in Western Europe and America until an early twentieth-century Russian Nobel laureate, Ilya Ilyich Mechnikov, began to suspect the unusually long life span of Bulgarian peasants was due to regular doses. Theorizing that its two bacteria were responsible for that extraordinarily strong health, the eminent biologist devoted the remainder of his career at the Institut Pasteur to promoting yogurt as a daily essential, and his enthusiasm may have inspired a Sephardic Jewish émigré from the Ottoman Empire to industrialize its manufacture. In 1919, Isaac Carasso started a yogurt business in Barcelona that, in honor of his son "little Daniel," he named

Danone—which, as anybody who has ever been in a grocery store knows, also thickened into something quite long-lived.

Yogurt was widely prescribed in Ayurvedic medicine and venerated in ancient India long before the Buddha was born. Its cornucopia of nutrients and its power to stimulate digestion and also cure diarrhea made it a metaphor for spiritual nourishment that could cleanse negative karma. Its eye-dazzling whiteness made it the perfect symbol of purity. For millennia it has been used in yogic rituals, along with its siblings milk and butter or ghee, as the "three white substances" offered by the sacred cow and accepted as the precious, tangible manifestation of solar and plant energy.

In ancient India, yogurt was included as one of the eight *astamangaladravya*, bringers of good fortune. When Buddhism took hold, the eight evolved into the "Eight Auspicious Substances" (see page 243), each representing one virtuous step on the Buddha's Eightfold Path to enlightenment. Yogurt was chosen to signify right livelihood because it is created without harming anything that is alive, even bacteria, which we are usually quick to exterminate. Yogurt prompts us to realize not only our dependence on what seems disgusting or insignificant, but the way seemingly unpleasant or inconsequential activity can become positive. Bacteria's work becomes an excellent example of what our own livelihood should entail: cleansing impurities to prevent suffering.

Yogurt may have played a role in the enlightenment of the Buddha. What exactly the dairymaid Sujata offered the emaciated Gautama Siddhartha to eat that restored his body, enabled him to meditate, and propelled him to enlightenment has never been identified with certainty—whether milk and honey, or milky rice porridge, or actually curd—but yogurt is traditionally used to epitomize it. In India, curd was believed to contain the nectars of longevity, vitality, and wisdom: precisely what the Buddha gained from breaking his ascetic fast by ingesting it, and exactly the qualities every meditator strives to attain. That is why the interior of the bowl in the hands of many a pictorial Buddha glows white, and sometimes why the contents are equally white, signifying yogurt.

When presented for eating, yogurt is neither extravagant nor paltry; my teacher, the renowned scholar Thrangu Rinpoche, calls it the ideal food to typify the Buddha's insistence on the Middle Way, the path that avoids veering to one side or another. "In order to practice Dharma properly," he says, "we need to abandon or transcend two extremes in lifestyles. One of these is hedonism...the other is self-mortification, because the attempt to attain something through tormenting or depriving your physical body of what it needs does not lead to enlightenment."

In ancient India curd—being creamy, heavy, and cool—was categorized in Ayurvedic medicine as *kapha*, the phlegmatic water element, and so was avoided during the hot rainy season. This tradition was carried to Tibet where monks remained cloistered in retreat annually during monsoon, then celebrated the end of *Yarne*, the "rains retreat," by eating lots of nutritious yogurt. Huge Tibetan monasteries like Drepung and Sera actually turned this "hundredth day" into the *Shoton* or *Zhoton*, "Curd Festival." In Lhasa, an enormous thangkha of the Buddha was traditionally unfurled for the public as part of a massive celebration that included picnics and dancing. *Shoton* continues today as a yearly spectacular of Tibet's performing arts and cooking.

Yogurt continues to be celebrated around the world with differing names that highlight the diverse roles it plays in the kitchen. Watered down into a salty drink, it's *lassi* or *ayran* or *shenina*. It's *kumiss* when the drink is made from mare's milk whose high sugar content adds alcoholic kick, and it's kefir when additional bacteria and yeast join the ferment. It's labeled "cream top" when made from unhomogenized milk. It's *labneh* when strained into a cheese-like texture in the Middle East and *chanklich* when hardened further. It's *srikhand* when strained in India or Nepal and mixed with fragrant spices like cinnamon and cardamom into a "pudding" served over fruit. Mixed with cucumber and garlic, it's the Greek spread *tzatziki* or, with a little water added, the Turkish soup *cacik*. Mixed with cucumber and mint it's Punjabi *raita*. Mixed with jam, fruits, or added sweeteners, it's all over the supermarket shelves of the Western world, or oozing out of stainless steel tanks as though it were soft ice cream.

Ironically, yogurt's newest claims to fame come from twenty-first-century medical scientists who picked up where the Russian biologist Mechnikov left off and have tried to supersize it into a magic bullet wonder drug: *Protein! Calcium! B vitamins 6 and 12! Probiotics!* Advertisements and articles—even from the high towers of the Ivy League—continue to assert that it fortifies the immune system, prevents yeast infections, lowers cholesterol, strengthens bones, increases fat loss, prevents arthritis, protects against ulcers, reduces the risk of colorectal cancer, reduces plaque, prevents gingivitis, and freshens the breath.

THE EIGHT AUSPICIOUS SUBSTANCES

(1) a mirror, (2) medicine, (3) yogurt, (4) a kind of grass known as *durva*, (5) a fruit called a *bilva*, (6) a white conch shell, (7) cinnabar or vermillion powder, and (8) mustard seed. These correspond to steps on the Noble Eight-fold Path of right view (the mustard), right thought (the mirror), right speech (the shell), right action (the fruit), right livelihood (the yogurt), right effort (the grass), right mindfulness (the medicine), and right meditation (the cinnabar).

Kashmiri and Pakistani Walnut Chutneys

These are essentially yogurt condiments, refreshing in heat or with spicy food. The differences between them and also the Mustang recipe that follows shows how a dish changes as it crosses mountains and cultures but also how much different cultures have in common.

SERVES 6–8 AS A CONDIMENT.

The Kashmiri Version

½ small onion, peeled and halved

2 serrano chilies or an equivalent hot pepper

⅔ cup toasted walnut pieces or halves

¼ tsp. ground cayenne
or other hot pepper

⅛ tsp. salt

6 oz. plain yogurt

GARNISH

¼ cup chopped fresh cilantro

1 whole walnut half

▶ In the bowl of a small food processor or by hand, grind together the onion and chilies as finely as you can. Add the walnuts and grind to almost paste.

▶ Add the cayenne, salt, and yogurt and process just long enough to blend into a smooth sauce; you can also do this part by hand with all ingredients in a mixing bowl.

▶ Pour into a serving bowl and garnish with the chopped cilantro. Be sure to put a walnut half clearly on top to ward off those highly allergic to nuts.

The Pakistani Version

¾ cup shelled walnuts, lightly toasted

2 small garlic cloves, peeled

2 serrano chilies, seeded and chopped

½ tsp. salt

2 cups fresh mint leaves, washed

juice of 1 lemon

¼ cup (4 oz.) very thick plain yogurt
(strain it for two hours if you have to)

GARNISH

¼ cup chopped fresh mint

1 whole walnut half

▶ Combine walnuts, garlic, chilies, salt, mint, lemon juice, and 1 Tbs. water in a food processor or blender. Process into a smooth paste, stopping to scrape down the sides. Add one additional Tbs. water if the mix is too dry to form a paste.

▶ Put the thick yogurt in a serving bowl. Using a fork, stir in the walnut paste.

▶ Serve garnished with chopped mint and a shelled walnut.

Mustang Yogurt
with Greens and Cayenne

Two women from the high and ancient Himalayan kingdom of Mustang told me everyone up there makes this dish with the green shoots of buckwheat, but when they went down to the Kathmandu valley to school, they couldn't find buckwheat so they made it with spinach. And that's what they continue to do now that they live in California, where they like to spoon this onto a naan or into a pita and eat it as sandwich filling.

SERVES 6–8.

1 lb. fresh spinach, stems off and washed clean

½ tsp. timur
(fragrant Nepali peppercorns),
or their close but not so aromatic relative Szechuan peppercorns, or regular black peppercorns soaked in ¼ tsp. rose water or mixed with ⅛ tsp. dried lavender; each will provide a distinct fragrance

¼ tsp. salt

¼ tsp. ground cayenne
(heaping if you like heat)

½ bunch cilantro, cleaned (about 1 very loosely packed cup)

16–17 oz. thick plain yogurt ("thick" means it doesn't move when you put a spoon in; drain thinner yogurt through a sieve lined with cheesecloth or paper towels)

▶ Put spinach leaves in a large bowl and pour 2 cups boiling water over them. Cover bowl and let sit 1–2 minutes. Drain and rinse spinach under cold water.

▶ Drain again. Squeeze spinach into a ball, wrap it in a towel, and squeeze it dry. Let it rest in the towel while you proceed with the recipe.

▶ Make a paste of the timur (or timur substitute), salt, cayenne, and cilantro by grinding them together in a small processor, coffee grinder, or mortar and pestle.

▶ Blend this paste into the yogurt. Taste and adjust seasonings to taste.

▶ Chop the spinach as finely as you can and stir it into the spiced yogurt.

▶ Serve immediately or store covered in the refrigerator up to 24 hours.

The Wisdom of
Being Spoiled Rotten

A<small>T THE START</small> of the 1990s, I participated in a Radcliffe College seminar that launched a new academic discipline called food history, and one of its sectors required us to research fermented food, an assignment that provoked faces of mock disgust and jokes about sauerkraut. The following week, we returned profoundly chastened. We had discovered that fermentation is alchemy, the magic of transcendence right here in daily life. It is grapes smashed and left to become wine—or longer to sour into vinegar, an excellent solvent and antiseptic. It's milk encouraged to spoil into cheese, from the softest curds like German *quark* to the dried tooth-breaking *churpi* of Tibetan nomads, pure white paneer to yellow English cheddar and the moldy blue Roquefort, Gorgonzola, and Stilton created by abandonment in dank caves. Legend has it that 7,500 years ago when goats were domesticated in Mesopotamia, the milk taken from them was stored in gourds and forgetfully left in the sun where it went sour and solidified into yogurt, which someone discovered was delicious and, better yet, not toxic. Milk has since then also been happily spoiled into the Slavic *smetana* or sour cream, Bulgarian kefir, and Mongolian *kumis*.

Scientifically known as *zymology*, fermentation in the kitchen is known as the good news about bacteria, at least the anaerobic kind. Given a pinch of salt or yeast or sometimes even nothing more than time, these energetic spoilers invade molecular bonds and create good things. Asian peoples transform the mildly toxic soybean into tofu, miso, soy sauce, *natto*, and tempeh. They let bacteria rot rice into wine and vinegar, tea into *kombucha*, black beans into a pungent seasoning. Indians ferment lentils into dosas and *idlis*; Filipinos turn coconut water and seaweed into the jellied *nato de coco*. Persians transform pomegranate arils into molasses and northern Pakistanis convert the pomegranate seeds into the sour *anardana*. Romanians ferment millet into *boza*; Hawaiians taro into *poi*; the ancient Romans, modern Vietnamese, and Thais ferment anchovies into fish sauce (*garum* in old Rome, *nuoc mam* in Vietnam, and *nam pla* in Thailand)—even very British Worcestershire sauce supposedly starts with a base of fermented anchovies. Northern Europeans let honey go into mead, apples into cider, potatoes into vodka. Cabbage fermented by salt is sauerkraut in Germany and kimchi in Korea. The Newars of Nepal let greens blacken in summer heat to become their winter condiment *gundruk* and Tibetan people let cooked rice ferment for two weeks from congee into their New Year drink *chang*.

Our pantries are full of ferment. The obvious yogurt, cheese, soy sauce, tofu, wine, and vinegar are likely to be joined by ketchup, bread, beer, olives, pickles, capers, salsa, relishes—even vanilla and chocolate, both beans that must be broken down to be edible.

Why all this ferment? The answer emerged in a twentieth-century debate set off by archeological findings from ancient Sumer. The big question: did the Sumerians who so smartly domesticated plants to create agriculture go to all the trouble of figuring out how to infect their new wheat harvest with wild yeast in order to bake bread or brew beer? The Victorian archeologists who'd unearthed shards of recipe cuneiforms insisted the Sumerians wanted bread because "it's the staff of life," an argument that went unchallenged until the late 1980s when beer brewers launched their archeological research, complaining that the Victorians had shamelessly projected their own cultural values onto a vanished civilization. The brewers pointed out that while Victorian England certainly valued bread, the ancient people of Sumer didn't make sandwiches or take high tea. The Sumerians were compelled to make bread, they reasoned, simply to get enough fermentation going to brew beer—and not necessarily for drunken orgies. Scientists then proved them right. Their research indicated beer is more nutritious and more helpful to digestion than bread.

No preindustrial culture would have been surprised. For millennia, cooks have mastered microbiology to hurdle obstacles to survival: preserving food for times of scarcity (pickled foods like sauerkraut, rotted foods like *gundruk*), preparing it to be portable and enduring on the trail (curdled foods like cheese and yogurt, dried foods like jerky), preventing it from being poisonous or indigestible (*poi*, soy). They figured out that fermentation cuts cooking time and therefore the need for fuel, while at the same time it adds taste sensations and textures to a menu. Above all, the Sumerians and everybody else discovered the real gold in all that bacterial alchemy was healthier eating, and more of it.

Fermentation enriches food with protein, essential amino acids, fatty acids, and vitamins that might not have been present in the raw state. It also enhances whatever was there. Mongolian nomads, British journalist Sarah Murray reported in *Movable Feasts*, eat such a diverse range of fermented dairy products, they don't need vegetables for vitamins or other vital nutrients.

Fermentation triggers enzymes that go to work fracturing nutrients so we digest food faster. They even make some food easier to digest. People who can't tolerate milk, for instance, can enjoy yogurt because the inherent bacteria break down the problematic lactose. Yogurt is often recommended to accompany antibiotics because it injects these same beneficial bacteria, probiotics, into our intestines to replace the meaningful microbes inadvertently wiped out by the medication. Because its bacteria attack the foreign ones that cause intestinal havoc, it's a traditional remedy for "Montezuma's revenge" or "Delhi belly" or whatever you want to call the diarrhea you get from dinner.

The alcohol created by the fermentation of grapes and hops is an even more potent antibiotic. This I learned the hard way in my midtwenties in a hot Saharan oasis of Tunisia when I—the lone American in a small group of French vacationers—drank icy soda while riding a camel to a Berber encampment for dinner, and contracted such severe and fevered dysentery that I blacked out. I regained consciousness a day later in a hotel bed with my roommate, a Parisian airline stewardess, hovering over me anxiously with a local doctor at her side.

"You did not do as the rest of us," Marie France said sadly, referring to our French companions who never touched soda, "and now you have to suffer. You must remember to drink wine or beer when you are eating because alcohol kills *les microbes*."

I have fanatically followed that advice at almost every foreign meal since, except for breakfast, and in the ensuing years, I have yet to suffer another incident of intestinal upheaval. I think of that as an example of transcendence through fermentation.

Pickled Beets

You make this up to a week ahead and store in Mason jars. It's a Persian version with different spices than we're used to.

SERVES 8–10.

2 lb. red beets with all but 1 inch of the stems and roots removed (to prevent beets from bleeding when boiled)

4 whole cloves

6 whole black peppercorns

1 tsp. ground allspice

1 short cinnamon stick or piece of cinnamon bark

1½ cups white vinegar

2 Tbs. granulated sugar

1⅛ Tbs. kosher salt

▶ Cook the beets until tender either by wrapping them in foil and roasting them or boiling them in salted water. Cool and peel. Slice the beets into thin disks.

▶ Sterilize the jars by submersion in boiling water. While still hot, fill them with the sliced beets, cloves, peppercorns, allspice, and about ¼ inch of cinnamon bark per jar.

▶ In a small saucepan, bring the vinegar and sugar to a boil over medium-high heat. Stir in the salt to dissolve. Pour the hot brine over the beets, filling to almost the top of the jar (leave a tiny space so it doesn't overflow). Immediately seal the jar.

▶ Store in the refrigerator for 3 to 7 days. Serve at room temperature.

Through abundant giving

Of the best food and drink

Your glorious hands and feet will be soft

…your body will be big.

—NAGARJUNA

Romesco Sauce

This is the pride of Catalonia, a vivid red-orange puree with the consistency of ketchup, served over or beside a huge platter of grilled vegetables that includes potatoes, eggplant, artichoke, and zucchini. Grilled fennel and onion are also options. Spaniards relish dipping stalks of grilled spring garlic and scallion in this sauce. It can be served over scrambled eggs or omelets, on a baked potato (in place of sour cream), or served with warm bread, especially Indian naan or a crusty round European-style peasant loaf.

SERVES 6.

2 large red bell peppers

5 medium tomatoes

½ head garlic or 6 cloves peeled

⅓ cup hazelnuts, lightly toasted

⅛ cup almonds, lightly toasted

1 tsp. salt

¼ tsp. smoked paprika
(best substitute: pinch chipotle chili powder and ⅛ tsp. paprika)

1 tsp. wine vinegar

1 Tbs. olive oil

pinch ground cayenne

pinch freshly ground black pepper

▶ Roast the peppers, tomatoes, and garlic at 450°F for 20–25 minutes, being careful not to burn them.

▶ Cool the roasted vegetables and remove skins.

▶ Combine all ingredients in a blender and puree. Taste and adjust for salt and black pepper.

▶ Serve at room temperature.

Tomato *Achar*

This all-purpose, much-loved Nepali sauce beats ketchup. I was so obsessed with the tomato *achar* served at my hotel in Rumtek, Sikkim, that for three days I ordered anything on the menu that came with it. Then I pestered all the Nepalis I knew until a family gave me their recipe. Serve this with scrambled eggs, dumplings, corncakes, fritters, grits, grilled vegetables, pasta, just about anything.

SERVES 6–8.

1 lb. ripe tomatoes, cored

3 dried arbol chilies or 1 fresh serrano or Thai chili

2 garlic cloves, peeled and halved

½ tsp. ground turmeric

½-inch piece fresh ginger, peeled and minced or ¼ tsp. ground ginger

2 Tbs. chopped fresh cilantro

¼ tsp. salt

▶ Either boil the tomatoes in salted water for 10 minutes, until they are soft, or roast them at 375°F for 15–18 minutes until they are ready to burst. Cool, and remove skin if the tomatoes are large ones.

▶ Meanwhile, quickly sear the dried or fresh chilies in a small nonstick frying pan or skillet— heat the pan, put them in, and cook 1 minute over high heat, shaking the pan. This adds roasted flavor to the *achar*.

▶ In a blender or food processor, combine all ingredients and puree into a thick dipping sauce.

Special Effects: Dishes Beyond Category

The Bushman loved honey. He loved honey with a passion that we,
with a sweet-shop on every corner, cannot hope to understand. Bitterness is to the
tongue what darkness is to the eye; darkness and bitterness are forms of one another.
And the taste of honey to the Bushman was like the light of the fire to his eye,
and the warmth of its ruby flame in the black night of Africa.

—LAURENS VAN DER POST, *The Lost World of the Kalahari*

If with kindly generosity
One merely has the wish to soothe
The aching heads of other beings,
Such merit has no bounds.

—SHANTIDEVA

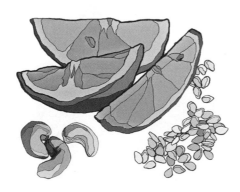

The Carrot Bodhisattva

IN MARCH 2004, over dinner in Kathmandu, the headmistress of my Rinpoche's boarding school told me the volunteer doctor who'd just performed checkups on the schools' children found their eyesight surprisingly weak. The word "carrots" shot out of my mouth. "The school needs to serve carrots." The headmistress agreed, but we both knew from experience that carrots would never be purchased or served unless I—the *American cook*, as the children called me—broke the kitchen inertia by doing it myself.

The next day I asked every Nepali I encountered—the statue maker, a taxi driver, the Internet café *wallah*, a money changer, even two Burmese nuns when it turned out they operated a local orphanage—what their favorite way to eat carrots was. Everybody's turned out to be the same: *gajarko haluwa*, carrot pudding. Everyone had their own way to make it, but the gist always boiled down to carrots, cardamom, and milk.

A day or two later I found free time and hailed a taxi, telling the driver to go to Chabahil, the neighborhood that abuts the boarding school's. Four years before when I'd first volunteered to cook meals for the children, believing richer nourishment the cure for their rashes, gawky thinness, and runny noses, monks had guided me to Chabahil's frenetic markets to buy a truckload of food. The driver grunted. We lurched into thick, noxious traffic, his tiny white Indian-made Maruti bouncing over stony dirt roads while I clung to the frayed and dusty backseat, hunting for familiar landmarks. "Where in Chabahil?" he growled as we got close.

"A market where I can buy carrots. *Garaj*," I added, thinking this the Nepali word for carrot.

His head whipped around. "What you want?"

"*Garaj*, for *ga-raj haluwa*."

He scowled, muttering to himself so unhappily I tensed as we drove down a narrow cobblestone street. He continued muttering. I continued worrying about this ride coming to a bad end. Suddenly his head swiveled toward me.

"*Gajar!*" he blurted triumphantly. "*Gajar!* How much?"

"Maybe ten kilos."

He shot an accusing look at me through the rearview mirror. "What for?"

"For three hundred children who live at a school with no mother, no *ama*. Doctor say bad here." I pointed to my eyes. "Carrots good for here, so I want to cook *gajar haluwa*."

The taxi stopped so short, I was hurled to the floor. The driver made a U-turn, slapped off the meter, and drove like a bat out of hell down streets and alleys I had never seen. Every time he glanced at me in his rearview mirror, I prayed to all the Buddhist deities for protection, certain this really was going to end badly. Finally, after crossing almost the entire Kathmandu valley, the tiny white taxi turned into a vast, trash-strewn parking lot crowded with trucks. In front of us was a cement depot. "You wait," he barked. "I go. For me less money than you." After maybe five minutes, he came out lugging a huge sack of carrots. We were, I later learned, at Kathmandu's wholesale vegetable market.

The driver shoved the carrots in the narrow space behind the back seat, got behind the wheel, and with a squeal of tires hurtled us into the sooty, honking traffic. It turned out we were headed for the national dairy in Lainchar. Prices here were fixed, so I was allowed to go inside to pay for the liters of milk the driver was piling on the seat beside him. "Where school?" he demanded when I came out.

"Boudha," I said.

The white Maruti tottered onto the road. We reached Chabahil with its meter still not running when the driver pulled over, parked, and jumped out of the cab, grunting, "*Suji. Gajarko haluwa* not good no *suji*." He disappeared into one store, then another. He was still not smiling when he reappeared, crossing the street to the cab. He took his seat before handing me a small brown paper bag. It was full of semolina. "Now we go," he said, whoever he was, and turned the motor but not the meter on. "You have everything to make children happy."

There is no love sincerer than the love of food.

—George Bernard Shaw

Gajarko Haluwa: Carrot Pudding

It's been my experience that although the word for pudding in India and Nepal where this recipe comes from is *kir*, and although *haluwa* or *halva* is fudge, people mean pudding when they talk about *gajarko haluwa*. I loaned this recipe to a friend whose son presented about Nepal at his fifth-grade show-and-tell assignment, and the morning after he offered it, she phoned from Marin County to tell me all the mothers at the presentation had flocked around her trying to get the recipe to take home. This is dessert but leftovers make a terrific breakfast.

SERVES 6.

2½ Tbs. unsalted butter

2 cups finely grated carrots, about 4 large (you can also chop them finely in a food processor if you stop long before they puree)

1 quart whole milk

½ tsp. ground cardamom

½ cup white raisins

½ cup confectioner's sugar (use regular granulated sugar if you don't have this; I use it because it thickens faster)

¼ cup cashews, split and lightly toasted (optional)

2 Tbs. unsweetened shredded coconut, lightly toasted (optional)

▶ In a large sauté pan over medium heat, melt butter. Add carrots and cook until they're buttery and very mushy.

▶ Meanwhile, in a large heavy-bottomed saucepan or medium casserole, put milk over high heat and bring it to a boil. Immediately lower heat just enough so the milk continues to boil but does not bubble over. The aim is to boil it down without burning it or losing it over the top of the pot.

▶ When it's ready, pour and scrape the contents of the carrot mush into the milk. Add cardamom and raisins. Stir to blend. Continue to boil over the highest heat at which it will not boil over, and stir occasionally to determine if the mix is thickening and to keep anything from sticking to the bottom. Do this until you start to feel it thicken against the spoon, which could be up to 30 minutes.

continued on next page

- ▶ Stir in sugar and continue cooking another 10 minutes or as long as it takes for the mixture to stick to the spoon. You should be able to see the bottom of the pan as the spoon passes through the pudding.

- ▶ Pour into a serving bowl and cool. It will thicken a little more. To serve, top with the toasted coconut and cashews if desired.

Granny Smith Indian Pudding

This quintessential New England dish of cornmeal and molasses is the way colonists merged native ingredients into a cooking style that favored "puddings." This modern version is not only gussied up with apples and raisins; it's baked as a "cake" you ice with whipped cream and slice. That makes it more festive than the original, which is simply spooned out of a bowl. Leftovers make a good breakfast. Also, if you omit the whipped cream icing, you can serve slices with a vegetable salad as lunch or Sunday supper.

SERVES 12.

5 cups milk

1 cup yellow cornmeal

2 Tbs. butter

2 extra large or jumbo eggs

⅓ cup light brown sugar

½ cup molasses

3 Tbs. real maple syrup

pinch salt

¼ tsp. ground ginger

1 tsp. ground nutmeg

½ tsp. ground cinnamon

1 cup raisins
(dark ones show up easier)

2 Granny Smith apples, peeled, cored, and diced

GARNISH

vanilla ice cream or fresh whipped cream

ground cinnamon or freshly grated ginger

▶ Preheat oven to 325°F. Butter a 3-quart soufflé dish or charlotte mold or other deep ovenproof baking dish.

▶ In a very large saucepan or medium casserole, bring the milk to a boil quickly over high heat so a skin forms and bubbles appear. Whisk in cornmeal and over medium or medium-high heat (depending on the strength of your stove) continue to whisk until the mixture thickens. This will take anywhere from 90 seconds to 3 minutes.

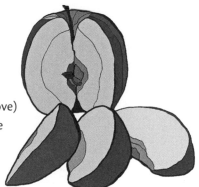

continued on next page

▶ Remove from heat. Whisk in butter, then eggs, carefully. Whisk in brown sugar, molasses, and maple syrup. Whisk in salt and spices.

▶ Stir in raisins and apples, distributing evenly.

▶ Pour mixture into baking dish and shake to level. Bake at 325°F in the center of the oven for 40–50 minutes, or until the center of the pudding is firm when you shake the pan. Remove from oven and cool.

▶ To serve: spoon from the baking pan and top with vanilla ice cream. Or invert the pan onto a cake stand or serving platter and "ice" with whipped cream. Sprinkle with cinnamon or freshly grated ginger to serve.

Muhamarra:
Persian Red Pepper Spread

This is an addictive Persian dip or spread whose haunting flavor comes from pomegranate molasses, and whose superb nutrition comes from nut protein and vegetable vitamins.

MAKES AROUND 2–3½ CUPS.

5 large firm red bell peppers

2 cups shelled walnuts (whole, halves, or pieces)

⅛ tsp. salt

1½ tsp. ground cumin

⅛ tsp. ground allspice

⅛ tsp. ground cinnamon

1 large garlic clove, minced

1 Tbs. pomegranate molasses*

juice of ½ lemon

3–4 Tbs. high-quality olive oil

GARNISH

chopped and roasted walnuts

breadcrumbs fried in olive oil

▶ Roast the red peppers for 10 minutes at 450°F to blister the skins (you can do this in a large toaster oven or regular oven). Remove from heat and put immediately into a brown paper bag. Fold down the top of the bag to stop steam from escaping and leave the bag on the counter for 10 minutes. Remove the peppers and peel off the thin skin membrane that started to detach in the blistering process.

▶ Chop the skinned peppers into ¾-inch cubes, put in a saucepan, and cover slightly more than halfway with water (about 1½ cups). Bring the water to a boil and boil hard for 5–10 minutes to soften the peppers. Add water if necessary.

▶ Pour the pot contents into a food processor and puree the peppers. Return the puree to the pot, put over medium heat, and boil uncovered to reduce the puree to a spreadable

continued on next page

✳ Pomegranate molasses is available in Middle Eastern stores and online and increasingly in gourmet food emporiums. Still it is the hardest-to-find ingredient in this book and there is no adequate substitute. It can be made by boiling down 1 cup of pomegranate juice with 1 Tbs. sugar and 1 tsp. lemon juice for about 30–40 minutes until you get a thick syrup. Or you can just omit it altogether without much harm to the final dish.

jam-like thickness (about 25 minutes), stirring frequently to be sure nothing burns. The pepper paste is thick enough when a spoon opens a clear path along the bottom of the pot. Remove from heat.

▶ Meanwhile, roast the walnuts on a baking sheet at 350°F for 8–10 minutes until they are golden brown and release a nutty aroma. Grind them in a food processor or grinder until they resemble tiny splinters.

▶ When the pepper sauce has thickened and been removed from the heat, stir in the salt and spices, garlic, molasses, lemon juice, and ground walnuts. Combine well. Now stir in olive oil to create your desired spreadable consistency.

▶ Taste and adjust seasonings. Pour into a serving bowl and surround with thick cucumber disks or pita triangles. Garnish with either option.

Sesame Chews

These are popular in one form or another in the broad swath of old trade routes from India and Nepal to Sicily. They're a mighty healthy snack, and a great alternative to sugary cookies.

MAKES ABOUT 3 DOZEN.

½ tsp. sesame oil

2 cups sesame seeds (white or brown)

½ tsp. grated lemon zest

¼ cup sugar

¾ cup best-quality honey (I recommend Greek Attiki)

¼ tsp. combined spices: ground nutmeg, cloves, and cardamom

▶ Coat the bottom and sides of a small cookie sheet, baking tray, or square baking dish with the sesame oil.

▶ Combine remaining ingredients in a small saucepan, stir to blend well, and cook over medium heat until the sesame seeds are toasted, about 15–18 minutes.

▶ Pour onto the oiled surface and spread so that the mixture is uniformly just under ½ inch thick. Smoothe the top. Let cool an hour or more.

▶ Cut into bite-sized squares. Store in a tightly sealed container.

As earth and the other elements, together with space,

eternally provide sustenance in many ways for countless sentient beings

So may I become sustenance in every way for sentient beings.

—SHANTIDEVA

Why Buddhist Monks Are Called Beggars

OF ALL THE WORDS in the considerable Sanskrit vocabulary of his time, the one the Buddha chose to describe individuals who abdicated the comforts of home to follow him toward liberation was *bhikshu*, beggar. And when Tibetans imported the Buddha's teachings, and painstakingly set about crafting a language that would reveal their subtle essence, they chose to call their monastic faithful *gelong*, an elision of two words, *gewa* and *long*, which together mean "asking—or begging—for a meritorious offering."

To decode this message, it's helpful to know Shakyamuni Buddha did not call himself a Buddhist. Buddhism is a Western word created maybe three hundred years ago to relate his teaching to familiar schools of thought like Judaism, Catholicism, Stoicism, Zoroastrianism, and "Mohammedanism." The Buddha only called himself a realist, a teacher of the truth underlying all existence.

To help his disciples understand this reality, he used a scientific manual, the *Abhidharma*, which begins: *All beings exist on food.* The *Abhidharma* explains that while there might be ways to skirt weather, avoid geography, or alter a karmic pattern, there is no way to circumvent the need to eat. Therefore, of all the influences on our existence, food is the primal and most powerful fact of life.

The Buddha's own experience had validated this. When at twenty-nine he abandoned the physical abundance of a princely existence to seek the meaning of life, he sacrificed the human essentials—shelter, clothing, and food—to follow the prevailing spiritual seekers, yogis convinced that denying the body was the proper prescription for unlocking the soul. For six years, Prince Siddhartha dutifully participated in self-mortification. Covered only by a loincloth, he meditated in forests until the absence of nourishment consigned him to death, no wiser than when he was a youth gallivanting around a palace. "I claim to have lived on a single bean a day," he later said, "on a single sesame seed a day, or a single grain of rice a day.... Never did this practice ... or those dire austerities bring me to ennobling fits of superhuman knowledge and insight." The sight of such a decimated man with knotted joints and ribs piercing through his skin so spontaneously filled a passing milkmaid, Sujata, with compassion that she stopped to offer the yogurt (sometimes described as "milk porridge" or "milk and honey") she carried in a bucket. With nothing left to lose, Siddhartha broke the rules and accepted it. Every biography emphasizes how reinvigoration of his body gave him strength to meditate under a fig tree and become a buddha, one who is awake.

The Buddha struggled with his realization of Dharma, the ultimate truth. For days he sat in silence, foreseeing and fearing that no one would understand. Eventually, he concluded all he could do was describe the path he had just taken and hope others could follow, step by step, until they too reached enlightenment. Consequently his disciples, like all seekers of realization, had to uproot themselves, abandoning all comforts and certainties to become homeless, which represents being open in every respect. One of the obvious comforting certainties to be abdicated was mealtime, but the Buddha understood pursuit of the spiritual dared not ignore the reality of the physical. The body is still the only vehicle the mind has. His disciples were thus welcome to two necessities: robes to cover themselves and a bowl to beg others for food. The begging bowls were uniform in every detail, one indistinguishable from another, to symbolize equality among those seeking truth, nobody superior to anybody else. The whole idea was so unique, the concept so surprising, that over the centuries in diverse parts of Asia, nearly all images of Shakyamuni Buddha featured the bowl front and center as the device that differentiates him and his teachings.

A significant portion of the Buddha's disciplinary rules, the Vinaya, choreographed every action related to that begging bowl. As the sun rose, disciples were required to take theirs firmly in hand and leave their meditation seat to wander in search of sustenance. They were not allowed to make requests or indicate preference or express opinion, only to accept whatever came to be offered and to eat all of it—exactly what we are supposed to do with whatever life serves to us. This is known as the practice of One Taste. Once the body was nourished and the bowl cleaned, the day could be devoted to nurturing the mind. This daily routine still continues across the southern strip of Asia from Sri Lanka to Singapore where at sunrise streams of uniformly robed monks pour out of monastery gates to snake through towns and villages, each with an identical begging bowl, keenly aware their survival will be—as Prince Siddhartha's ultimately was—totally dependent on the kindness of others.

By making monks into beggars like this, Buddha ingeniously turned the inevitable need for food into a vehicle that drives ordinary people toward Dharma. Every morning that monks fan out to eat, they invite householders to become indispensible participants in the Dharma's survival, offering them the opportunity to recreate the role of Sujata who spontaneously gave food to a starving Siddhartha, sustaining the life of a savior. The good deed gives its doer merit, a gold star on the karma report card. Thanks to the Buddha's great skill, that scene has been replayed every day for almost 2,600 years and remains so powerful that every morning those who live in monastery precincts, regardless of financial means, still prepare more rice, tea, and/or vegetables than they can eat in order to participate. Their key to earning merit is realizing that while these particular beggars are indigent, they are not ignorant. The monks accept food as the Buddha did: to sustain the body so that it will support the mind. Since any passing *bhikshu* can attain buddhahood, any offering of food will narrow the chasm between the worldly suffering of samsara and the nirvana of freedom from it.

This ritual shows food to be transformational, its offering a form of transcendence for everyone involved. Giving, or more accurately giving away, something to eat expresses what the Buddha called ultimate generosity, defined in part as relieving others from fear, particularly of their own demise. It is a momentary liberation from suffering, a taste of paradise.

In the mind's eye, the ritual represents sublime possibility for all of us. Every monk requesting a meritorious offering from a stranger reinforces the strength of the Buddha's three pillars of Dharma: compassion, wisdom, and the skillful means to unite them. A monk requesting and getting food provides an indelibly vivid picture of how compassion feeds wisdom so that wisdom survives to spread compassion. The begging bowl skillfully forges a bond between those dedicated to discovering liberation from suffering and those who, sooner or later, will end up begging for exactly that.

Obediently, Rechungpa returned to retreat in the mountains, practicing and having
a very hard life. Sometimes he would do the particular practice of "one taste" which
means begging for food and being grateful for whatever you get. You might find a good
honor and get very nice food along with a request for dharma teachings with a nice
clean chair and place to stay. Or you might get someone shouting at you:
"Why are you always coming around here begging for food? Go away."
They may even try to hit you. The practice is to accept whatever happens,
good or bad, as being all the same, one taste, so you develop equanimity through
both good and bad situations. Begging is a path to realization.

—KHENCHEN THRANGU RINPOCHE,
The Spiritual Biography of Rechungpa

Squash Begging Bowls with Jamaican Rice and Peas

What the Jamaicans call "peas" are really beans: kidney, pinto, or the original pigeon peas. In El Salvador, the mix of rice, beans, and coconut is called *casamiento*.

SERVES 8.

8 small acorn or dumpling winter squash

1 Tbs. olive or corn oil

1 medium-large onion, peeled and finely diced

½ tsp. dried thyme

1 small hot red pepper, seeded and minced

1 tsp. ground allspice

⅛ tsp. freshly ground or cracked black pepper

1 cup long grain rice

1 cup coconut milk
(or a reduced-fat version, if desired)

1⅛ tsp. salt, plus 8 pinches

1 (15-oz.) can pinto or red kidney beans, drained

¼ cup apple cider or pure apple juice, divided

8 pinches ground cinnamon

GARNISH

½ bunch cilantro, chopped

▶ Slice the point off the bottom of each squash to flatten it so it sits steady on its own. Put the squashes in a microwave on medium for around 90 seconds to slightly soften. Let sit 5 minutes. Then neatly cut about ¼ inch off the top. Scoop out any remaining pulp at the top to get to the cavity. Clean out the seeds and strings. Preheat the oven to 350°F.

▶ Heat the oil in a large saucepan that has a cover. Add onion and sauté until soft and golden, maybe 5 minutes over medium heat. Add thyme, hot red pepper, allspice, black pepper, and rice, and stir to blend.

▶ Add coconut milk. Add enough water to cover the rice by 1 inch. Add 1⅛ tsp. salt and beans. Bring to a boil, then cover, and reduce heat to simmer. Simmer for 20 minutes, checking and, if necessary, adding ¼ cup of water at a time to prevent burning.

▶ Put ½ Tbs. apple cider/juice in the bottom of each hollowed out squash. Add a pinch of ground cinnamon and a pinch of salt. Swirl the seasoned liquid around so it reaches all the squash. Fill the squash to the top with the rice and beans, heaping it no more than ¼–½ inch from the top.

▶ Fill a 9" x 13" baking pan with ½ inch water and arrange squash in it. Cover tightly with foil and bake at 350°F until squash is tender, 45–60 minutes.

▶ Garnish the top of each squash with a few chopped cilantro leaves to serve.

When you eat with awareness, you find that there is more space, more beauty.

You begin to watch yourself, to see yourself, and you notice how clumsy

you are or how accurate you are. You notice the way you pick up your

fork and knife, and the way you put the food in your mouth.

When you practice awareness, everything becomes majestic and good.

—Chögyam Trungpa Rinpoche

Winter Salad

This bright blend of nuts, fruits, and greens with cheese combines eye-catching colors that delight the appetite. It also combines most of the food groups, and you can add grain by serving it with bread.

SERVES 6.

SALAD

¼ lb. (about 3 handfuls) baby spinach leaves, washed and dried

Freshly ground black pepper to taste

1 Fuyu persimmon, stemmed and peeled

1 small Asian pear or 1 medium bosc pear, stemmed and seeded

1 small avocado, peeled, pit removed

¾ cup toasted pecans or walnuts

¼ lb. Gorgonzola dolce, Roquefort, or Stilton cheese

¼ cup pomegranate arils

DRESSING

pinch salt

½ tsp. orange juice
(a sour orange like Valencia is best)

½ tsp. fresh lemon juice

1 tsp. balsamic vinegar

2 Tbs. plus 1 tsp. fruity olive oil

pinch ground cloves (optional)

▶ Make the dressing by combining all of the ingredients.

▶ Arrange spinach leaves to cover the bottom of serving bowl or platter. Season with black pepper to taste.

▶ Slice persimmon into thin wedges. Coarsely chop the pear into ½-inch chunks and slice the avocado into thin wedges. Or vice versa.

▶ Compose the fruits on the bed of spinach by either laying the wedges around the exterior and making an inner circle of the chunks, or mixing all three together and spreading the blend evenly atop the spinach.

▶ Sprinkle nuts atop the fruits. Crumble cheese and sprinkle it evenly across the salad. Top with the pomegranate arils.

▶ Pour as much dressing as you prefer evenly over the salad and serve.

Tutti Frutti

Fruits always form part of any offering that we make whether to the spirit house or to Buddha. If there is a special occasion such as the blessing of an altar in a new house, then the visiting monks will be offered whatever is best in season. On all occasions that involve a party, fruits… will be set out in pretty patterns on raised dishes.

—Vatcharin Bhumichitr, *The Taste of Thailand*

Fruits of Desire

O F ALL THE WORLD's edibles, fruit is most frequently chosen to symbolize human desires. An apple for the teacher is supposed to put us in good standing. We use the phrase *forbidden fruit* as a metaphor for taboo, talk about *plum* jobs, and describe somebody attractively rosy tempered and generous as a "peach." The bite of a seductively shiny red apple launched the sexual awakening of the fairy tale princess Snow White—just as in another tale Western civilization is launched by the bite into a forbidden apple. Then come the admonitions to be "fruitful" and multiply, to revere the fruit of the vine, and later the directive to imagine wine produced by grapes as the blood of salvation. In Asia, fruit frequently represents the sense of taste and is piled high on altars to epitomize the fertility and ripeness of life, which birth invites us to taste. We sing, "Life is just a bowl of cherries."

Indian monks who brought Buddhism to China also brought the fragrant, bizarrely shaped citron known as Buddha's Hand, *Citrus medica* var. *sarcodactylis*, whose golden color prompted the Chinese to adopt it as a symbol of happiness, wealth, and longevity. They still carry it in their hands, place it on tables in their homes, and present it at temple altars as an offering. Its dried peel is prescribed in traditional medicine as a stimulant or tonic. The fruit was later imported with Chinese Buddhism to Japan where the population also interpreted its bright yellow color and pleasing aroma as a sign of good fortune. It remains a popular New Year's gift and a substitute for flowers in a household's sacred alcove.

Three round fruits graphically clustered into a stylized triangle often signify a trinity such as past, present, and future. Or they stand for the ingredients of the plenty we desire: abundance, maturity, and ripeness. The Chinese version of life's three greatest blessings is pictorially depicted as a pomegranate (happiness) with a peach (longevity) and a citron (wealth). In Buddhist iconography, a trio of round fruits dangling from a single stem or sticking out of a small bowl represents the Three Jewels: Buddha, the teacher; Dharma, the teachings; Sangha, the community that protects the teachings.

Among fruits sacred to Buddhists, the one most likely to be used in any depiction of those blessed jewels is the *bilva* or *bael*, misnamed by confused Victorian British botanists both as "wood apple" and "Bengal quince." It is neither an apple nor a quince. Round as an orange and hard as bark, *bilva* is a bitter, citrus-like fruit with intense astringency that seems to ameliorate or actually cure a plethora of physical problems. Three thousand years ago, it was so widely prescribed for Ayurvedic medicine that it became revered as the perfect panacea, the ideal symbol of purification—spiritual as well as physical. As the most venerated fruit on the Indian subcontinent, *bilva* was ritually offered by laypeople to temple gods in hope that their bodies would remain clear of disease. Similarly Brahma, the Vedic God of creation, is supposed to have presented one to Shakyamuni Buddha as a gesture of humble surrender to a more purified being. The fruit continues to be used medicinally in South and Southeast Asia, and dried for herbal tea like *mak toum* in Laos.

The second sacred fruit whose unusual astringency remains traditionally esteemed in South Asia as a potent antibiotic and tonic is the Indian gooseberry, emblica, called *amala* in Nepali. Medicinal richness made its tree sacred to Hindus who associate it with the wealth goddess Lakshmi, and the tree is rapidly becoming important to Western medical scientists who find its fruits, leaves, and bark surprisingly effective in treating afflictions as diverse as diabetes, inflammation, cancer, and rheumatoid arthritis. The berry-like fruits are a wealth of vitamin C but are so bitter that they're normally dried into powder or pickled with salt and spice. The tiny fruit is sacred to Buddhists in Nepal and India because, as emblica ripens, its skin gets more and more translucent until it becomes totally transparent, making it possible to see inside and out at the same time—an exceptional power possessed only by the omniscient, all-seeing Buddha.

The plum-like *arura*, the *Terminalia chebula* myrobalan, that grows from India to northern Vietnam, is the third astringent prized as the ideal antidote for a wide range of physical ailments. Its skin was boiled into a tea that stopped intractable coughing, its bitter pulp eaten as an anti-inflammatory heart tonic or blood cleanser. The fruit was supposed to remedy both flatulence and constipation. The Tibetans so venerated *arura* as a panacea for just about any conceivable ailment, they called it "king of all medicines," the very epithet ascribed to the Medicine Buddha himself. Consequently the *arura* plant is usually featured in portraits of the Medicine Buddha, clasped in his right hand, to emphasize his miraculous healing prowess. Tibetan monasteries still plant and rely on *arura* for medications. Its potency, like that of olive-like emblica, appears to come from a prevalence of tannin. This explains why in addition to exceptional healing properties, *arura* yields incomparable dye. Mixed with alum, it produces bright yellow; yet when parts of it are combined with iron, they create the intense black historically famed as India ink.

Specifically the eleventh aspiration of the Medicine Buddha...

is to free beings from the suffering of lacking the necessities of life—

from the sufferings of hunger and thirst.... This aspiration

is to free beings from lack of food and drink, and

from the need to struggle to acquire them.

—Khenchen Thrangu Rinpoche,

on the meaning of Medicine Buddha practice

Berber Date Bars

The Berbers are an ancient tribal people thought to predate the Arabs who settled along the North African coast. Although most have traditionally been farmers, they're popularly pictured as nomads in the Sahara, crossing it in trade caravans from one date palm oasis to the next. These sweets are ideal for those of us on the go today: they don't have to be baked.

MAKES ABOUT 24, WHICH IS NEVER ENOUGH.

corn oil or canola oil

1 Tbs. lightly toasted shredded coconut, divided (optional)

1½ cups whole almonds or walnuts

pinch ground cinnamon

4 cups pitted dates (about 1 lb.)

½ cup ghee

splash of rose water or orange flower water (optional)

2 Tbs. sesame seeds, lightly toasted

▶ Line an 8" x 8" square pan with parchment or waxed paper. Make sure the edges are high enough along the pan's sides so that you will be able to grab the paper easily when the pan is full. Very lightly grease the paper with oil. If you are using coconut, sprinkle ½ Tbs. around.

▶ Toast the nuts on a baking sheet at 350°F for 5 minutes or until you can smell their aroma. While warm, coarsely chop and sprinkle with ground cinnamon.

▶ Coarsely chop dates (you can use the pulse button on a food processor).

▶ Melt ghee in a large heavy-gauge pot over medium heat. Lower heat and add chopped dates and fragrant water, if desired, stirring to blend. Cover and cook over low heat for 10 minutes or until the dates soften into a thick paste.

▶ Put half the date mixture into the square pan. Run cold water on an icing spatula or large spoon and use the cold, damp instrument to spread the hot dates evenly in the pan.

▶ Pour chopped nuts on top. Put the spatula or spoon under cold water again and use it to spread them evenly and lightly push them down into the dates.

▶ Cover the nuts with a layer of the remaining date paste, spreading it evenly with a cold, wet spatula or spoon. Push this layer down into the nut layer.

▶ Sprinkle sesame seeds and optional remaining coconut on top and lightly press them down into the dates.

- ▶ Set the pan aside to cool for at least 1 hour. Pull the parchment or waxed paper up so the date bars come out of the pan and can be put on a flat cutting surface. Cut into small bars or squares.

- ▶ Sometimes these bars will stick to the paper, in which case pull up the paper and peel it off once the bars are released from the pan. Sometimes the layers may separate but this can be quickly fixed by pressing the top date layer back down onto the nuts. It is flexible.

When I was very young, I developed a close attachment to the Master of the Kitchen.

So strong was it that he had to be in my sight at all times, even if it was only

the bottom of his robe visible through a doorway.... I have often wondered

since about our relationship. I see it now as being like the bond

between a kitten or small animal and the person who feeds it.

—THE DALAI LAMA, *Freedom in Exile*

New England Fruit Soup

This is an ode to the intrepid farmers of New England who coax fruits from forbidding soil and to that magical moment when all these ingredients, except the banana, are piled high at their markets.

SERVES 5–6.

1 banana, peeled

1 apple, cored, peeled, and quartered

1 peach, peeled and quartered

½ cantaloupe, peeled and chunked

2–3 Tbs. honey or real maple syrup

1 cup plain yogurt

½ tsp. ground nutmeg

handful fresh mint leaves

1 Tbs. fresh lime juice

1¼ cup unsweetened apple juice or orange juice

GARNISH

fresh blueberries

▶ Combine everything but the apple juice in a blender or food processor. Start to puree and, after a few seconds, pour the apple juice in a steady stream to make a soup. It should be thick enough to eat with a spoon but not too thick to pour.

▶ Chill for at least 45 minutes.

▶ Serve garnished with fresh blueberries.

For many people may not know what they think
about politics in the Balkans,
or the vexed question of men and women,

but everyone has a definite opinion
about the flavor of shredded coconut.

—LOUIS SIMPSON

Kashmiri Compote

This warm Himalayan comfort food, rich with the scents and sense of Kashmir, will please anyone with a sweet tooth. Delicious served over oatmeal or pancakes.

SERVES 6.

2 Tbs. ghee or butter

¼ cup whole almonds

¼ cup cashews, lightly toasted

½ cup raisins

⅓ cup coconut, chopped or shredded

8 dried dates, pitted

10 dried small apricots

1 tsp. whole black peppercorns

¼ cup brown sugar

½ cup granulated or turbinado sugar

1 tsp. fresh orange peel, minced

pinch ground cinnamon

½ tsp. ground cardamom or 6 crushed cardamom pods

½ tsp. saffron

1 Tbs. fresh lemon juice

GARNISHES

candied ginger, fresh mint leaves, or fried cheese

▶ In a medium saucepan, heat the ghee over medium heat. Add almonds, cashews, raisins, coconut, dates, apricots, and peppercorns. Lightly sauté for 1 minute.

▶ Add ½ cup water, sugars, orange peel, cinnamon, and cardamom. Stir until the water boils. Lower heat and cook for 5 minutes.

▶ Soak the saffron in 2 tsp. of hot water for 3–4 minutes, crush it, and pour into the fruits.

▶ Stir in lemon juice and continue cooking another 5 minutes, until the juice has become syrupy. Remove from heat. Fish out the cinnamon stick.

▶ Serve warm, plain or garnished.

Nepali Pomelo with Yogurt Pudding

Pomelos, ancestors of our grapefruit, grow wild in the Nepali Himalayas and people in Kathmandu make this pretty and pretty nutritious winter dessert from them. The tart citrus is refreshing and the rich "yogurt pudding" less sweet and caloric than ice cream: win-win! This can also be served for breakfast.

SERVES 6–8.

10.5 oz. plain thick yogurt (you don't have to be exact)

pinch saffron

1 tsp. rose water or orange flower water

¼ tsp. ground cardamom

¼ tsp. ground cloves

¼ tsp. ground cinnamon

⅛ tsp. freshly ground black pepper

⅓ cup granulated sugar

1 pomelo or large grapefruit, peeled, segmented, and cleared of pith

½ cup cashew halves, roasted

GARNISH

½ tsp. chopped fresh mint

▶ Drain the yogurt in a strainer lined with cheesecloth, muslin, or paper towel for at least 3 hours.

▶ Put the saffron and rose water in a small bowl and let sit for at least an hour so the saffron dissolves.

▶ Put drained yogurt in a medium bowl. Stir in the saffron rose water.

▶ Combine the spices and sugar and stir into the yogurt. You now have what the Nepalese call "yogurt pudding."

▶ To assemble for serving: on a round platter, arrange the pomelo sections like spokes or daisy petals pointing out to the rim of the plate and meeting in the center. Spoon the yogurt pudding over the pomelo and top with toasted cashews, then optionally with mint.

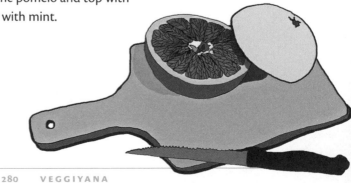

Arabic-Style Stuffed Apples

4 dried figs

3 Tbs. granulated sugar

2 very large Granny Smith apples, halved and cored

1 cup shredded coconut (unsweetened is best), divided

1 Tbs. unsalted butter, melted

⅓ cup chopped walnuts or blanched almonds

1 Tbs. dried currants

¼ cup light brown sugar

1 Tbs. honey

1 tsp. rose water

⅛ tsp. ground cinnamon

⅛ tsp. ground nutmeg

6 whole cloves

2 Tbs. fresh lemon juice, divided

1 cup apple juice, divided

4 dried apricot halves

GARNISH

sliced almonds or additional grated coconut

▶ Combine figs, granulated sugar, and 1½ cups water in a medium saucepan and bring to a boil over medium heat. Reduce heat and cook 5–10 minutes until figs are soft. Remove figs from the juice and leave juice in the pot. Chop figs.

▶ Preheat oven to 325°F. Ready a shallow baking dish.

▶ Carefully remove as much of the fruit of the apple as you dare without piercing the skin. Chop the fruit and put it into the pot with the fig juice. If the hollowed apple halves do not sit straight up, carefully slice a tiny piece off the bottom without breaking through to the center.

▶ Put half the coconut in a small shallow bowl. Brush skin side of apples with melted butter and roll them in the coconut to cover their skins, pressing down as you do. Put coated apples in the baking dish.

▶ Add remaining coconut, nuts, currants, brown sugar, honey, rose water, spices, and 1 Tbs. lemon juice to the pot with the apples and fig juices. Add ½ cup apple juice and stir to blend. Bring pot to a boil over medium heat, reduce to low, and simmer 5 minutes or until the liquid has mostly evaporated and everything sticks together.

continued on next page

- Stuff the apple halves thickly. Place a dried apricot on top of each one. Sprinkle 1 Tbs. lemon juice over them. Pour ½ cup apple juice in the bottom of the pan. If this doesn't cover the whole pan, add ½ cup water. Cover the apples tightly.

- Bake at 350°F for 1 hour or until apples are tender enough to be eaten with a spoon. Alternatively, place stuffed apples in a steamer, cover and steam until tender, 30–40 minutes.

- Garnish with sliced almonds or grated coconut. Serve warm or cold, maybe with yogurt spiced with cinnamon and nutmeg or maybe with vanilla ice cream.

With mindfulness, the simple act of eating an apple becomes a profound experience. It opens up our awareness that the apple is a manifestation of our world and that it cannot come into being in isolation. The apple is dependent on everything else for its existence, reminding us that we too are constantly supported by the effort of many beings so that we can enjoy the apple.

—THICH NHAT HANH AND DR. LILLIAN CHEUNG,

Savor: Mindful Eating, Mindful Life

Thai "Nun" Bananas

This is a simple Thai dessert made at home for family and named for Thai Buddhist nuns whose faces, sticking out from white robes, are thought to look like these bananas in coconut milk.

Serve warm or cold. If cold, the coconut milk congeals more into a pudding.

SERVES 6.

2 Tbs. mung beans

5 bananas, peeled and quartered

1 tsp. orange flower water or 2 tsp. rose water (optional)

1½ cups thick coconut milk (a 13.5–15 oz. can will do it)

1 Tbs. sugar (2 if you like dessert sweet)

⅛ tsp. ground cardamom or nutmeg (your choice of flavor)

½ tsp. salt

▶ Roast mung beans on a baking sheet at 350°F for 6–8 minutes or until they turn slightly brown. Cool, and then grind and set aside.

▶ In a large saucepan or medium casserole, combine all ingredients except the mung beans. Bring to a boil, lower heat, and simmer 3 minutes.

▶ Arrange in serving bowls and top with a sprinkle of ground mung beans.

By means of water, sunlight, wind, earth, time and space, the necessary conditions,

the tree grows from within the narrow shroud of the fruit of a banana or mango.

Similarly, the fertile seed of the Perfect Buddha, contained within the

fruit-skin of the mental poisons of beings, also grows from virtue

as its necessary condition, until the shoot of Dharma is seen

and oriented toward perfection.

—UTTARATANTRA SHASTRA

Oryoki:
Just the Right Amount

O NE OF THE RULES of the Buddha's code of discipline still in effect today—the Dalai Lama adheres to it carefully—forbids eating after twelve noon. Life-saving logic is believed to be behind this prohibition: in the drastic heat of India, food collected by the begging monks in the early morning light could easily turn toxic if left in their bowls until evening. It was safer to eat everything as soon as possible, dividing it into two meals at most. Another rationale advanced for this strict regimen is that it prevents going to bed on a full stomach, taxing the digestive system as well as the body's need for rest. Anyone who has gorged on late night dinner or midnight snacking knows how it feels to sink into the mattress and toss uncomfortably, waking up lethargic and sickly in the morning, instead of alert to face the day. Not eating after noon also allows a long, uninterrupted period of meditation.

Specific eating times were one way the Buddha and his disciples came to grips with the most endlessly debatable issue about food: what is enough? Where is that elusive line between necessity and gluttony? Fasting was, and still is, seriously discouraged. "Practice," the early Indian master Nagarjuna cautioned, "does not mean to mortify the body." Even today Asian monasteries display horrifying bronze statues of a severely emaciated Buddha, ribs clearly countable under sagging skin, as a warning against despising or ignoring your body. Eating is encouraged like the taking of medicine to remedy an ailment is encouraged, and Buddhists found a way to keep food from becoming showy and supersized. They made a rule of the ancient Ayurvedic wisdom that for optimum functioning a stomach should only be two-thirds full, giving that famed Buddhist emptiness—sublime spaciousness—a whole new meaning.

As this stricture moved with Dharma into China, Tibet, and Japan—areas in which monks did not stream out into nearby villages to collect alms but ate collectively in a monastery dining room, supplied by villagers who donated sacks of grain and produce—it evolved into distinct rituals designed to impede stuffing. Instead of receiving only one bowl at ordination, Chinese monks got a set of bowls: the largest for rice, the smaller for vegetables. They held them out in the manner of a monk asking for alms as they received what the cook dropped in. Tibetan monks came to their prenoon meal with one bowl that servers filled in stages to the rhythm of long chants that kept them moving quickly down the rows, and the final offering was strong milk tea to keep the monks awake through the afternoon. In Japan, Zen Buddhists exquisitely codified meals into an elaborately choreographed ceremony called *oryoki*, which means "just the right amount," or "just enough"—referring to the portions one receives and takes in. As practiced today in American Zen and some Tibetan Buddhist centers, it starts with servers entering the room to the boom of a drum. The cook appears to make an offering to the Buddha on the altar, a reminder of the sacred feast offering that is this food. Everyone in the hall waiting to eat unwraps their *oryoki* set—a series of nesting bowls wrapped in a napkin and, using that napkin as a place mat, sets them out in a very specific pattern: the large rice bowl in the center surrounded by the protein bowl, the vegetable bowl, and the smaller condiment bowl. As the servers move along the rows, each participant raises the appropriate bowl in both hands, the way the Buddha taught his monks to present their begging bowls, and signals the server to start and then, with a slight nod, to stop filling it. That is the moment of truth, for those accepting the food must be mindful of their own limit, knowing they have to consume absolutely every morsel taken into every bowl. The final phase of the ceremony is scraping the contents of each bowl into a single bowl, which the next server fills with boiling water. The diner must drink it, food scraps and all. This cleans the dishes, which are then wrapped back up in the napkin, leaving what campers and Zen Buddhists alike call "no trace."

This lesson in not biting off more than you can chew was designed to teach how special our food is, to be the practice of appreciating—without squandering—our riches. The information manual of the Sonoma Mountain Zen Center in Santa Rosa, California, says: "The styles of Oryoki may vary but the spirit of gratitude and receiving food medicinally for the benefit of the Dharma remains the core of this practice. When the monks received food from the villagers, and thus expounded the Dharma in exchange, it was in the same spirit of gratitude and appreciation."

We are creating our world, and we are appreciating

our world in that way. We are also making sure that our world

doesn't create any further nuisance for others, but in fact provides

tremendous vision and inspiration for people to clean things up.

—Chögyam Trungpa Rinpoche

Rice

It grew in the black mud.
It grew under the tiger's orange paws.
It seems thinner than candles, and as straight.
Its leaves like the feathers of egrets, but green.
The grains cresting, wanting to burst.
Oh, blood of the tiger.

I don't want you to just sit down at the table.
I don't want you just to eat, and be content.
I want you to walk out into the fields
where the water is shining, and the rice has risen.
I want you to stand there, far from the white tablecloth.
I want you to fill your hands with the mud, like a blessing.

—Mary Oliver

Acknowledgments

BEFORE THERE WAS THIS BOOK, there was me as a crazed cook, careening around Kathmandu to learn and buy its food so I could feed children there. What subsequently bloomed from that "outrageousness," as some called it, is due to those who actually made it possible. So here's to the quiet generosity of my friend Sushil Lama, the courageous energy of the steward monk Karma Lekshey, the unceasing compassion of the talented flutist Manose, and the patient wisdom of Khenpo Chonyi Rangdrol, first fan of my *emadhasi* and *desi*.

Along the way, my main teachers of Himalayan cooking and culture became in Kathmandu Manju Newa and in America Damtsik Beckham, through whose grace I was able to make cheesecake for His Holiness the Karmapa. Also, big time, Tashi Chodron who operates the Himalayan Pantry in New York City and is the official Language Line Tibetan interpreter. She's the one who translated "dishpan hands" into my Tibetan name, Hayong Trukhen Lakpa.

Josh Bartok, senior editor of Wisdom Publications, is the reason there is this book, and Janet-Ruth Young, aka Hypergeek, in Brooklyn, New York, is how there was a Veggiyana website that led him to imagine the possibility. Hearing that news, my beloved and incredibly busy teacher Thrangu Rinpoche compassionately made special time to give me private teachings, like why the cow is sacred and why monks are called beggars.

The warm-hearted Wayne Ng in San Francisco made himself available as a resourceful and tireless guide to Chinese and Japanese customs and recipes, and the exquisite Sonia Serrano Subirano forthrightly shared secrets from her family's successful food business in Barcelona. Ram Maharjan and Rakita Singh somehow found time between their jobs and baby preparation to cook with or for me. Lynn Kay in Maine, once the treasurer for the Culinary Historians in Boston, was a treasury of books and contacts, and is still talking to me even after she burned herself testing the grit soufflé. My precious Mahamudra Study Group in Novato, California, turned their monthly lunch table over to recipe tasting, which led two members, Nancy Long and Chuck Reed, to become vital recipe testers, and which also encouraged photographer Peter Sutherland to volunteer his skills for author photos. Joan Grant in Maine and Corena Chase in Manhattan were blunt and insightful essay critics. I have Joan, who speaks Turkish, to thank for saying over the years after eating at my house, "Health to your hands," and Corena to thank for encouraging me to keep on after she read "Yogurt" by saying, "I am getting a good feeling about this book."

Wisdom editor Laura Cunningham's enthusiastic attention to detail has guaranteed the recipes, for she painstakingly caught left out and leftover ingredients. Ari Goldfield graciously let me transcribe and use his oral teaching on eating chocolate, right after he gave it to a small class I attended. And I think in the end we are all incalculably indebted to designers Gopa & Ted2 and illustrator Michelle Antonisse who had the verve to serve up the teachings and recipes with thrilling crispness and cheer.

By this merit may beings be freed from suffering.

Permissions

New and Selected Poems: Volume One by Mary Oliver
Copyright © 1992 by Mary Oliver
Reprinted by permission of Beacon Press, Boston.

"Plant A Radish" (from *The Fantasticks*)
Lyrics by Harvey Schmidt, music by Tom Jones
Copyright © 1960, 1963 (Renewed) by Tom Jones and Harvey Schmidt
Publication and allied rights assigned to Chappell & Co.
All rights reserved. Used by permission.

Selction from "Nevertheless" reprinted with the permission of Scribner, a division of Simon & Schuster, Inc., from The Collected Poems of Marianne Moore by Marianne Moore. Copyright © 1944 by Marianne Moore, renewed 1972 by Marianne Moore. All rights reserved.

Louis Simpson, excerpt from "Chocolates" from *The Owner of the House: New Collected Poems 1940–2001*. Copyright ©1980 by Louis Simpson. Reprinted with the permission of The Permissions Company, Inc. on behalf of BOA Editions Ltd., www. boaeditions.org.

Select Bibliography

Bays, Jan Chozen. *Mindful Eating*. Boston: Shambhala Publications, 2009.

Brillat-Savarin, Jean Anthelme. *The Physiology of Taste or Meditations on Transcendental Gastronomy*, translated and annotated by M .F. K. Fisher. San Francisco: North Point Press, 1986.

Chang, K. C., ed. *Food in Chinese Culture*. New Haven: Yale University Press, 1977.

Dilgo Khyentse Rinpoche. *Enlightened Courage*. Ithaca: Snow Lion Publications, 1993.

Dogen and Uchiyama. *Refining Your Life: From the Zen Kitchen to Enlightenment*, translated by Thomas Wright. New York: Weatherhill, 1987.

Eat, Drink and Be Merry: Poems about Food and Drink. New York: Alfred A. Knopf, 2005.

Garson, Sandra. "How the Buddha Came into Your Kitchen," *The Maine Scholar*. University of Maine: Autumn 2001.

Goldstein, Darra. *A La Russe: A Cookbook of Russian Hospitality*. New York: Random House, 1983.

Harris, Marvin. *The Sacred Cow and the Abominable Pig: Riddles of Food and Culture*. New York: Simon & Schuster, 1985.

Khenchen Thrangu Rinpoche. *Medicine Buddha Teachings*, translated by Lama Yeshe Gyamtso. Ithaca: Snow Lion Publications, 2004.

——————. *The Spiritual Biography of Rechunga*, translated by Peter Roberts. Boulder: Namo Buddha Publications, 1999.

Kijac, Maria Baez. *The South American Table*. Boston: Harvard Common Press, 2003.

Majupuria, Indra. *Joys of Nepalese Cooking*. Lashkar, Gwalior: S Devi, 2002.

Manual of Abhidharma, translated by Maha Thera Narada, edited by Bhikkhu Bodhi. Sanghardja, Sri Lanka: Buddhist Publication Society, 1993.

Moore, Christopher J. *In Other Words: A Language Lover's Guide to the Most Intriguing Words Around the World*. New York: Walker & Company, 1985.

Murray, Sarah. *Moveable Feasts, From Ancient Rome to the 21st Century, the Incredible Journeys of the Food We Eat*. New York: St Martin's Press, 2007.

Powell, Stewart M. "The Berlin Airlift," *Air Force Magazine*. Washington, DC: June 1998.

Shabkar, Rinpoche. *Food of the Bodhisattavas*, translated by the Padmakara Translation Committee. Boston: Shambhala Publications, 2004.

Sotetsu, Fujii. "Culinary Fundamentals: Shojin Ryori," *Nipponia*, vol. 2. Japan, 1997.

Tannahill, Reay. *Food in History*. Rev. ed. New York: Crown Publishing, 1988.

Turner, Jack. *Spice, the History of a Temptation*. New York: Alfred A. Knopf, 2004.

Visser, Margaret. *Much Depends on Dinner*. New York: Macmillan, 1986.

Wolfert, Paula. *Couscous and Other Good Food from Morocco*. New York: Harpercollins, 1973.

Zane, Eva. *Middle Eastern Cookery*. San Francisco: 101 Productions, 1974.

Index of Major Ingredients

Index of Quote Citations

About the Author

SANDRA GARSON is dedicated to the profound spiritual practice of caring for our bodies and healing others through the power of food and community. A long-time practitioner of Tibetan Buddhism, her work has appeared in *The New York Times, Tricycle, Boston Globe, Yankee,* and *Down East: The Magazine of Maine.* She has worked as a professional caterer, has transformed the nutritional value of the diets of many monasteries in Nepal, and is regularly called upon to consult on the food for visiting Tibetan dignitaries. Sandy is the founder and president of the charity Veggiyana, which provides food, kitchen gardens, and nutritional education to monks, nuns, and children in monastery schools. She studied food history at Harvard University and is the author of *How to Fix a Leek and Other Food from Your Farmers' Market.* She lives in San Francisco.

About Wisdom Publications

Wisdom Publications is dedicated to offering works relating to and inspired by Buddhist traditions.

To learn more about us or to explore our other books, please visit our website at www.wisdompubs.org.

You can subscribe to our e-newsletter or request our print catalog online, or by writing to:

Wisdom Publications
199 Elm Street
Somerville, Massachusetts 02144 USA

You can also contact us at 617-776-7416, or info@wisdompubs.org.

Wisdom is a nonprofit, charitable 501(c)(3) organization and donations in support of our mission are tax deductible.

Wisdom Publications is affiliated with the Foundation for the Preservation of the Mahayana Tradition (FPMT).